GREAT CAREERS

IN 2 YEARS

The Associate Degree Option

High-Skill and High-Wage Jobs
Available Through Two-Year Programs

PAUL PHIFER

Ferguson Publishing Company
Chicago, Illinois

S

Editor: Andrew Morkes
Additional Editorial Assistance: Paula Garner
Proofreader: Anne Paterson
Indexer: Debra Graf

Library of Congress Cataloging-in-Publication Data

Phifer, Paul.
    Great careers in two years: the associate degree option/by
        Paul Phifer.
      p. cm.
    Includes bibliographical references and index.
    Summary: Presents an overview of careers that can be
    obtained by earning an associate degree and discusses the
    pros and cons of such a degree.
    ISBN 0-89434-285-1
    1. Vocational guidance--United States. 2. High school stu-
    dents--Vocational guidance--United States. 3. Associate in
    arts degree. 4. College majors--United States.
    [1.Vocational guidance. 2. Associate in arts degree.]
    I. Title

HF5382.5.U5 P447 1999
331.7˙0233 21--dc21

                        99-041448

TABLE OF CONTENTS

- A family of four is driving to their favorite amusement park in a nearby city when their car breaks down. They'd been planning this trip for months, and now it looks like everything is ruined. Suddenly, another driver, who happens to be an *Automobile Service Technician,* pulls over and offers to help. The technician opens the hood, and after making several adjustments, announces to the family that everything should now be okay. The family is soon on its way, and is able to enjoy a fun-filled day at the amusement park.

- A young expectant mother waits on an examination table, her forehead creased with worry lines. It seems like weeks since she last felt the sharp kick of her baby. She is worried that something has gone wrong with the development of her child. A *Diagnostic Medical Sonographer* enters the room and greets the woman. She explains the imaging procedure, then directs the high-frequency sound waves toward the fetus. An image of a healthy boy appears. The sonographer shows the mother the baby's beating heart on the monitor. She also points out the babies head and hands and feet. The mother is overwhelmed with happiness and relief.

- The new highway is a success. Redesign and expansion of the lanes have reduced gridlock and travel times. The on-ramps offer clearer lines of vision. And the new highway doesn't flood in heavy storms. The new state-of-the-art drainage system has the pavement bone-dry in no-time after a storm. Little do the commuters stop to think that *Civil Engineering Technicians* played a large role in making the new highway a success.

- A college student has pulled an "all nighter" to finish an English paper. From her window, she can see the horizon gradually growing lighter as the sun begins to rise. Her class begins in less than an hour. As she finishes typing the last paragraph, the monitor on her personal computer suddenly "freezes." She pounds on the keyboard unmercifully, but to no avail. She calls her college's computer hotline, and 15 minutes later a *Computer Service Technician* arrives, "unfreezes" the computer and helps the student to retrieve her paper. The student is elated and, with a sense of relief, completes her project.

- A young man notices water on the floor of his basement but cannot, initially, find the cause. After a closer inspection, he discovers water dripping from an overhead pipe, but he is unable to reach it or determine how to repair it. The water on the floor inches closer to his home office. He quickly moves a few items to safety, then calls a local plumbing firm who immediately sends out a licensed *Plumber.* The leak is quickly repaired and the man proceeds to "dry out" his basement, thankful that the problem has been corrected without significant damage being done.

- It's the height of summer in the Texas Panhandle. Temperatures are in the 90s and rising. A Severe Heat Warning has been issued. A woman with a chronic respiratory ailment, who can only get around the house with a walker, has a problem. Her air conditioner has broken down. She can already feel her house heating up. Fortunately, she has the number of a qualified *Heating and Cooling Technician.* Within a half hour, the technician has the air back on, thus helping her to avoid a health emergency.

THESE EXAMPLES REPRESENT JUST A SMALL NUMBER OF SITUATIONS THAT WE ENCOUNTER IN OUR DAILY LIVES. We rely on trained workers of all kinds to keep us safe, healthy, and productive at home, school, and work. You might think that jobs like these require a bachelor's degree or higher. In fact, the workers in these examples became qualified to do their jobs by completing educational programs which granted less than a bachelor's degree. Most likely, each worker received all or a significant portion of his or her preparation from an associate degree granting institution. Such institutions have become crucial to the preparation of workers for high demand occupations which are currently experiencing severe labor shortages. This shortage is expected to continue for some time. Therefore, it is not too farfetched to conclude that associate degree granting institutions may eventually become the preferred postsecondary choice for millions of Americans. This belief, in part, derives support from a growing number of scholars and business leaders who have expressed the concern that too many of America's colleges and universities have, for too long, concentrated primarily on exposing their students to a four-year liberal arts experience.

Consequently, these institutions have failed to keep pace with a society that appears to increasingly need workers who have technical skills. Such skills not only require a different curriculum content, but are often more practical, and quite often, require less time to learn. Still others have expressed the additional concern that, in general, both high school and colleges have seriously neglected the fact that most high school graduates will never earn a bachelor's degree. According to the report, "Counseling For High Skills" (compiled by researchers at Kansas State University), 83 percent of parents hope their children will become a four-year college graduate. However, only about 30 percent of high school graduates eventually obtain a bachelor's degree.

Many communities and educational institutions have realized the need for more practical connections

> The Department of Labor predicts that almost two-thirds of the 18.6 million new jobs between 1996 and 2006 will require less education than a bachelor's degree.

between school and work. The proliferation of School-To-Work, Tech Prep, "applied" education, and other similar programs, clearly attests to this fact.

The U.S. Department of Labor predicts most of the jobs in the future will require education and training similar to what community and technical colleges have traditionally attempted to provide. Most community colleges tend to offer a comprehensive array of courses and programs beyond what School-To-Work and Tech Prep programs can provide. Such variety gives students the opportunity to take courses which prepare them to complete an associate degree or certificate program, or to transfer to a four-year institution. The steady rise in tuition at the average four-year college, along with a number of other factors, is expected to make the community college option more attractive to a growing number of individuals.

Not many will argue that education is one of the most important "keys" to personal success in America. Millions of dollars are regularly allocated by national, state, and local government officials for education, from the elementary level through adulthood. In addition, industry is reported to be spending larger sums on inservice, retraining, and education of both current and incoming employees. Effective community agencies and organizations, as well as many religious institutions, have traditionally been committed to providing strong educational initiatives for the clients they serve. At the same time, our nation continues to experience increased global competition, economic fluctuation, rapid technological changes, an overwhelming explosion of knowledge, and, what appears to be a growing scarcity of effective leadership. Never before in America's history has

> According to the American Association of Community Colleges, there were 5.4 million students (in credit programs) enrolled in community colleges in Fall 1997.

the need for appropriate education for each citizen appeared to be so acute as it seems today. Change is now occurring at such a rapid pace that many of us as career counselors are advising our clients to prepare for change, not constants, and to brace themselves for increasing ambiguity and uncertainty, in the job market.

Therefore, in light of these realities, there is an urgent need for practical answers to the following questions.:

- What type of education do many, if not most, Americans need in a society such as ours? Who can best deliver these services?

- How, and in what form, should and can such services be provided?

- What occupations will help employers to effectively compete and meet their needs for today, and hopefully, tomorrow?

I firmly believe this nation's two-year colleges can contribute significantly, and in a practical way. Increasingly, evidence seems to support the belief that community colleges will become "key players" in America's economic future. The community college's unique and comprehensive mission, which has traditionally placed emphasis on flexibility and outreach, is particularly suited to a society in need of rapid, customized responses. It should be noted that communities all across the country, as well as businesses and industries, have for some time relied on cooperative efforts with nearby community colleges to effectively deliver their economic planning and development endeavors. Nothing on the horizon seems to indicate such cooperative efforts will not continue to occur.

It is important for current and future college students, parents, and educators to take a closer look at

> According to the National Center for Education Statistics, there were 1,132 community colleges in the United States in 1998.

how the two-year institution, and its associate degree and programs, can possibly provide for millions, a viable and fulfilling educational option. Therefore, in order to heighten awareness for both current and potential students of two-year institutions, we have written *Great Careers in 2 Years: The Associate Degree Option* to highlight the advantages of acquiring an associate degree in a growing number of high demand areas; address the question of whether one should attend a two-year institution or not; introduce some important considerations; and offer suggestions for preparation. In addition, *Great Careers in 2 Years* identifies and describes 100 high-need occupational areas. Each career article provides a description of job duties; certification, licensing, and personal requirements; ways to enter the field after students complete their education; salary information; an employment outlook; and sources of additional information to contact to learn more about the career.

We hope that *Great Careers in 2 Years* will expand your knowledge of the associate degree option and help you to make informed career decisions.

A word about the employment predictions

For the most part, the Employment Outlook information is based on the most recent U.S. Department of Labor predictions through the year 2006, and is supplemented by information taken from professional associations. Job growth terms follow those used in the *Occupational Outlook Handbook:*

- growth described as "much faster than the average" means an increase of 36 percent or more;

- growth described as "faster than the average" means an increase of 21 to 35 percent;

- growth described as "about as fast as the average" means an increase of 10 to 20 percent;

- growth described as "little change or more slowly than the average" means an increase of 0 to 9 percent.

ASSOCIATE DEGREES...AND MORE

TWO-YEAR INSTITUTIONS HAVE UNIQUE MISSIONS WHICH ARE ESPE-
CIALLY GEARED TO MEET THE SERVICE AND WORKFORCE LABOR
NEEDS OF THEIR LOCAL COMMUNITY. Included among these are
community and junior colleges as well as technical colleges or institutes. For the sake of clarity, after a brief definition below of each of
the above, I will refer to such institutions as two-year colleges.

Junior Colleges, traditionally, have focused on providing for their
students the first two years of a bachelor's degree program. However,
many junior colleges have expanded their missions and changed their
name to community college. Few restrict their curriculum offerings
to transfer programs only.

Technical Colleges or *Institutes* are primarily occupational readiness
oriented although many are essentially community colleges with an
emphasis on technical high-demand employment areas. They tend
to provide specialized and intense training in trade or skill areas, such
as electronics, computers, dental assisting, and respiratory therapy.

Students who desire a "no extras" approach, and want to only learn
the essentials of a certain trade/skill area in the shortest period of time,
may prefer a technical college experience.

Community Colleges are probably the most popular among two-year
institutions. Most usually offer a wide variety of curriculum offerings.
Community colleges present an attractive, economical, and realistic
option for many in our society who would not otherwise be able to
attend college. For a significant number of students, being able to attend
a community college constitutes a bridge which moves them closer
to acquiring occupational suitability and personal fulfillment.

Community colleges are usually well respected in their local
areas. Typical curriculum offerings include the first two years of a variety of four-year bachelor's degree programs as well as one- and

11

two-year occupational programs. In addition, most community colleges offer an array of community-oriented options such as continuing education classes, remedial and support endeavors, community service outreach, and customized training for local businesses and industries. Many of the disabled, minorities, women, veterans, immigrants, and economically disadvantaged students have found in the past, as well as the present, the community college's "open door policy" to be their only avenue to higher education.

Two-year colleges usually grant at least two documents that officially recognize a student's successful completion of a program of study; the certificate (which we will cover a bit later) and the associate degree.

An *Associate Degree* is awarded when a student has successfully completed the minimum academic and related graduation requirements of a particular curriculum area. Normally, it is the equivalent of two years of study beyond the high school level. While most associate degrees are usually said to be the equivalent of two years, the actual time spent can vary greatly. For some students it may take less time due to the student having "tested out" of some courses prior to or during college. Others may take longer than expected due to a delayed major selection, curriculum requirements, or personal interruptions. The following represent the most common associate degrees granted by most two-year colleges.

ASSOCIATE IN APPLIED SCIENCE (or ASSOCIATE IN APPLIED ARTS AND SCIENCES)—A curriculum of study which prepares one for immediate employment or advancement after successful completion. Many or most courses may be transferable to selected four-year colleges—often referred to as occupational programs.

ASSOCIATE IN ARTS—A curriculum of study which constitute the first two years of a liberal arts four-year bachelor's degree or pre-professional program.

ASSOCIATE IN SCIENCE—A curriculum of study which constitute the first two years of a science-related four-year bachelor's degree program.

Other popular degrees, just to name a few, are the Associate Degree in Nursing; Associate in Business; and the Associate in Music.

Associate degree programs have been developed for almost every interest. If you want to take an associate degree program in Professional Pilot Technology, you might want to attend Miami-Dade Community College (http://www.mdcc.edu/). If you prefer, instead, to become proficient in the paper industry, then the Pulp & Paper Technology curriculum at Bay de Noc Community College (http://www.baydenoc.cc.mi.us/) in upper Michigan may be just the answer. Or; maybe you are more interested in the outdoors and backpacking, and that is why the Wilderness Studies program at Colorado Mountain College's (Alpine campus—http://www.coloradomtn.edu/campus_alp/) sounds attractive to you. Or you may choose to enroll in a Boat Maintenance and Repair program at Honolulu Community College (http://www.hcc.hawaii.edu/) while a friend of yours, hundreds of miles away, completes her associate degree in Instrumentation & Controls at Northern Maine Technical College (http://www.nmtc.net/). The above represent only the "tip of the iceberg" when it comes to the rich variety of associate in science or associate in applied arts and science degree options. The following is a sampling of other possibilities.

Alcohol and Other Drug Abuse Associate, Accounting, Administrative Assistant, Aquaculture, Arboriculture (Urban Forestry), Computer Programming, Communication Technologies, Civil Engineering Technician, Culinary Arts, Chiropractic Technician, Diesel Equipment Technology, Equine Studies (Horses-Harness Racing), Entrepreneurship, Fire Protection, Funeral Service Education, Food Service Management, Fish & Wildlife Technology, Farm & Ranch Management, Golf/Recreational Management Technology, Gerontology, Graphic Design, Gunsmithing Technology, Horticulture Technology, Human Services, Health Insurance Claims Management, Interpreter Training Technology, Occupational Therapy Assisting, Physical Therapy Assisting, Registered Nurse, Ski Area Management, Sports Management, Water Technology, Welding

While the main focus of this book is on the associate degree, two-year colleges offer a variety of other programs. A brief description of each follows.

CERTIFICATE—Certificates are awarded when a student has successfully completed the minimum academic and related requirements of a particular curriculum area, usually equivalent to one year of study beyond the high school level. However, in a growing number of colleges, a variety of certificates of completion may be awarded for special or customized training which require shorter periods of time. Also, while most certificates are usually said to be the equivalent of one year, the actual time spent can vary greatly depending on a variety of personal and educational factors.

APPRENTICESHIP—An apprenticeship is a written agreement between an employer and an individual (referred to as an apprentice) whereby the apprentice agrees to be trained and supervised by a skilled craft person(s) for a period of time (roughly three to five years, although this can vary). Apprenticeship experiences combine classroom instruction and on-the-job training which must add up to a minimum number of required hours. During this time the apprentice is paid at a progressively higher rate of pay. If successfully completed, the apprentice usually applies for and receives his or her Journey Worker's (Person's) Card, which represents full status as a skilled craftsperson in the particular area of training. Apprenticeship

Median Earnings for Persons 18 or Older by Educational Attainment, 1996

No high school diploma—$17,148

High school graduate—$22,502

Some college, no degree—$26,090

Associate degree—$29,547

Bachelor's degree—$36,525

Master's degree—$45,053

Professional degree—$65,916

Doctorate—$56,758

Source: U.S. Bureau of the Census, 1997

training has long been a vehicle used by thousands of manufacturing and construction firms to help meet the continuing scarcity of highly skilled, technically-trained workers. Not only is the demand for such training still prevalent, it is expected to continue in the foreseeable future.

The academic courses required to successfully complete apprenticeship programs are frequently taken at a local two-year college. Several advantages of being in an apprenticeship include the opportunity to acquire high demand skills while possibly earning college credit, and receiving an income which increases each year of the program. The number of possible apprenticeship programs are too numerous to list here but a sampling has been provided.

Automotive-Body Repairer, Automotive Mechanic, Baker, Barber/Cosmetologist, Boilermaker, Butcher, Bricklayer, Carpenter, Cement Mason, Ceramic Layer, Construction Electrician, Drywall Finisher, Firefighter, Glazier, Industrial Electrician, Industrial Millwright, Insulation Worker, Iron Worker, Machinist, Operating Engineer, Painter, Patternmaker, Pipefitter, Plasterer, Plumber, Roofer & Waterproofer, Sheet Metal Worker, Sprinkler Fitter, Tool & Die Maker, Welder

BUSINESS & INDUSTRY CENTERS/PROGRAMS—are geared to meet the immediate and short-term needs of private businesses, industries and special interests groups, as well as nonprofit and governmental agencies. Partnerships or contracted agreements typically entered into by two-year colleges range from crisis intervention strategies to professional development. Although private businesses and industries are often the "other party" in such partnerships, agreements are also made with economic development groups, high school districts, labor unions, and other colleges. Delivery of these outreach efforts come in various customized forms and could be conducted on or off campus. They may include highly specialized seminars; workshops and professional development inservices or short-term classes; structured off-campus experiences; and one-time presentations.

LICENSURE—Although licensure is not considered a "program," it is mentioned here because a number of occupational and transfer curriculum students will be required to obtain a license before being able to legally work in the area they have been prepared for. Many occupational programs not only prepare student graduates to proficiently perform in an occupation, but to also be successful on licensure exams.

Occupational licensure is a form of legal authorization and recognition which permits an individual to "practice" a trade or perform a service within a particular area, region or, in most instances, state. Although it may not be true in all situations, it is relatively safe to say it is a positive indicator of the quality of a program, if there is regular publicity about the success former graduates have, in terms of license or certification acquirement.

Be sure to find out if the occupation you plan to enter requires or recommends a license or certification in order to practice or perform. The department chairperson or an informed counselor should be able to provide you with this information. In addition to meeting other criteria for acquiring a license, students are usually required to pass an exam (sometimes referred to as "Boards"). College catalogs or departmental publications may include general information about licensure requirements for certain career areas. When inquiring, you should remember to ask if there are statistics available on how well past graduates have done on licensure.

The following represent a sampling of the various licenses two-year college occupational programs prepare their students to take exams for:

Certified Shorthand Reporter (Court Reporter), Dental Assistant, Dental Hygienist, EMT (Emergency Medical Technician), Fire Fighter, Insurance Agent, Occupational Therapy Assistant, Optician Technician, Practical Nurse, Real Estate Appraiser, Registered Nurse, Social Work Technician, Veterinary Technician

For more information, contact your state department of labor, bureau of occupational licensing, or contact the state government headquarters (ask for the office which can provide occupational license information).

I have only "scratched the surface" of some of the basic characteristics of two-year colleges. In light of the current and predicted challenges, the future looks bright, especially if the thousands of

American workers who will need to be trained or retrained become actively motivated to prepare for the future. Therefore, on the eve of the 21st century, the two-year college, if it maintains its unique mission, can make a major impact, in regards to helping to meet the critical needs of the type of students who will seek their assistance.

Notable Community College Alumni

- Gwendolyn Brooks, Pulitzer Prize-winning author and poet (City Colleges of Chicago, Illinois)

- Billy Crystal, actor and comedian (Nassau Community College, New York)

- Emory Cunningham, president/publisher of *Southern Living* magazine (Mississippi Gulf Coast Junior College, Mississippi)

- Walt Disney, film producer (Metropolitan Junior College, Missouri)

- Thomas Donovan, president/CEO, Chicago Board of Trade (City Colleges of Chicago, Illinois)

- Morgan Freeman, actor (Los Angeles City College, California)

- Dennis Hayes, Earth Day co-creator (Clark College, Washington)

- Jeanne Kirkpatrick, educator, stateswoman (Stephens College, Missouri)

- Jim Lehrer, broadcast journalist (Victoria College, Texas)

- John Cougar Mellencamp, singer, musician (Vincennes University Junior College, Indiana)

- Natalie Merchant, singer (Jamestown Community College, New York)

- Kweisi Mfume, president-NAACP, former U.S. Congressman (Baltimore City Community College, Maryland)

- H. Ross Perot, corporate executive, 1992 Presidential Candidate (Texarkana Junior College, Texas)

Source: American Association of Community Colleges

The Ten Best Community Colleges in the United States (according to *Rolling Stone*)

1. **Bellevue Community College,** 3000 Landerholm Circle, SE, Bellevue, Washington 98007-6484, Tel: 425-641-0111, Web: http://www.bcc.ctc.edu/.

2. **Brookhaven College,** 3939 Valley View Lane, Farmers Branch, Texas, 75244-4997, Tel: 972-860-4700, Web: http://www.dcccd.edu/bhc/index.htm.

3. **Cuyahoga Community College,** 2900 Community College Avenue, Cleveland, Ohio, 44115, Tel: 216-987-4000, Web: http://www.tri-c.cc.oh.us/Metro/INDEX.htm.

4. **De Anza College,** 21250 Stevens Creek Boulevard, Cupertino, California 95014, Tel: 408-864-5678, Web: http://www.deanza.fhda.edu/.

5. **John A. Logan College,** 700 Logan College Road, Carterville, Illinois 62918, Email: logan@jal.cc.il.us, Web: http://www.jal.cc.il.us/.

6. **Johnson County Community College,** 12345 College Boulevard, Overland Park, Kansas 66210, Tel: 913-469-8500, ext 3120, Email: jhaas@jccc.net, Web: http://www.johnco.cc.ks.us/.

7. **Miami-Dade Community College** (6 campuses in Florida) Web: http://www.mdcc.edu/.

8. **Nassau Community College,** Garden City, New York 11530, Tel: 516-572-7501, Web: http://www.sunynassau.edu/.

9. **Northern Virginia Community College** (5 campuses in Northern Virginia), Web: http://www.nv.cc.va.us/.

10. **Santa Monica College,** 1900 Pico Boulevard, Santa Monica, California 90405, Tel: 310-434-4000, Web: http://www.smc.edu/.

Source: ***Rolling Stone,*** September 29, 1998

Chapter II

SHOULD I ATTEND AN ASSOCIATE DEGREE GRANTING INSTITUTION?

"Anybody can get through a junior college."

"My grades were terrible in high school and our technical college was the only place I could get in!"

"Community college gave me a solid first two years compared to what some of my friends received who went to four-year colleges."

"I'll go anyplace except a community college."

"I don't have to quit my job if I go to a community college."

"I want to experience dorm-life and just being away."

"I only wanted to go to school for a year or two."

"The community college provided me with a few extra years to mature."

THE STATEMENTS ABOVE, BOTH PRO AND CON, ARE SIMILAR TO THOSE OFTEN VOICED BY STUDENTS WHEN THEY ARE ASKED ABOUT ASSOCIATE DEGREE GRANTING INSTITUTIONS, PARTICULARLY COMMUNITY COLLEGES. It is little wonder if, after reading over the statements, you might say: How confusing! Or, which statements are actually true? How can you know if a two-year associate degree institution is right for you? The ability to accurately answer the latter question is certainly a difficult one for many people.

At this time, you might be asking yourself: What is an associate degree granting institution? An associate degree granting institution is a two-year community, junior, or technical college which grants associate degrees and certificates for the majority of its program offerings. The decision to attend or not attend such an institution should start with a basic awareness of your life direction. Not only is this important awareness often overlooked by thousands of students each year, but the lack of accurate life direction may be responsible for millions of dollars being misdirected along with countless weeks, months, and even years of wasted time and energy.

Learning how to establish your life direction usually requires a deep scrutiny and introspection. Career counselors call this process a SELF-ASSESSMENT. A self-assessment, if honestly and thoroughly conducted, can help you uncover very helpful personal information which, too often, remains abstract and non-directive. Learning such information will more realistically help you decide whether you should join the military, attend a four-year college, apply for a job, or enroll in a two-year institution.

Contrary to what too many educators might suggest, students should not be encouraged, in general, to simply "take a variety of exploratory courses" as a strategy for discovering a major direction. Educators who advise this approach probably mean well, but I have personally witnessed the frustration and discouragement of too many students after they have "explored" a number of courses with no success.

Several years ago, I sat in on my son's freshmen orientation session, and was rather disappointed to hear the college official recommend to the incoming freshman that they should probably delay taking a career development class until at least their second semester, and possibly even wait until the first semester of their sophomore year.

Top 5 "Hot Programs" Reported by Community College Administrators, 1997

Program Name	Average Starting Salary
Dental hygiene	$31,750
Manufacturing process technology	$30,675
Telecommunications/interactive information specialists	$29,268
Physical therapy assisting	$28,782
Registered nursing	$28,777

Source: AACC Hot Programs Survey, 1997

This statement would have been somewhat understandable had he encouraged each student to engage in career development activities on their own or at least avail themselves of the campus career services. I do not recall this being mentioned. He went on to say, in essence, that most students usually take five or more years to graduate and that there was plenty of time, and to not rush. It is no wonder we have a growing number of what appears to be "professional students."

Imagine how you might feel if the results of your self-assessment, along with other important factors, strongly suggests that a two-year technical program, rather than the four-year art curriculum you are currently in, would be most appropriate for you? Imagine further that you had already taken classes, part-time, for roughly three years and had accumulated 72 credit hours during this "exploratory" time period!

The following SELF-ASSESSMENT SURVEY AND PROFILE SHEET should help you to determine exactly who you are and what you want do with your future.

SELF-ASSESSMENT SURVEY AND PROFILE SHEET

Note: Feel free to duplicate any of the following self-assessment sheets for your own personal use. Responses can also be simply written on a sheet of paper.

PERSONALITY ATTRIBUTES: GENERAL

Personality attributes (sometimes referred to as traits) are qualities which help to distinguish one individual from another. A partial list of attributes appears on the next few pages. Carefully look over this list and identify those attributes you believe to reflect yourself (place an "S" beside those you believe are STRONG FOR YOU, and a "W" beside those you are PARTICULARLY WEAK IN). It is often helpful to have someone who knows you well provide his or her opinion of which of the attributes fit best. Feel free to add attributes not listed which you believe may be more representative. After careful consideration, PLACE IN THE BLANKS BELOW THOSE ATTRIBUTES YOU BELIEVE TO BE YOUR 5 STRONGEST. . . AS WELL AS THOSE YOU BELIEVE TO BE YOUR 5 WEAKEST.

Able	Comforting	Forgiving	Loving
Active	Convincing	Frank	Loyal
Adaptable	Conscientious	Friendly	Mannerly
Admirable	Consistent	Frugal	Materialistic
Adventurous	Considerate	Gentle	Mature
Affectionate	Cooperative	Go-getter	Merciful
Aggressive	Courageous	Good listener	Methodical
Alert	Creative	Graceful	Moody
Aloof	Critical	Grateful	Motivated
Ambitious	Cruel	Gullible	Musical
Amiable	Curious	Handsome	Negative
Analytical	Deceptive	Helpful	Naive
Anxious	Decisive	Honest	Neat
Apathetic	Dedicated	Hospitable	Nonconforming
Argumentative	Dependable	Humble	Obedient
Articulate	Determined	Humorous	Objective
Artistic	Disciplined	Imaginative	Obnoxious
Aspiring	Discreet	Impatient	Observant
Assertive	Dishonest	Impulsive	Open-minded
Athletic	Disorganized	Inconsistent	Optimistic
Beautiful	Disrespectful	Independent	Orderly
Boastful	Distrustful	Industrious	Original
Capable	Domineering	Inflexible	Organizer
Caring	Earnest	Initiating	Outgoing
Casual	Efficient	Inquiring	Overbearing
Cautious	Emotional	Insensitive	Passive
Cheerful	Encouraging	Insightful	Panicky
Charming	Energetic	Intuitive	Patient
Clever	Enthusiastic	Intelligent	Peaceful
Clumsy	Envious	Integrity	Perfectionist
Cocky	Expressive	Intense	Persistent
Commanding	Extroverted	Intolerant	Persuasive
Committed	Fair-minded	Irresponsible	Pessimistic
Compassionate	Faithful	Joiner	Picky
Competent	Fearful	Judgmental	Planner
Competitive	Flexible	Kind	Pleasant
Condescending	Flippant	Lazy	Poised
Confident	Forceful	Liar	Practical
Conforming	Forgetful	Logical	Precise

Prejudiced	Responsible	Serious	Systematic
Procrastinator	Rigid	Sharing	Tactless
Promiscuous	Rude	Shy	Tactful
Punctual	Sacrificing	Sickly	Talented
Purposeful	Sarcastic	Smart	Thoughtful
Pursuing	Secretive	Sociable	Tolerant
Quiet	Self-Confident	Spontaneous	Trustworthy
Reliable	Selfish	Steady	Uncouth
Reserved	Self-directed	Strong-willed	Understanding
Resourceful	Sensitive	Stubborn	Unselfish
Respectful	Serene	Sulky	

5 STRONGEST ABILITIES

_____

_____

_____

_____

_____

5 WEAKEST APTITUDES

_____

_____

_____

_____

_____

TEMPERAMENTS

Temperaments are personality attributes which relate to your way of thinking, feeling and behaving and determine whether you are comfortable or uncomfortable in a given situation. Please read the directions and complete the temperaments profile below.

Directions: Weigh each of the temperaments below on a comfort scale of 1-12 (12 being the situation in which you feel the MOST COMFORTABLE). Place your rating on the black line beside the appropriate letter. If you feel equally comfortable about more than one, do not hesitate to use the same number twice.

___**A.** Situations involving a VARIETY of duties often requiring frequent CHANGE (doing different activities).

___**B.** Situations involving REPETITION or REPEATING SOMETHING FREQUENTLY according to set procedures or sequences (doing the same task over and over).

___**C.** Situations involving DOING THINGS only UNDER SPECIFIC INSTRUCTION, allowing little or no room for independent action or judgment in working out job problems (little or no personal input required).

TEMPERAMENTS (continued)

__D. Situations which involve DEALING WITH PEOPLE in actual job duties beyond giving and receiving instructions (high degree of interaction and cooperation with people).

__E. Situations which involve DIRECTING, CONTROLLING, and PLANNING of entire activities or the activities of others.

__F. Situations involving WORKING ALONE and apart from others although the activity may be integrated with that of others (doing most or all of your work by yourself although it may be done around others).

__G. Situations which involve INFLUENCING PEOPLE in their opinions, attitudes, or judgments about ideas or things (being able to persuade others in the way they think, act, and behave).

__H. Situations involving PERFORMING ADEQUATELY WHILE WORKING UNDER PRESSURE or when confronted with the critical or unexpected or when taking risks (being challenged and coming through).

__I. Situations wherein one makes an evaluation based on PERSONAL JUDGMENT (making decisions based on personal experiences and through the use of one's senses, e.g., sight, smell, hearing, taste, or touch).

__J. Situations requiring you to make a decision using MEASURABLE OR VERIFIABLE CRITERIA (making decisions based on something that has been or can be measured based on facts, rules, or standards).

__K. Situations in which one INTERPRETS AND EXPRESSES FEELINGS, IDEAS, OR FACTS IN A PERSONALLY CREATIVE WAY (such as through song, acting, writing, painting, etc.).

__L. Situations involving PRECISENESS in terms of set limits, tolerances or standards (being detailed and exact).

PRIMARY SOURCES: *Dictionary of Occupational Titles;* Vol. 2, 3rd Ed., 1965

STRENGTHS AND WEAKNESSES (Optional)

Obtaining another opinion can be very helpful. The strengths and weaknesses cited below represent a partial list of the many personality attributes which characterize the behavior of people. Many are similar to the personality attributes you were previously asked to look over and respond to. Please have someone who knows you well and in whom you can trust indicate with an "S" those 5 points he or she believes to be your strongest. In addition, ask this person to place a "W" beside those believed to be your weakest points. Remember, other strengths and/or weaknesses can be substituted if it is believed they would be more representative of you.

Before placing your strengths and weaknesses on the SELF-ASSESSMENT PRO-FILE SHEET, it is suggested that you compare your list with how the other person rated you. After considering both lists, select those strengths and weaknesses you believe are most representative of you.

■ STRENGTHS

Active	Encouraging	Independent	Punctual
Ambitious	Enduring	Industrious	Respectful
Analytical	Energetic	Intelligent	Self-Confident
Assertive	Enthusiastic	Joiner	Sense of humor
Affectionate	Expressive	Kind	Sensitive
Caring	Fair	Like challenges	Sharing
Charming	Faithful	Logical	Speak well
Cheerful	Flexible	Loyal	Spontaneous
Comforting	Forgiving	Mannerly	Steadfast
Compassionate	Friendly	Neat	Tactful
Competent	Generous	Objective	Talented
Cooperative	Gentle	Observant	Team player
Courageous	Good listener	Open-minded	Thoughtful
Creative	Good w/hands	Optimistic	Thrifty
Dedicated	Good-natured	Organized	Tolerant
Dependable	Graceful	Patient	Trustworthy
Determined	Helpful	Peacemaker	Understanding
Disciplined	Honest	Persistent	Unselfish
Discreet	Hospitable	Poised	Witty
Efficient	Humble	Productive	

■ WEAKNESSES

Apathetic	Cocky	Fearful	Insensitive
Argumentative	Confronter	Flippant	Intolerant
Aggressive	Deceptive	Gullible	Irresponsible
Bossy	Dependent	Hateful	Jealous
Braggart	Dishonest	Hostile	Judgmental
Can't say no	Disorganized	Indecisive	Lazy
Clumsy	Disrespectful	Impatient	Liar
Cruel	Domineering	Impulsive	Moody
Complainer	Drug abuser	Inflexible	Negative

WEAKNESSES (continued)

Obnoxious	Prejudiced	Sarcastic	Uncouth
Overly critical	Prideful	Secretive	Undependable
Overweight	Promiscuous	Selfish	Swear a lot
Perfectionist	Put things off	Shy	Wasteful
Pessimistic	Quick to anger	Stingy	Whiny
Poor listener	Racist	Stubborn	Wimpy
Poor loser	Rude	Sulky	Worry a lot

5 STRONGEST: 5 WEAKEST:

_____   _____

_____   _____

_____   _____

_____   _____

_____   _____

SKILLS (Abilities & Aptitudes)

Skills can be divided into 2 major categories:

ABILITIES—An ability can be defined as something you can do as a result of rehearsal and/or practice. Abilities and skills are often thought of as having the same meaning; being skilled, though usually implies that one can do something well. Specific knowledge of your strongest abilities can greatly increase your sense of confidence.

APTITUDES—Aptitudes are those activities you have the potential to perform well and seem to come easily and naturally. Some people have aptitudes they are either unaware of or have been unable to develop to their fullest. Becoming aware of your aptitudes can help you to better understand who you are on the inside.

DIRECTIONS: Place an "A" in front of the area(s) in which you believe you have ABILITY. Place a "P" in front of the area(s) in which you believe you have an APTITUDE. Feel free to write in any ability/aptitude you may have in addition to or instead of the sampling listed. Leave blank any area you are not sure of. As you go through, keep in mind that you will be asked when finished to list your 5 strongest abilities as well as 5 strongest aptitudes.

___ Understanding instructions, facts and underlying reasoning; being able to reason and make judgments

___ Understanding the meaning of words and ideas; being able to present information or ideas clearly

___ Doing arithmetic operations quickly and correctly

__ Looking at flat drawings or pictures of objects and forming mental images of them in three dimensions or in terms of height, width, and depth (such as in reading blueprints, patterns, etc.)

__ Observing details in pictorial or graphic material and effectively making visual comparisons; good at noticing differences in shapes, shading, etc.

__ Observing details and recognizing errors in numbers, spelling and punctuation in written materials, charts and tables; good at avoiding errors when copying

__ Moving the eyes and hands or fingers together to perform a task rapidly and correctly

__ Moving the fingers to work with small objects rapidly and correctly

__ Moving the hands with ease and skill, as in placing and turning

__ Moving hands and feet together in response to visual signals, etc.

__ Seeing likenesses and differences in colors or shades; matching colors

__ Finding errors in writing

__ Asking the right questions

__ Following instructions

__ Improving what others have done

__ Explaining things clearly

__ Planning and organizing

__ Operating mechanical equipment

__ Expanding on what others have started

__ Exploring and doing research

__ Budgeting

__ Being exact and to the point

__ Spelling

__ Accepting constructive advice

__ Being creative

__ Getting along with others

__ Counseling others

__ Doing artistic things

__ Keeping records

__ Leading and supervising others

__ Teaching others

__ Gardening

__ Typing

__ Giving others helpful advice

__ Being flexible

__ Drawing or designing things

__ Mechanical things

__ Training others to do things

__ Driving vehicles

__ Performing in front of others

__ Taking risks

__ Solving conflicts

__ Noticing shapes, sizes, etc.

__ Staying with a task until done

__ Repairing and servicing computers

__ Getting others to believe in something

__ Making good decisions during emergencies

__ Simplifying what appears to be complex

__ Learning from mistakes and past experiences

__ Working alone for long periods of time

__ Understanding and reading blueprints, maps, drawings, etc.

__ Listening or picking up on what others say

ABILITIES AND APTITUDES (continued)

__ Seeing the underlying reasons for behavior or events

__ Estimating costs

__ Interpreting the feelings and emotions of others

__ Reading articulately

__ Doing activities that require heavy physical work

__ Writing

__ Copying things or activities done by others

__ Collecting things

__ Constructing things out of wood or metal or other materials

__ Speaking in public

__ Working with numbers/solving accounting-type problems

__ Operating computers

__ Motivating others to perform or do something

__ Being thorough

__ Expressing feelings

__ Managing time

__ Distinguishing sounds

__ Doing things for others

__ Communicating to others

__ Controlling own emotions

__ Thinking before acting

__ Team sports (basketball, football, etc.)

__ Individual sports (tennis, golf, etc.)

__ Leading and supervising people and activities

__ Using your fingers to work with small objects or instruments

__ Studying English or related subjects

__ Studying Social Studies or related subjects

__ Studying Science or related subjects

Other _____

Other _____

Other _____

Other _____

Other _____

Other _____

Other _____

Other _____

NOTE: The 8 spaces above have been left blank for you to include any additional or alternative skills.

5 STRONGEST ATTRIBUTES

_____

_____

_____

_____

_____

5 WEAKEST ATTRIBUTES

_____

_____

_____

_____

_____

The aforementioned represent just a sampling of possibilities. For a more comprehensive and personalized listing, you may want to read Richard Bolles' *How To Create A Picture of Your Ideal Job or Next Career.*

LIFE VALUES

Life values are those deeply cherished things, activities, or relationships you place the most importance on and aspire to obtain or engage in. Life values provide us with the necessary motivation to endure many of life's hardships. Please read the directions and complete the life values survey below.

Directions: First, read through the entire list. After reading, go back and circle each value's level of importance to you. Next, place an "M " beside those values which are most important. (Identify at least 5 but no more than 7.)

ACHIEVEMENT (accomplishment; being able to see or experience results which have been brought about by persistence or hard work)

Not very important Important Very important

AESTHETICS (the appreciation and enjoyment of beauty for beauty's sake, as in the arts and/or in nature)

Not very important Important Very important

ALTRUISM (having a special regard for or dedication to the welfare of others; service to others)

Not very important Important Very important

AUTONOMY (independence; the ability to make one's own decisions; self-directed; not being dependent on others)

Not very important Important Very important

CREATIVITY (being able to try out new ideas; to differ from the traditional; being innovative)

Not very important Important Very important

EMOTIONAL WELL-BEING (having peace of mind and inner sense of security; able to identify and resolve inner conflict; relatively free from anxiety)

Not very important Important Very important

HEALTH (maintaining an acceptable condition in terms of one's physical body; being relatively free from pain, discomfort, sickness, etc.)

Not very important Important Very important

HELPING MANKIND (engaging in activities or inventing, developing or producing something which will positively influence the lives of many; making a significant contribution of lasting or continuing value)

Not very important Important Very important

HONESTY (being frank, genuine and truthful with yourself and others)

Not very important Important Very important

LIFE VALUES (continued)

JUSTICE (treating others fairly or impartially; holding to truth or reason)

Not very important   Important   Very important

KNOWLEDGE (desire to learn or know; to seek truth; to acquire information about)

Not very important   Important   Very important

LOVE (warmth, caring, and unselfish devotion which freely accepts others without conditions)

Not very important   Important   Very important

LOYALTY (maintaining allegiance to a person, group or institution; not abandoning; sticking with during difficult times)

Not very important   Important   Very important

MORALITY (believing and keeping ethical standards; personal honor; integrity; doing what you truly believe is right)

Not very important   Important   Very important

PHYSICAL APPEARANCE (concern for your attractiveness; being neat, clean and well-groomed)

Not very important   Important   Very important

PLEASURE (having satisfaction, fun, joy, gratification)

Not very important   Important   Very important

POWER (having possession or control; authority or influence over others)

Not very important   Important   Very important

RECOGNITION (to be regularly recognized and positively noticed; receive attention)

Not very important   Important   Very important

RELIGIOUS FAITH (having religious beliefs; having a personal relationship with God)

Not very important   Important   Very important

SECURITY (to be sure of most endeavors or involvements in life; having visible or concrete support or back-up before taking risks)

Not very important   Important   Very important

SKILL (being very good at something; being better than average; performing at a high proficiency level)

Not very important   Important   Very important

WEALTH (having many possessions and plenty of money)

Not very important   Important   Very important

WISDOM (having mature understanding; deep insight; good sense and judgment; being able to make appropriate and effective decisions)

Not very important Important Very important

WORK VALUES

Work values are those things, activities and relationships you place the most importance on and aspire to obtain or engage in, relative to an occupation. While work values are often similar to life values, many are specifically related to an occupational setting. Work values tend to reflect much of who you are on the INSIDE. Please read the directions and complete the work values survey that follows.

Directions: Read through the entire list. After reading, go back and place in the blank to the left of each value the code which best describes its level of importance to you (see codes below).

NVI = Not Very Important I = Important VI = Very Important

Next, place a "M" at the end of the definition of each value you consider MOST IMPORTANT (Identify at least 5 but no more than 7).

__ **ADVANCEMENT** able to advance and move up; opportunity for higher position or training or education, etc.

__ **ACHIEVEMENT** accomplishing something everyone can't do or will not do; doing something that requires considerable effort and/or difficulty

__ **ASSISTING OTHERS** being directed and supervised by others; prefer not to have the responsibility of leading or directing people or activities

__ **BENEFITS** having good hospital and life insurance (etc.); unemployment, and vacation benefits

__ **COMPETITION** being in an environment wherein one has to compete or be matched against in rivalry; being challenged to produce or perform

__ **CREATIVITY** being able to try out new ideas; to be innovative

__ **ENVIRONMENT** physical or social surroundings which are suitable to your temperaments and values (e.g., beauty, neat, friendly, warm, etc.)

__ **HANDS-ON CONTACT** working with things, objects and/or equipment; use of hands and other body parts to perform tasks and activities which are primarily of a physical nature

__ **HELPING OTHERS** engaging in activities which directly aid and assist others

__ **INDEPENDENCE** having little or no supervision; freedom to guide one's own activities and make one's own decisions

WORK VALUES (continued)

___ INDUSTRY work which keeps one busy and active continuously (could include physical and/or mental tasks); having little or no "down time"

___ INTERESTING being positively excited and motivated most of the time in what you are doing; not likely to be bored for any significant span of time; doing something you can continuously enjoy with few exceptions

___ LEADERSHIP MANAGEMENT being in a leadership, supervisory, or managerial position; being in charge of others

___ LEARNING using mental abilities; gaining knowledge and understanding; being intellectually stimulated

___ MONEY earning a very high salary

___ NUMBER CONTACT working with numbers; charting; doing statistical reports and summaries

___ POSITIVE RELATIONSHIPS being able to get along very well with co-workers and supervisors; working with people who you generally like; being in an environment which is characterized by warm and cooperative relationships

___ PRESTIGE having a position that is recognized as being very important and influential by most; being in a position that commands great respect

___ PEOPLE CONTACT high interaction and cooperation with people; being around people most of the time

___ RELIGIOUS FAITH work that is in line with one's religious beliefs; work which does not interfere with one's ability to practice his or her religious principles

___ SECURITY being relatively free from the fear of frequent layoffs, job loss, reduced hours, etc.

___ SELF-DIRECTION able to determine what you are going to do and how you are going to do it in terms of work tasks, procedures, pace, etc.

___ SKILL having the ability to perform one or more tasks at an extremely high proficiency level; being able to do something which requires special effort or training or education

___ SUPPORT work environment wherein you receive emotional support, praise, and backing

___ TRAVEL being able to travel within a local community as well as from city to city as a part of your job responsibilities; having a travel budget

___ VARIETY doing different things or activities; not doing repetitive tasks

___ WHOLE LIFE SENSITIVITY work situation which allows or provides reasonable flexibility and choice in terms of overtime, time off, vacation selection, length of workday, family priorities and outside concerns; being able to engage in non-job related activities without hindrances

__ **WORDS/IDEAS/INFORMATION** working with oral, visual and written information, knowledge, facts, ideas and/or symbols (may include numbers)

__ **OTHER** _____

_____

_____

(any value you want to include that has not already been mentioned . . . if you desire to add more, please feel free to do so)

INTERESTS

Interests are those things, activities and experiences you enjoy and are excited about. Much of what we do during our leisure time tends to reflect our interests. Interests often reveal some of our most important values. Also, one can be interested in, without being actually involved with, an activity, experience, etc. A selected list of interests and/or leisure-time activities has been included on the next several pages. Please read through the directions and complete the interests survey.

Directions: Go through the entire list and while doing so, circle those things, activities or experiences which represent a STRONG INTEREST for you. Keep in mind that you will be asked when you finish to list your 5 strongest likes as well as your 5 strongest dislikes.

being the leader

cooking

acting

gardening

solving math problems

visiting museums/art galleries

organizing community events

working with people

water sports & games

canoeing, sailing

doing hard physical work

working with words or ideas

church activities

drawing

helping the poor

hunting, trapping

biology, life science, etc.

working on cars

team sports

individual sports

reading

writing

selling things

going to plays

music

teaching

parenting

earning money

competing with others

talk shows

video/computer games

listening to the radio

watching TV/movies

eating out

INTERESTS (continued)

bowling

arts & crafts

traveling

antiques

talking

foreign languages

politics

collections

Internet

interior decorating

backpacking

birdwatching

camping

exploring

hiking

horseback riding

sailing

sightseeing

walking

Big Brother/Big Sister programs

charitable drives

counseling others

Peace Corps

military involvement

Red Cross

spending time with the elderly

visiting the sick & shut in

YMCA/YWCA

conferences/conventions

debating

editing

organizing activities

researching

science exhibits

studying & going to school

working in a day care center

writing in a diary

auto shows

Bible study

singing in a choir

playing or singing with a group

circuses

macrame/needlepoint/knitting

photography

pottery

dancing

entertaining others

fairs/festivals

nightclubs/parties

poetry

talent/variety shows

visiting libraries

zoos/planetariums

4-H

conservation

health/nutrition

investments

Junior Achievement

motorcycles

scouting

sororities/fraternities

broadcasting

doing housework

exercising

learning new things

magazines/newspapers

sleeping

shopping

teaching a craft or sport

gymnastics

ice skating

skiing

weight lifting

cross country

In the blanks below, write any interests or leisure-time pursuits that you strongly enjoy but were not included in the sampling.

_____

_____

_____

What do you like the most? Write your 5 strongest likes (interests or leisure-time pursuits) below.

1. _____

2. _____

3. _____

4. _____

5. _____

Are there any things, activities or experiences which have been included (or not included) that you strongly dislike? If so, write these in the blanks below.

1. _____

2. _____

3. _____

4. _____

5. _____

SELF-ASSESSMENT PROFILE SHEET (SAPS)

Directions: A Self-Assessment Profile Sheet appears on the next pages. On these pages record the summary information you were asked to identify in each section. If you feel there are some which should be added to the number requested because you believe they are of equal weight (or tied in terms of rank order) please feel free to do so. A sample of a completed SAPS has been included.

After completing your SAPS you will probably want to identify the occupation and/or college major you believe the results most realistically reflect (minus the weaknesses and dislikes, of course). You can generate your own list of occupations and majors to pick from or take a Career Interest Survey such as the Kuder or Strong-Campbell (see page 38 for contact information) from a career counselor. It is our hope that after you complete the reading and exercises in this book, as well as follow the suggestions given, you will be well on your way toward a more directed and fulfilling life.

Temperaments (Most Comfortable) (pp. 23-24)

1. _____
2. _____
3. _____
4. _____
5. _____

Skills (pp. 26-28)

5 Strongest Abilities

1. _____
2. _____
3. _____
4. _____
5. _____

5 Strongest Aptitudes

1. _____
2. _____
3. _____
4. _____
5. _____

Strengths (p. 25)

1. _____
2. _____
3. _____
4. _____
5. _____

Weaknesses (pp. 25-26)

1. _____
2. _____
3. _____
4. _____
5. _____

Likes (5 Strongest) (pp. 26-28)

1. _____
2. _____
3. _____
4. _____
5. _____

Dislikes (pp. 26-28)

1. _____
2. _____
3. _____
4. _____
5. _____

Work Values (pp. 31-33)

1. _____
2. _____
3. _____
4. _____
5. _____

Life Values (pp. 29-31)

1. _____
2. _____
3. _____
4. _____
5. _____

SELF-ASSESSMENT PROFILE SHEET (Sample of Completed Form)

Temperaments (Most Comfortable) (pp. 23-24)
1. Directing, controlling
2. Influencing people
3. Dealing with people
4. Interpreting
5. Handling pressure

Skills (pp. 26-28)

5 Strongest Abilities
1. Leading/supervising
2. Motivating others
3. Interpreting feelings
4. Learning from mistakes
5. Teaching children

5 Strongest Aptitudes
1. Physical work
2. Working with numbers
3. Copy things done by others
4. Working with small objects
5. Mechanical things

Strengths (p. 25)
1. Honest
2. Punctual
3. Like challenges
4. Dedicated
5. Tactful

Weaknesses (pp. 25-26)
1. Stubborn
2. Aggressive
3. Overly critical
4. Bossy
5. Disorganized

Likes (5 Strongest) (pp. 26-28)
1. Church activities
2. Antiques
3. Activities with children
4. Drawing/reading books
5. Volunteer work

Dislikes (pp. 26-28)
1. Being supervised
2. Snakes
3. Being quiet
4. Golf
5. Hot weather

Work Values (pp. 31-33)
1. Leadership/management
2. Achievement
3. Helping others
4. Variety
5. Independent
6. People contact

Life Values (pp.29-31)
1. Honesty
2. Love
3. Loyalty
4. Autonomy
5. Altruism
6. Knowledge

Remember your profile is subject to change in time due to Significant Influencing Factors (SIF). SIF can and often do influence your life/career direction. SIF are situations, events, or incidents which significantly alter your thinking patterns, activities, and relationships beyond the temporary (and consequently, motivate you to make adjustments in terms of important occupational decisions). Several examples of SIF are sickness, a disease or accident, flood, famine, war, change in religious beliefs, a divorce, drug abuse problem, loss of a job or acquiring a new job, new legislation, etc. The list could go on and on. Therefore, it is suggested that you periodically review this profile and, whenever necessary, update.

While this self-assessment should provide you with a good start in determining your interests and abilities, there is no one test or survey that I am aware of that would measure all the factors which must be considered. This is why most career counselors rely on a battery of surveys, tests and instruments, both developed and commercial to assist clients with life direction. Some other surveys and tests which may be useful include:

Kuder Career Search (Measures Occupational Interest), National Career Assessment Services, Inc., 601 Visions Parkway, Adel, IA 50003, Tel: 800-314-8972, Web: http://www.ncasi.com/.

Strong Interest Inventory (Measures Occupational Interests), Consulting Psychologist Press, 3803 East Bayshore Road, Palo Alto, CA 94303, Tel: 800-624-1765, Web: http://www.mbti.com/cpp4.htm.

Self-Directed Search (SDS) (Measures Personality Environments/Interests), Psychological Assessment Resources, Inc., 16204 North Florida Avenue, Lutz, FL 33549, Tel: 813-968-3003, Web: http://www.sdstest3.com/.

Myers-Briggs Type Indicator (Measures Personality Types), Consulting Psychologist Press, 3803 East Bayshore Road, Palo Alto, CA 94303, Tel: 800-624-1765, Web: http://www.mbti.com/cpp4.htm.

The following pages contain some practical considerations you may want to carefully weigh before making a final decision.

An Associate Degree Granting Institution May Be Right For You If...

■ *You are very good in math and/or science but cannot and will not spend three or four years doing a lot of reading, writing papers, and exercising continuous focus in courses that may not be directly related to what you want to do as a career*

■ *You are the type of person who will work hard for a year or two for those things that are visible, practical, and hands-on*

■ *You need to see concrete and short-term results of what you do; you want to have a more secure occupational future, but do not qualify and/or want to apply for financial aid or take out a loan; or you have no scholarship possibilities and have very little money*

■ *The curriculum you are most realistically suited for is only offered at an associate degree granting institution*

■ *Going to a four-year college would put you into significant debt, which you cannot afford to have at this time in your life*

■ *You really don't want to attend college but it is required by your current employer in order to advance or keep your position*

■ *Either because of illness (you or one or more family members) or some other personal problem, you need to stay close to home and work full-time while attending school*

■ *You are seeking an attractive option to the high cost of many four-year institutions*

■ *You want to acquire training which requires less than an associate degree at a highly reputable, accredited institution*

■ *You are applying for an apprenticeship program at a local company, and if accepted, it will require you to take classes at a local community college*

■ *You want to obtain both an associate and bachelor's degree, and the four-year college you plan to transfer to does not award associate degrees*

■ *You are very weak academically, primarily because you didn't apply yourself in high school; however, now that you have worked several years on a job which pays low wages and offers no benefits, you are strongly motivated to find something better*

AN ASSOCIATE DEGREE GRANTING INSTITUTION MAY NOT BE RIGHT FOR YOU IF...

- *For personal reasons, you need to "go away," in order to leave a family or other situation which, if you remained, would be harmful to your academic, emotional, and/or physical health*

- *You have a strong desire to leave home, live on campus, and experience what you consider a 24 hours-a-day, seven-day a week comprehensive college experience*

- *The major that you are interested in is only offered in a four-year institution, and very few, if any, courses at the two-year technical/vocational college closest to you would transfer or apply*

- *Your values and personality configuration (self-assessment) is more suitable to a typical four-year military academy*

- *You have a scholarship to a four-year institution and, everything else appearing to be equal, you believe it would save you and your parents a large amount of money*

- *There are no associate degree granting institutions close to where you live, or the closet one to you is not accredited, or has a poor reputation*

- *Your father or mother works at a nearby four-year institution, and you could realize a significant savings on tuition each semester (a benefit for offspring of university and college loyees); in addition, the college offers your major*

The aforementioned are only a few of the many possible influencing situations a person might have to consider. It is more than likely that a combination of these situations, rather than just one, will eventually help you make a decision. I truly believe that many two- and four-year institution students become discouraged and eventually drop or flunk-out, due to, at least indirectly, the consequences of having selected the wrong curriculum or institution.

Putting all of this together might sound like an overwhelming task, but it doesn't have to be done alone. Most community colleges will be able to offer you help or provide references of professionals qualified to give you assistance with career direction. Ultimately, though, the choice is up to you.

Chapter III

ACCREDITATION

■ Mary attended a small community college in Washington State
for approximately one year. During this time, it was necessary
for her to work two part-time jobs in order to pay car, rent, and
other miscellaneous expenses. Although Mary's hometown is
thousands of miles away in Georgia, she was motivated to attend
this college after reading an attractive advertisement she received
in the mail. The ad claimed that new enrollees could earn an
associate degree in a popular health field in less than two years.
Unfortunately, Mary developed an unexpected illness after being
in the program for 12 months, causing her to withdraw from
classes and return to her hometown to live with her parents.
Shortly after returning, Mary's health began to improve to the
point where she decided to enroll at a nearby community college.
Mary was shocked to find out during the process of enrollment
that the community college she had previously attended was not
accredited. Consequently, none of her credits would be accepted.
Understandably, Mary was extremely discouraged and somewhat
bitter as she faced the reality of "starting all over again!"

■ Raphael had just completed an associate degree program at an
electronics institute located in a community roughly 500 miles
from where he grew up. He was very excited because he had read
(and been told by a number of friends) there was a shortage of
workers in the electronics field. Raphael's grades had been consistently good and he had graduated near the top of his class. He
did have one concern, though, which seemed to nag at him the
entire time he was in the program. This concern was how he
always seemed to know more than his instructors and their frequent replacements. Upon graduation, he applied for a number of
jobs at some of the area's most prestigious firms, only to be

repeatedly rejected. Eventually, Raphael was hired, but at a less desirable company, and at a significantly lower salary/benefit package than what he had hoped for. Being disappointed and puzzled as to why he had not been hired by the more desirable firms, Raphael contacted a few and inquired as to why he had not been selected. To his surprise, he discovered the electronics institute he had attended had a long-standing reputation in the local community of graduating students of poor quality, hiring non-certified instructors, and not being accredited. Unfortunately, he did not know much about nor had he become involved in the local community. Furthermore, he had not even researched or took the time to visit the school prior to his enrollment.

THE SCENARIOS ABOVE, OR SITUATIONS SIMILAR TO THEM, OCCUR FAR TOO OFTEN FOR TOO MANY UNPREPARED STUDENTS. They frequently neglect the important task of researching to determine, prior to their enrollment, whether a college is properly accredited. It is simply incomplete to conduct a thorough and accurate self-assessment, consider and apply all appropriate significant influencing factors that apply, and then neglect to check on the credentials of the institution you decide to attend.

What is ACCREDITATION?

Accreditation is the official stamp of approval given by a committee of evaluators (usually a non-governmental agency affiliated with a national association) to an educational or training institution or program which demonstrates that a minimum standard of quality or service has been met (e.g., has adequate number of faculty with advanced degrees; adequate equipment; appropriate course offerings). Lack of accreditation sometimes, although not always, can result in a two-year college having a less than favorable public image and possible loss of potential students. In short, accreditation is a systematic way a college elects to, periodically and continuously, evaluate itself in order to assure students, employees, and the community of the quality of services being provided.

Accreditation is voluntary and usually consist of two types—institutional and special programs. *Institutional Accreditation* is concerned more with the adequate human, financial, and physical resources, educational purposes, effectiveness, and integrity of the institution. *Special Program Accreditation* focuses on specialized technical or professional programs within an institution (such as nursing, automotive technology, electronics, dental hygiene, and occupational therapy). Normally, accredited special programs will need to meet the minimum quality standards of other recognized agencies. Areas evaluated usually include program course content; conditions; equipment used; length and experiences students will be exposed to, and so on. A brief summary of the five criteria used by the North Central Association Commission on Institutions of Higher Education (NCA-CIHE) to evaluate and grant accreditation to higher education institutions (including two-year colleges) appear below.

Criterion 1
The institution has clear and publicly stated purposes consistent with its mission and appropriate to an institution of higher education.

Criterion 2
The institution has effectively organized the human, financial, and physical resources necessary to accomplish its purposes.

Criterion 3
The institution is accomplishing its educational goals and other purposes.

Criterion 4
The institution can continue to accomplish its purposes and strengthen its educational effectiveness.

Criterion 5
The institution practices integrity in its practices and relationships.

Advantages (of attending an accredited college)

1. Usually gives you a sense of confidence that you are being trained and educated well

2. If you attend a reputable and accredited college, the credits are more likely to transfer

3. In addition, employers will be more likely to hire you if you come from a college known for its high quality of education/training.

4. Will give you piece of mind that you are receiving quality training for the career you are interested in

Disadvantages (of attending an unaccredited college)

1. You probably will not be able to transfer credits

2. You may have trouble finding the type of job you want due to the poor reputation of the college you attended

3. You will possibly waste money and time

4. You might feel resentment toward the college and embarrassment that you did not research its accreditation before you enrolled

5. If the institution that you attended was not accredited, you may have received a poor education and thus might not be able to perform the trade or service you were "prepared" for (This is a generalization. Not all non-accredited colleges produce poor quality; some do quite well...on the other hand, some accredited colleges still produce questionable quality.

A sampling of the better known accreditation agencies along with some helpful addresses have been listed below.

Accredits degree-granting colleges and universities in the following states and U.S. territories: Delaware, Maryland, New Jersey, New York, Pennsylvania, District of Columbia, Puerto Rico, U.S. Virgin Islands.

■ **Middle Atlantic Association of Schools and Colleges**
   3624 Market Street
   Philadelphia, PA 19104
   Tel: 215-662-5603

Accredits degree-granting colleges and universities in the following states: Connecticut, Maine, Massachusetts, New Hampshire, Rhode Island, Vermont.

■ **New England Association of Schools and Colleges**
209 Burlington Road
Bedford, MA 01730-1433
Tel: 781-271-0022
Web: http://www.neasc.org/

Accredits degree-granting colleges and universities in the following states: Alabama, Florida, Georgia, Kentucky, Louisiana, Mississippi, North Carolina, South Carolina, Tennessee, Texas, Virginia.

■ **Southern Association of Colleges and Schools**
1866 Southern Lane
Decatur, GA 30033-4097
Tel: 800-248-7701
Web: http://www.sacscoc.org/

Accredits degree-granting colleges and universities in the following states and U.S. territories: California and Hawaii, and the territories of Guam; American Samoa; Commonwealth of the Northern Marianas Islands.

■ **Western Association of Schools and Colleges**
Accrediting Commission for Community and Junior Colleges
3402 Mendocino Avenue
Santa Rosa, CA 95403
Tel: 707-569-9177
Web: http://www.wascweb.org/

Accredits degree-granting colleges and universities in the Navajo Nation and the following states: Arkansas, Arizona; Colorado; Iowa; Illinois; Indiana; Kansas; Michigan; Minnesota; Missouri; North Dakota; Nebraska; Ohio; Oklahoma; New Mexico; South Dakota; Wisconsin; West Virginia; Wyoming.

■ **North Central Association of Colleges and Schools**
30 North LaSalle Street, Suite 2400
Chicago, IL 60602
Tel: 800-621-7440
Web: http://www.ncacihe.org

Accredits degree-granting colleges and universities in the following states: Alaska, Idaho, Montana, Nevada, Oregon, Pennsylvania, Utah, Virginia, and Washington.

■ **Northwest Association of Schools and Colleges**
1910 University Drive
Boise, ID 83725-1060
Tel: 208-334-3210
Web: http://www2.idbsu.edu/nasc/

You can check to see if the two-year college of your choice is accredited by contacting the appropriate regional accreditation agency listed in the last few pages. Accreditation can and does have tremendous impact as it relates to helping you acquire a desirable career; determine what credits will transfer; gauge the amount of money and time you will spend; and meet your life goals.

Top 10 Community College Associate Degrees

1. Liberal/general studies & humanities

2. Health professions & related sciences

3. Business management & administrative services

4. Engineering-related technologies

5. Protective services

6. Mechanics and repairers

7. Education

8. Visual and performing arts

9. Multi/interdisciplinary studies

10. Computer and information services

Source: National Center for Education Statistics, IPEDS data files (data for 1996-97 school year)

Adult Day Care Coordinators

School Subjects: Family and Consumer Science, Psychology, Sociology
Personal Skills: Helping/teaching, Leadership/management
Work Environment: Primarily indoors, Primarily one location
Salary Range: $18,000 to $31,000 to $45,000
Certification or Licensing: Required for certain positions
Outlook: Much faster than the average

The Job

Adult day care coordinators direct adult day care centers. They oversee various staff members who provide care, such as nurses, physical therapists, social workers, cooks, and several aides. Coordinators are responsible for staff hiring, training, and scheduling.

Coordinators schedule daily and weekly activities for the clients and oversee meal planning and preparation. They work closely with client family members to make sure that each individual is receiving care that best fits his or her needs.

Adult day care coordinators may have other duties, such as developing and adhering to a budget for the center. In centers licensed or certified by the state, coordinators may ensure that their centers remain in compliance with the regulations and have all necessary documentation. They may also be responsible for general bookkeeping, bill payment, and office management.

Professional and Personal Requirements

No certification or licensing is required to become an adult day care coordinator. In some cases, however, the agency that a coordinator works for may be licensed or certified by the state health department. Any adult day care center that receives payment from Medicare or from other government agencies must be certified by the state department of health. In these cases, licensing requirements may include requirements for coordinators and other staff members. The trend is toward stricter standards.

Coordinators need compassion and an affinity for the elderly and disabled, as well as patience and the desire to help others.

Starting Out

Candidates should contact programs in their areas. Checking the local yellow pages under "Nursing Homes," "Residential Care Facilities," "Aging Services," or "Senior Citizens Services" should provide a list of leads. Prospective coordinators should also watch for job openings listed in area newspapers.

Another means of finding job leads is to become affiliated with a professional association, such as the American Geriatrics Society, the American Association of Homes and Services for the Aging, the Gerontological Society of America, or the National Council on Aging. Job seekers who have received associate degrees should also check with the career placement offices at their schools.

Earnings

According to the Association for Gerontology in Higher Education, beginning annual salaries range from $18,000 to $31,000 for persons with a bachelor's degree and little experience. Generally, coordinators who do not have a bachelor's degree can expect to earn somewhat less than this. Experienced coordinators with a bachelor's degree employed in large, well-funded centers may earn from $20,000 to $45,000 annually.

In addition to salary, some coordinators are also offered a benefits package, which typically includes health insurance, paid vacation and sick days, and a retirement plan.

Employment Outlook

The career outlook for adult day care coordinators, as for all human services workers, is expected to be excellent through the year 2006. According to the U.S. Department of Labor, the number of human services workers is projected to double between the years 1992 and 2006, due in large part to the aging population, and adult day care is expected to be one of the fastest-growing human service areas.

According to the National Adult Day Services Association, there were as few as 15 adult day care centers in existence in the 1970s; today, there are more than 3,000. This growth should continue as Americans become increasingly aware of the diverse needs of the elderly and the various service options available to them. Adult day care is expected to be used more frequently as a cost-efficient and preferable alternative to nursing homes.

For More Information

The following organizations offer information on aging, services for the elderly, and careers in gerontology.

- **American Geriatrics Society**
  770 Lexington Avenue, Suite 300
  New York, NY 10021
  Tel: 212-308-1414
  Web: http://www.americangeriatrics.org

- **Association for Gerontology in Higher Education**
  1030 15th Street, NW, Suite 240
  Washington, DC 20005-1503
  Tel: 202-289-9806
  Web: http://www.aghe.org

- **Gerontological Society of America**
  1030 15th Street, NW, Suite 250
  Washington, DC 20005-1503
  Tel: 202-842-1275
  Web: http://www.geron.org

- **National Adult Day Services Association**
  National Council on Aging
  409 Third Street, SW, Suite 200
  Washington, DC 20024
  Tel: 202-479-6682
  Web: http://www.ncoa.org/nadsa

Aerobics Instructors

School Subjects: Health, Physical education, Theater/Dance
Personal Skills: Helping/teaching, Leadership/management
Work Environment: Primarily indoors, Primarily one location
Salary Range: $15,000 to $30,000 to $50,000+
Certification or Licensing: Required for certain positions
Outlook: Faster than the average

The Job

Three general levels of aerobics classes are recognized today: low-impact, moderate, and high-intensity. A typical class starts with warm-up exercises—slow stretching movements to aid flexibility—followed by 35 minutes of nonstop activity to raise the heart rate and ending with a cool-down period of stretching and slower movements.

Aerobics instructors choose exercises to work different muscles and music to motivate students during each phase of the program. Instructors demonstrate each step of the routine until the class can follow along. They then incorporate the routines into a sequence that is set to music. Many aerobics instructors also lead toning and shaping classes. Although the emphasis is not on aerobic activity but on working particular areas of the body, the instructor begins the class with a brief aerobic period followed by stretching exercises that warm and loosen the muscles and thereby prevent pulled or strained muscles or other injuries.

Professional and Personal Requirements

Most serious aerobics instructors become certified. Certification is not required in most states, but it is a requirement of many employers. Certifying agencies include the following: Aerobics and Fitness Association of America (AFAA), American College of Sports Medicine

(ACSM), American Council on Exercise (ACE), and National Academy of Sports Medicine (NASM). Aerobics instructors also must be certified in CPR (cardiopulmonary resuscitation).

Aerobics instructors and fitness trainers are expected to be physically fit, but not specimens of human perfection. For example, members of an aerobics class geared to overweight people might feel more comfortable with a heavier instructor; a class geared towards the elderly may benefit from an older instructor.

Starting Out

Students should use their schools' placement offices for information on available jobs. Often the facility that provided their training or internship will hire them or can provide information on job openings in the area. Students can also find jobs through classified ads and by applying to health and fitness clubs, YMCAs, YWCAs, Jewish Community Centers, local schools and colleges, park and recreation districts, church groups and organizations, and any other likely sponsor of aerobics classes or fitness facilities.

Earnings

Aerobics instructors are usually paid by the class and generally start out at about $10 per class. Experienced aerobics instructors can earn up to $50 or $60 per class. Health club directors usually earn about $30,000 per year.

Employment Outlook

Because of the country's ever-expanding interest in health and fitness, the U.S. Department of Labor predicts that the job outlook for aerobics instructors should remain strong through the year 2006. As the population ages, more opportunities will arise to work with the elderly in retirement homes. America's much talked-about "weight problem" will also have an effect on the popularity and demand for aerobics instructors. As communities, schools, and individuals attempt to shed the pounds, the need for fitness instructors and motivators will continue.

For More Information

For free information materials about sports medicine topics, contact:

- **American College of Sports Medicine**
  PO Box 1440
  Indianapolis, IN 46206-1440
  Tel: 317-637-9200
  Web: http://www.acsm.org/

For information about personal fitness trainer certification, contact:

- **National Athletic Trainers' Association**
  2952 Stemmons Freeway, Suite 200
  Dallas, TX 75247-6916
  Tel: 214-637-6282, ext. 108
  Email: suzannec@nata.org
  Web: http://www.nata.org

For more information about careers in fitness, contact:

- **American Council on Exercise**
  5820 Oberlin Drive, Suite 102
  San Diego, CA 92121-3787
  Tel: 619-535-8227
  Web: http://www.acefitness.org

Aeronautical and Aerospace Technicians

School Subjects: Mathematics, Physics, Technical/Shop
Personal Skills: Mechanical/manipulative, Technical/scientific
Work Environment: Primarily indoors, Primarily one location
Salary Range: $20,000 to $32,000 to $50,000
Certification or Licensing: Required for certain positions
Outlook: About as fast as the average

The Job

Aeronautical and aerospace technicians design, construct, test, operate, and maintain the basic structures of aircraft and spacecraft, as well as propulsion and control systems. They work with scientists and engineers. Many aeronautical and aerospace technicians assist engineers in preparing equipment drawings, diagrams, blueprints, and scale models. They collect information, make computations, and perform laboratory tests. Their work may involve aerodynamics, structural design, flight-test evaluation, or propulsion problems. Other technicians serve as manufacturers' field service technicians, write technical materials, and estimate the cost of materials and labor required to manufacture the product.

Professional and Personal Requirements

Only a few aerospace technician positions require licensing or certification. Certification is usually required of those working with nuclear-powered engines or testing radioactive sources, for those working on aircraft in some test programs, and in some safety-related positions.

Aeronautical and aerospace technicians must be able to learn basic engineering skills. They should be proficient in mathematics and the physical sciences and able to visualize size, form, and function. They should have an understanding of manufacturing and statistics and be able to work with computers.

Starting Out

The best way for students to obtain an aeronautical or aerospace technician's job is through their college or university's job placement office. Many manufacturers maintain recruiting relationships with schools in their area. Jobs may also be obtained through state employment offices, newspaper advertisements, applications for government employment, and industry work-study programs offered by many aircraft companies.

Earnings

Starting salaries for most aerospace technicians generally ranged from $20,000 to $23,000 per year in 1996, according to the Bureau of Labor Statistics. Beyond that, salaries varied depending on specialty. For aircraft mechanics, including engine specialists, the average salary was $35,000 in 1996, with starting pay at about $23,000 and pay for more experienced mechanics at over $44,000. Engineering technicians averaged $32,700 per year. Beginning aeronautical drafters earned about $20,500 per year in 1995, with more experienced drafters earning $31,250. For all specialties, those with years of experience and continuing education earned $40,000 to $50,000 per year.

Benefits depend on employers, but usually include paid vacations and holidays, sick pay, health insurance, and a retirement plan.

Employment Outlook

After a difficult period in the 1980s and 1990s, the aerospace industry seems to be rebounding slowly as it expands into new markets. With growth predicted in many areas, and losses in others, the U.S. Department of Labor predicts that the overall job growth for aerospace technicians should be about as fast as the average through the year 2006.

The Aerospace Industries Association of America (AIAA) predicts aerospace companies will be looking for qualified technicians in fields such as laser optics; mission operations; spacecraft integrations; hazardous materials procedures; production planning; materials testing; computer-aided design; and robotic operations and programming. AIAA predicts that production workers, including some technicians, will fill the majority of new positions in the near future.

For More Information

For information on accredited training programs, contact:

- **Accreditation Board for Engineering and Technology, Inc.**
  111 Market Place, Suite 1050
  Baltimore, MD 21202
  Tel: 410-347-7700
  Web: http://www.abet.org

For general information about the aviation industry, contact:

- **Aerospace Industries Association of America**
  1250 Eye Street, NW
  Washington, DC 20005
  Tel: 202-371-8400
  Web: http://www.aia-aerospace.org/

For information on careers and scholarships, contact:

- **Aerospace Education Foundation**
  1501 Lee Highway
  Arlington, VA 22209-1198
  Tel: 703-247-5839
  Web: http://www.aef.org

For information on career pamphlets, books, lists of schools, and scholarships, contact:

- **General Aviation Manufacturers Association**
  1400 K Street, NW, Suite 801
  Washington, DC 20005
  Tel: 202-393-1500
  Web: http://www.generalaviation.org

Agricultural Equipment Technicians

School Subjects: Mathematics, Technical/Shop
Personal Skills: Mechanical/manipulative, Technical/scientific
Work Environment: Indoors and outdoors, Primarily multiple locations
Salary Range: $20,588 to $32,032 to $40,000
Certification or Licensing: None available
Outlook: About as fast as the average

The Job

Agricultural equipment technicians work with modern farm machinery. They assemble, adjust, operate, maintain, modify, test, and even help design it. This machinery includes automatic animal feeding systems; milking machine systems; and tilling, planting, harvesting, irrigating, drying, and handling equipment. Agricultural equipment technicians work on farms or for agricultural machinery manufacturers or dealerships. They often supervise skilled mechanics and other workers who keep machines and systems operating at maximum efficiency.

Agricultural equipment technicians work in a wide variety of jobs both on and off the farm. In general, most agricultural equipment technicians find employment in one of three areas: equipment manufacturing, equipment sales and service, and on-farm equipment management.

Specific jobs in this field include equipment manufacturing technicians, agricultural engineering technicians, and agricultural equipment test technicians.

Professional and Personal Requirements

There is no certification or licensing available in this field.

The work of the agricultural equipment technician is similar to that of an engineer. Agricultural equipment technicians must have a knowledge of physical science and engineering principles and enough mathematical background to work with these principles. They must have a working knowledge of farm crops, machinery, and all agri-cultural-related products. Technicians should be detail-oriented, and have people skills, as they work closely with professionals, other technicians, and farmers.

Starting Out

It is still possible to enter this career by starting as an inexperi-enced worker in a machinery manufacturer's plant or on a farm and learning machine technician skills on the job. However, this approach is becoming increasingly difficult due to the complexity of modern machinery.

The demand for qualified agricultural equipment technicians currently exceeds the supply. Operators and managers of large, well-equipped farms and farm equipment companies in need of employees keep in touch with colleges offering agricultural equipment programs. In general, any student who does well in a training program can expect employment immediately upon graduation.

Earnings

Agricultural technicians working for the government may be able to enter a position at GS-5 (government wage scale), which was $20,588 in 1999. Those with more education and specialized experience may be able to enter at GS-8, $28,242. The 1998 Bureau of Labor Statistics tables list the weekly median wage of engineering and related technologists and technicians as $616. The most experi-enced agricultural technicians may earn as much as $40,000 per year. Those working on farms often receive room and board as a supple-ment to their annual salary.

In addition to their salaries, most technicians receive fringe ben-efits such as health and retirement packages, paid vacations, and other benefits similar to those received by engineering technicians.

Employment Outlook

The demand for agricultural equipment technicians is strong and expected to increase. Agricultural equipment businesses now demand more expertise than ever before. A variety of complex specialized machines and mechanical devices are steadily being produced and modified to help farmers improve the quality and productivity of their labor. These machines require trained technical workers to design, produce, test, sell, and service them. Trained workers also are needed to instruct the final owners in their proper repair, operation, and maintenance.

In addition, the agricultural industry is adopting advanced computer and electronic technology. Precision farming will also require specialized training as agricultural equipment becomes hooked up to satellite systems.

For More Information

To read equipment sales statistics, agricultural reports, and other news of interest to agricultural equipment technicians, visit the EMI Web site:

- **Equipment Manufacturers Institute (EMI)**
  10 South Riverside Plaza
  Chicago, IL 60606
  Tel: 312-321-1470
  Web: http://www.emi.org

At the FEMA Web site, you can learn about their publications and read industry news:

- **Farm Equipment Manufacturers Association (FEMA)**
  1000 Executive Parkway, Suite 100
  St. Louis, MO 63141
  Tel: 314-878-2304
  Web: http://www.farmequip.org

Aircraft Mechanics

School Subjects: Computer science, Technical/Shop
Personal Skills: Mechanical/manipulative, Technical/scientific
Work Environment: Indoors and outdoors, One location with some travel
Salary Range: $23,000 to $35,000 to $52,000+
Certification or Licensing: Required for certain positions
Outlook: About as fast as the average

The Job

Aircraft mechanics adjust and repair electrical wiring systems and aircraft accessories and instruments; inspect, service, and repair pneumatic and hydraulic systems; and handle various servicing tasks, such as flushing crankcases, cleaning screens, greasing moving parts, and checking brakes.

Specific positions in this field include line maintenance mechanics, overhaul mechanics, airframe mechanics, aircraft powerplant mechanics, and avionics technicians.

Mechanics may work on only one type of aircraft or on many different types, such as jets, propeller-driven planes, and helicopters. For greater efficiency, some specialize in one section, such as the electrical system, of a particular type of aircraft. Among the specialists, there are airplane electricians; pneumatic testers and pressure sealer-and-testers; aircraft body repairers and bonded structures repairers, such as burnishers and bumpers; air conditioning mechanics; aircraft rigging and controls mechanics; plumbing and hydraulics mechanics; and experimental-aircraft testing mechanics.

Professional and Personal Requirements

Federal Aviation Administration (FAA) certification is necessary for certain types of aircraft mechanics and is usually required to advance beyond entry-level positions. FAA certification is granted only to aircraft mechanics with previous work experience: a minimum of 18 months for an airframe or power plant certificate and at least 30 months working with both engines and airframes for a combination certificate.

Aircraft mechanics must be able to work with precision and meet rigid standards. Their physical condition is also important. They need physical strength for lifting heavy parts and tools and agility for reaching and climbing.

Starting Out

High school graduates who wish to become aircraft mechanics may enter this field by enrolling in an FAA-approved trade school. These schools generally have placement services available for their graduates.

Another method is to make direct application to the employment offices of companies providing air transportation and services or the local offices of the state employment service, although airlines prefer to employ people who have already completed training. The field may also be entered through enlistment in the armed forces.

Earnings

Aircraft mechanics earned an average of $35,000 per year in 1996, according to the *Occupational Outlook Handbook*. The middle 50 percent earned between $29,000 and $44,000. The bottom 10 percent earned less than $23,000. Experienced mechanics can earn more than $52,000 per year. Flight engineers average around $38,000 per year, while avionics technicians average around $27,000 per year.

Mechanics who belong to a union generally earn more than those who don't, and their contracts usually include health insurance and often life insurance and retirement plans as well. An attractive fringe benefit for airline mechanics and their immediate families is free or reduced fares on their own and many other airlines.

Employment Outlook

The U.S. Department of Labor predicts that employment of aircraft mechanics is likely to increase about as fast as the average though the year 2006. The demand for air travel and the numbers of aircraft created are expected to increase due to population growth and rising incomes.

Job prospects will vary according to the type of employer. Less competition for jobs is likely to be found at smaller commuter and regional airlines, FAA repair stations, and in general aviation. These employers pay lower wages and fewer applicants compete for their positions, while higher paying airline positions, which also include travel benefits, are more in demand among qualified applicants.

For More Information

For information on careers in aircraft mechanics, contact:

■ **Aeronautical Repair Station Association**
121 North Henry Street
Alexandria, VA 22314
Tel: 703-739-9543
Web: http://www.arsa.org/

For career books and information about high school student membership, national forums, and job fairs, contact:

■ **Aviation Information Resources, Inc.**
1001 Riverdale Court
Atlanta, GA 30337
Tel: 800-AIR-APPS
Web: http://www.airapps.com

For information on scholarships and membership, contact:

■ **Professional Aviation Maintenance Association**
636 Eye Street, NW, Suite 300
Washington, DC 20001-3736
Tel: 202-216-9220
Web: http://www.pama.org/

Automobile Collision Repairers

School Subjects: Computer science, Technical/Shop
Personal Skills: Following instructions, Mechanical/manipulative
Work Environment: Primarily indoors, Primarily one location
Salary Range: $20,000 to $24,076 to $39,000
Certification or Licensing: Recommended
Outlook: About as fast as the average

The Job

Automobile collision repairers repair, replace, and repaint damaged body parts of automobiles, buses, and light trucks. They use hand tools and power tools to straighten bent frames and body sections, replace badly damaged parts, smooth out minor dents and creases, remove rust, fill small holes or dents, and repaint surfaces damaged by accident or wear. A range of skills is needed to repair body damage to vehicles. Some body repairers specialize in certain areas, such as painting, welding, glass replacement or air bag replacement. All collision repairers should know how to perform common repairs, such as realigning vehicle frames, smoothing dents, and removing and replacing panels.

A major part of the automobile collision repairer's job is assessing the damage and providing an estimate on the cost to repair it.

Professional and Personal Requirements

Certification, which is offered by the National Automotive Technicians Education Foundation, is voluntary, but it assures that students meet the standards employers expect.

Automobile collision repairers are responsible for providing their own hand tools at an investment of approximately $6,000 to $20,000 or more, depending upon the technician's specialty. Skill in handling both hand and power tools is essential for any repairer.

Starting Out

The best way to start out in the field of automobile collision repair is, first, to attend one of the many postsecondary training programs available throughout the country and, second, to obtain certification. Trade and technical schools usually provide job placement assistance for their graduates.

Although postsecondary training programs are considered the best way to enter the field, some repairers learn the trade on the job as apprentices. Their training consists of working for several years under the guidance of experienced repairers. Those who do learn their skills on the job will inevitably require some formal training if they wish to advance and stay in step with the changing industry.

Earnings

Most collision repairers earned annual salaries in the $20,000 to $30,000 range, with a median salary of $24,076 in 1996, according to the Bureau of Labor Statistics. Managers of repair shops earn between $34,000 and $39,000. In many repair shops and dealerships, collision repairers can earn more by working on commission.

Most repair technicians can expect health insurance and a paid vacation from employers. Other benefits may include dental and eye care, life and disability insurance, and a pension plan.

Employment Outlook

The collision repair industry is facing a labor shortage of skilled, entry-level workers in many areas of the country. Demand for collision repair services is expected to remain consistent, at the least, and will likely rise as the population increases and there are more vehicles on the road. The increased demand translates into a healthy job market for those willing to undergo the training needed.

Changing technology also plays a role in the industry's outlook. New automobile designs have body parts made of steel alloys, aluminum, and plastics—materials that are more time consuming to work with. In many cases, such materials are more prone to damage, increasing the need for body repairs.

For More Information

These industry associations can offer information on careers, training and technology:

- **Automotive Service Industry Association**
  25 Northwest Point Boulevard, #425
  Elk Grove Village, IL 60007
  Tel: 847-228-1310
  Web: http://www.aftmkt.com/asia

- **Inter-Industry Conference on Auto Collision Repair**
  3701 Algonquin Road, Suite 400
  Rolling Meadows, IL 60008
  Web: http://www.i-car.com

- **National Institute for Automotive Service Excellence**
  13505 Dulles Technology Drive, Suite 2
  Herndon, VA 20171-3421
  Tel: 703-713-3800
  Web: http://www.asecert.org

For more information on training and accreditation, contact:

- **National Automotive Technicians Education Foundation**
  13505 Dulles Technology Drive
  Herndon, VA 20171-3421
  Tel: 703-713-0100
  Web: http://www.natef.org

Automobile Service Technicians

School Subjects: Business, Technical/Shop
Personal Skills: Mechanical/manipulative, Technical/scientific
Work Environment: Primarily indoors, Primarily one location
Salary Range: $13,000 to $24,856 to $44,200+
Certification or Licensing: Recommended
Outlook: About as fast as the average

The Job

Automobile service technicians maintain and repair cars, vans, small trucks, and other vehicles. Using both hand tools and specialized diagnostic test equipment, they pinpoint problems and make the necessary repairs or adjustments. They also perform a number of routine maintenance procedures, such as oil changes, tire rotation, and battery replacement. Technicians interact with customers to explain repair procedures and discuss maintenance needs.

Generally, there are two types of automobile service technicians: generalists and specialists. Generalists work under a broad umbrella of repair and service duties, and their work is fairly routine and basic. Specialists concentrate in one or two areas and learn to master them for many different car makes and models.

Professional and Personal Requirements

Certification, which is currently voluntary but preferred, is available from the National Automotive Technicians Education Foundation in several different specific areas of focus.

Automobile service technicians must be patient and thorough in their work; a shoddy repair job may put the driver's life at risk. They must have excellent troubleshooting skills and be able to logically deduce the cause of system malfunctions.

Starting Out

The best way to start out in this field is to attend one of the many post-secondary training programs available throughout the country and obtain certification. Trade and technical schools usually provide job placement assistance for their graduates.

A decreasing number of technicians learn the trade on the job as apprentices. Their training consists of working for several years under the guidance of experienced mechanics. These technicians will inevitably require some formal training if they wish to advance and stay in step with the changing industry.

Earnings

According to the Bureau of Labor Statistics, the lowest paid automobile service technicians earn about $13,000 per year. The median salary for automobile service technicians was $24,856 in 1996. Technicians with experience and certification earn on average about $30,000 per year. Since most technicians work on an hourly basis and frequently work overtime, their salaries can vary significantly. Managers of service and repair shops earn between $34,000 and $39,000. The top 10 percent in the field earned over $44,200 a year in 1996. In many repair shops and dealerships, technicians can earn higher incomes by working on commission.

Most technicians can expect paid vacation, a pension plan, health insurance, and possibly dental, life, and disability insurance.

Employment Outlook

With an estimated 189 million vehicles in operation today, automobile service technicians should feel confident that a good percentage will require servicing and repair. Skilled and highly trained technicians will be in particular demand. Less skilled workers will face tough competition.

A concern for the industry is the automobile industry's trend toward developing the "maintenance-free" car. Manufacturers are producing high-end cars that require no servicing for their first 100,000 miles. In addition, many new cars are equipped with on-board diagnostics (OBD) that detect both wear and failure for many of the car's components, eliminating the need for technicians to perform extensive diagnostic tests.

Most new jobs for technicians will be at independent service dealers, specialty shops, and franchised new car dealers.

For More Information

For more information on the automotive service industry, contact the following organizations:

- **Automotive Service Industry Association**
  25 Northwest Point Boulevard, #425
  Elk Grove Village, IL 60007
  Tel: 847-228-1310
  Web: http://www.afmtkt.com/asia

- **Automotive Service Association**
  PO Box 929
  Bedford, TX 76095-0929
  Tel: 817-283-6205
  Web: http://www.asashop.org

- **National Institute for Automotive Service Excellence**
  13505 Dulles Technology Drive, Suite 2
  Herndon, VA 20171-3421
  Tel: 703-713-3800
  Web: http://www.asecert.org

For information on certification, contact:

- **National Automotive Technicians Education Foundation**
  13505 Dulles Technology Drive
  Herndon, VA 20171-3421
  Tel: 703-713-0100
  Web: http://www.natef.org

Biomedical Equipment Technicians

School Subjects: Biology, Technical/Shop
Personal Skills: Mechanical/manipulative, Technical/scientific
Work Environment: Primarily indoors, Primarily one location
Salary Range: $17,000 to $25,500 to $46,000
Certification or Licensing: Recommended
Outlook: About as fast as the average

The Job

Biomedical equipment technicians handle the complex medical equipment and instruments found in hospitals, clinics, and research facilities. This equipment is used for medical therapy and diagnosis and includes heart-lung machines, artificial-kidney machines, patient monitors, chemical analyzers, and other electrical, electronic, mechanical, or pneumatic devices.

The technician's main duties are to inspect, maintain, repair, and install this equipment. They disassemble equipment to locate malfunctioning components; repair or replace defective parts; and reassemble the equipment, adjusting and calibrating it to ensure that it operates according to manufacturers' specifications. Other duties of biomedical equipment technicians include modifying equipment according to the directions of medical or supervisory personnel, arranging with equipment manufacturers for necessary equipment repair, and safety-testing equipment to ensure that patients, equipment operators, and other staff members are safe from electrical or mechanical hazards. Biomedical equipment technicians work with hand tools, power tools, measuring devices, and manufacturers' manuals.

Professional and Personal Requirements

Certification is offered by the Association for the Advancement of Medical Instrumentation. This program provides an opportunity

68

to demonstrate overall knowledge of the field, and many employers prefer to hire technicians with this certificate.

Biomedical equipment technicians need mechanical ability and should enjoy working with tools. Because this job demands quick decision-making and prompt repairs, technicians should work well under pressure. They must have good communications skills and be extremely precise and accurate in their work.

Starting Out

Most schools offering programs in biomedical equipment technology work closely with local hospitals and industries, and school placement officers are usually informed about openings when they become available. In some cases, recruiters may visit a school periodically to conduct interviews. Also, many schools place students in part-time hospital jobs to help them gain practical experience. Students are often able to return to these hospitals for full-time employment after graduation.

Another effective method of finding employment is to write directly to hospitals, research institutes, or biomedical equipment manufacturers. Other good sources of leads for job openings include state employment offices and newspaper want ads.

Earnings

In general, entry-level salaries range from $17,000 to $20,500 for technicians working in hospitals and from $20,000 to $23,800 for technicians working for manufacturers or governmental agencies. Experienced technicians earn approximately $19,000 to $25,500 working in a hospital and approximately $25,000 to $36,000 working for a manufacturer. Senior technicians earn approximately $25,000 to $35,000 in hospitals and approximately $35,000 to $46,000 working for a manufacturer. Experienced and senior technicians working for government agencies earn from $25,000 to $35,500 a year. Biomedical equipment technicians are eligible for typical fringe benefits, including medical insurance, paid sick and vacation time, and retirement plans.

Employment Outlook

Because of the increasing use of medical electronic devices and other sophisticated biomedical equipment, the outlook for skilled and trained biomedical equipment technicians is good and should continue through the year 2006.

In hospitals the need for more biomedical equipment technicians exists not only because of the increasing use of biomedical equipment but also because hospital administrators realize that these technicians can help hold down costs. For the many biomedical equipment technicians who work for companies that build, sell, lease, or service biomedical equipment, job opportunities also should continue to grow.

For More Information

For general information on the career of biomedical equipment technician, contact:

- **Society of Biomedical Equipment Technicians**
  3330 Washington Boulevard, Suite 400
  Arlington, VA 22201-4890
  Tel: 800-332-2264

For information on certification, contact:

- **Association for the Advancement of Medical Instrumentation**
  3330 Washington Boulevard, Suite. 400
  Arlington, VA 22201-4598
  Web: http://www.aami.org/

Broadcast Engineers

School Subjects: Computer science, Mathematics
Personal Skills: Mechanical/manipulative, Technical/scientific
Work Environment: Indoors and outdoors, Primarily multiple locations
Salary Range: $12,000 to $30,251 to $53,655
Certification or Licensing: Recommended
Outlook: About as fast as the average

The Job

Broadcast engineers, also referred to as *broadcast technicians,* or *broadcast operators,* operate and maintain the electronic equipment used to record and transmit the audio for radio signals and the audio and visual images for television signals to the public. Broadcast engineers are responsible for the transmission of radio and television programming, including live and recorded broadcasts. Broadcasts are usually transmitted directly from the station; however, engineers are capable of transmitting signals on location from specially designed, mobile equipment. The specific tasks of the broadcast engineer depend on the size of the television or radio station. In small stations, engineers have a wide variety of responsibilities. Larger stations are able to hire a greater number of engineers and specifically delegate responsibilities to each engineer. In both small and large stations, however, engineers are responsible for the operation, installation, repair, and thorough knowledge of the equipment.

Professional and Personal Requirements

Certification from the Society of Broadcast Engineers is desirable, and certified engineers consistently earn higher salaries than uncertified engineers.

Broadcast engineers must have both an aptitude for working with highly technical electronic and computer equipment and great attention to detail to be successful in the field. They should enjoy both the technical and artistic aspects of working in the radio or television industry. They should also be able to communicate with a wide range of people with various levels of technical expertise.

Starting Out

In many towns and cities there are public-access cable television stations and public radio stations where high school students interested in broadcasting and broadcast technology can obtain an internship. An entry-level technician should be flexible about job location; most begin their careers at small stations and with experience may advance to larger-market stations.

Earnings

Larger stations usually pay higher wages than smaller stations, and television stations tend to pay more than radio stations. According to the 1996 National Association of Broadcasters survey, the salary for a radio station technician averaged $30,251 a year (this includes those with considerable experience; the lowest reported salary was $12,000). The salary for chief engineers averaged $46,602 a year. In television stations in 1995, an engineer's salary averaged $32,533 a year and a chief engineer's $53,655 a year.

Employment Outlook

Broadcasting technology is rapidly advancing in both radio and television broadcasting. According to the U.S. Department of Labor, the overall employment of broadcast technicians is expected to grow about as fast as the average through the year 2006. Growth in the number of stations and number of programming hours should increase demand.

However, due to increased technology, some positions may be eliminated due to laborsaving technical advances like computer programming and remote control transmitters. Many new jobs will result from the need to replace existing engineers who often leave the industry for other jobs in electronics.

For More Information

For information on its summer internship program, contact:

■ **The Association of Local Television Stations**
1320 19th Street, NW, Suite 300
Washington, DC 20036
Tel: 202-887-1970
Web: http://www.altv.com

Contact BEA for scholarship information and a list of schools offering degrees in broadcasting. Visit their Web site to sign up for a free monthly email newsletter that contains useful information about broadcast education and the broadcasting industry:

■ **Broadcast Education Association**
1771 N Street, NW
Washington, DC 20036-2891
Tel: 202-429-5354
Web: http://www.beaweb.org

For broadcast education and scholarship information, contact:

■ **National Association of Broadcasters**
1771 N Street, NW
Washington, DC 20036-2891
Tel: 202-429-5300
Web: http://www.nab.org

For job listings, college programs, and union information, contact:

■ **National Association of Broadcast Employees and Technicians**
501 3rd Street, NW, 8th Floor
Washington, DC 20001
Tel: 202-434-1254
Web: http://union.nabetcwa.org/nabet/

For information on membership, scholarships, and certification, contact:

■ **Society of Broadcast Engineers**
8445 Keystone Crossing, Suite 140
Indianapolis, IN 46240-2454
Tel: 317-253-1640
Email: kmoran@sbe.org
Web: http://www.sbe.org

Cardiovascular Technologists

School Subjects: Biology, Health
Personal Skills: Communication/ideas, Technical/scientific
Work Environment: Primarily indoors, Primarily one location
Salary Range: $15,200 to $20,200 to $33,600
Certification or Licensing: Voluntary
Outlook: Faster than the average

The Job

Cardiovascular technologists assist physicians in diagnosing and treating heart and blood vessel ailments. Depending on their specialty, they operate electrocardiograph machines, perform Holter monitor and stress testing, and assist in cardiac catheterization procedures and ultrasound testing. These tasks help the physicians diagnose heart disease and monitor progress during treatment.

Specific jobs within this field include EKG technologists; Holter monitoring and stress test technologists; cardiology technologists; vascular technologists; echocardiographers; and cardiac monitor technicians.

Cardiovascular technologists perform one or more of a wide range of procedures in cardiovascular medicine, including invasive, noninvasive, peripheral vascular, or echocardiography (ultrasound) procedures. In most facilities they use equipment that is among the most advanced in the medical field; drug therapies also may be used as part of the diagnostic imaging procedures or in addition to them. Technologists' services may be required when the patient's condition is first being explored, before surgery, during surgery (cardiology technologists primarily), or during rehabilitation of the patient. Some of the work is performed on an outpatient basis.

Professional and Personal Requirements

Right now, certification or licensing for cardiovascular technologists is voluntary, but the move to state licensing is expected in the near future. Many credentialing bodies for cardiovascular and pulmonary positions exist.

Technicians must be able to put patients at ease about the procedure they are to undergo. They should be pleasant, patient, and alert, and their manner should be calm, reassuring, and confident.

Starting Out

Because most cardiovascular technologists receive their initial training on their first job, great care should be taken in finding this first employer. High school vocational counselors may be able to tell you which hospitals have good reputations for EKG training programs. Applying directly to hospitals is a common way of entering the field.

For students who graduate from one- to two-year training programs, finding a first job should be easier. First, employers are always eager to hire people who are already trained. Second, these graduates can be less concerned about the training programs offered by their employers. Third, they should find that their teachers and guidance counselors can be excellent sources of information about job possibilities in the area.

Earnings

Beginning cardiovascular technologists earned starting salaries of approximately $20,200 a year in 1997, according to a Hay Group Survey. The average salary for cardiovascular technologists was about $33,600 in 1996. Average pay for all EKG technicians, who generally have a less extensive academic background than technologists, was $20,200 per year.

Cardiovascular technologists working in hospitals receive the same fringe benefits as other hospital workers, including medical insurance, paid vacations, and sick leave.

Employment Outlook

Employment of cardiology technologists, vascular technologists, and Holter monitoring technologists is expected to grow faster than the average through the year 2006, according to the U.S. Department of Labor. Growth will be due primarily to the increasing numbers of older people.

Openings for EKG technicians, on the other hand, are expected to decline through the year 2006; although there is an increased demand for EKGs, the equipment and procedures are currently much more efficient and easier to use than they were in the past.

For More Information

For general information about a career in cardiovascular technology, contact:

■ **Alliance of Cardiovascular Professionals**
910 Charles Street
Fredericksburg,VA 22401
Tel: 540-370-0102
Web: http://www.acp-online.org/

For information on credentials, contact:

■ **Cardiovascular Credentialing International**
4456 Corporation Lane, Suite 110
Virginia Beach, VA 23462
Tel: 800-326-0268

Carpenters

School Subjects: Mathematics, Technical/Shop
Personal Skills: Following instructions, Mechanical/manipulative
Work Environment: Indoors and outdoors, Primarily multiple locations
Salary Range: $11,960 to $30,800 to $50,440+
Certification or Licensing: Voluntary
Outlook: Much faster than the average

The Job

Carpenters cut, shape, level, and fasten together pieces of wood and other construction materials, such as wallboard, plywood, and insulation. Many carpenters work on constructing, remodeling, or repairing houses and other kinds of buildings. Other carpenters work at construction sites where roads, bridges, docks, boats, mining tunnels, and wooden vats are built. They may specialize in building the rough framing of a structure, and thus be considered a *rough carpenter,* or they may specialize in the finishing details of a structure, such as the trim around doors and windows, and be a *finish carpenter.*

Professional and Personal Requirements

The United Brotherhood of Carpenters and Joiners of America (UBC), the national union for the industry, offers certification courses in a variety of specialty skills. These courses teach the ins and outs of advanced skills—like scaffold construction—that help to ensure worker safety, while at the same time giving workers ways to enhance their abilities and so qualify for better jobs. Some job sites require all workers to undergo training in safety techniques and guidelines specified by the Occupational Safety and Health Administration. Workers who have not passed these courses are considered ineligible for jobs at these sites.

Carpenters need to have manual dexterity, good hand-eye coordination, and a good sense of balance. They need to be in good physical condition, as the work involves a great deal of physical activity. Stamina is much more important than physical strength. On the job, carpenters may have to climb, stoop, kneel, crouch, and reach as well as deal with the challenges of weather.

Starting Out

Information about available apprenticeships can be obtained by contacting the local office of the state employment service, area contractors that hire carpenters, or the local offices of the UBC, which cooperates in sponsoring apprenticeship programs. Helper jobs that can be filled by beginners without special training in carpentry may be advertised in newspaper classified ads, or with the state employment service. Aspiring carpenters also might consider contacting potential employers directly.

Earnings

According to the Bureau of Labor Statistics, the majority of carpenters who did not own their own businesses made between $20,780 and $40,039 in 1997, the most recent year for which statistics are available. Fifteen percent of the survey group made between $11,960 and $20,780. Seven percent had earnings above $50,440. The median annual wage was $30,800.

Starting pay for apprentices is approximately 40 percent of the experienced worker's median, or roughly $12,320. The wage is increased periodically so that by the fourth year of training apprentice pay is 80 percent of the journeyman carpenter's rate.

Fringe benefits, such as health insurance, pension funds, and paid vacations, are available to most workers in this field and vary with local union contracts. In general, benefits are more likely to be offered on jobs staffed by union workers.

Employment Outlook

The outlook for carpenters—and indeed the vast majority of construction trades—over the next 10 to 15 years is much faster than the average for other occupational fields, according to both the UBC and the Home Builders Institute. The industry is undergoing a severe shortage of qualified, well-trained, and experienced workers. Well-trained carpenters and other construction experts will be in high demand for the next several years.

For More Information

Visit the HBI Web site for information on apprenticeship and training services. The HBI also is a good resource for general information about trends in the industry.

■ **Home Builders Institute (HBI)**
1090 Vermont Avenue, NW, Suite 600
Washington, DC 20005
Tel: 202-371-0600 or 800-795-7955
Web: http://www.hbi.org

The NAHB offers quite a bit of information about careers in the construction trades. It also has student chapters for its younger members.

■ **National Association of Home Builders (NAHB)**
1201 15th Street, NW
Washington, DC 20005-2800
Tel: 202-822-0200
Web: http://www.nahb.com

The AGCA is a leading trade organization in the construction industry that offers some activities for young people interested in construction careers. It also sponsors student chapters at the college level.

■ **Associated General Contractors of America (AGCA)**
1957 E Street, NW
Washington, DC 20006
Web: http://www.agc.org

For information on certification and apprenticeships, contact:

■ **The United Brotherhood of Carpenters and Joiners of America**
101 Constitution Avenue, NW
Washington, DC 20001

Cartoonists and Animators

School Subjects: Art, Computer science
Personal Skills: Artistic, Communication/ideas
Work Environment: Primarily indoors, Primarily one location
Salary Range: $10,400 to $44,000 to $338,000+
Certification or Licensing: None available
Outlook: Faster than the average

The Job

Cartoonists draw illustrations for newspapers, books, magazines, greeting cards, movies, television shows, civic organizations, and private businesses. Cartoons most often are associated with newspaper comics or with children's television, but they are also used to highlight and interpret information in publications as well as in advertising. Sometimes cartoon ideas are original; at other times they are directly related to the news of the day, the content of a magazine article, or a new product. After cartoonists come up with ideas, they discuss them with their employers, who include editors, producers, and creative directors at advertising agencies. Next, cartoonists sketch drawings and submit these for approval. Employers may suggest changes, which the cartoonists then make.

Animators, or *motion cartoonists,* also draw individual pictures, but they must draw many more for a moving cartoon. Each picture varies only slightly from the ones before and after it in a series. When these drawings are photographed in sequence to make a film and then the film is projected at high speed, the cartoon images appear to be moving. (One can achieve a similar effect by drawing stick figures on the pages of a notepad and then flipping through the pages very quickly.) Animators today also work a great deal with computers.

Specific jobs within this field include animation checkers; story sketchers; comic strip artists; comic book artists; cel painters; prop designers; layout artists; editorial cartoonists; portraitists; and story-book artists.

Professional and Personal Requirements

There is no certification or licensing available in this field.

Cartoonists and animators must be creative. They must have a good sense of humor and an observant eye to detect people's distinguishing characteristics and society's interesting attributes or incongruities. Cartoonists and animators should also be flexible and able to take suggestions and rejections gracefully.

Starting Out

A few places, such as the Walt Disney studios, offer apprenticeships. To enter these programs, applicants must have attended an accredited art school for two or three years.

Formal entry-level positions for cartoonists and animators are rare, but there are several ways for artists to enter the cartooning field. Most cartoonists and animators begin by working piecemeal, selling cartoons to small publications, such as community newspapers, that buy freelance cartoons. Others assemble a portfolio of their best work and apply to publishers or the art departments of advertising agencies.

Earnings

Most cartoonists and animators average from $200 to $1,500 a week, although syndicated cartoonists on commission can earn much more. Cel painters, as listed in a salary survey conducted by *Animation World,* start at about $750 a week; animation checkers, $930 a week; story sketchers, $1,500 weekly. According to *U.S. News & World Report,* animators, depending on their experience, can earn from $800 to $1,800 a week. Top animators can command weekly fees of about $6,500 or more. Comic strip artists are usually paid according to the number of publications that carry their strip. Self-employed artists do not receive fringe benefits such as paid vacations, sick leave, health insurance, or pension benefits.

Employment Outlook

Opportunities in this field are expected to grow faster than average through the year 2006, according to the U.S. Department of Labor. *U.S. News & World Report* recently included the career of animator in its list of 20 Hot Job Tracks.

Cartoons are not just for children anymore. Much of the animation today is geared for an adult audience. Interactive games, animated films, network and cable television, and the Internet are among the many employment sources for talented cartoonists and animators.

For More Information

For education and career information, contact:

■ **National Cartoonists Society**
Columbus Circle Station
PO Box 20267
New York, NY 10023
Tel: 212-627-1550
Web: http://www.reuben.org

For an art school directory, a scholarship guide, or general information, contact:

■ **National Art Education Association**
1916 Association Drive
Reston, VA 20191-1590
Tel: 703-860-8000
Web: http://www.naea-reston.org

For scholarship information for qualified students in art school, have your instructor contact:

■ **Society of Illustrators**
128 East 63rd Street
New York, NY 10021-7303
Email: society@societyillustrators.org
Web: http://www.societyillustrators.org

Caterers

School Subjects: Business, Family and consumer science
Personal Skills: Artistic, Helping/teaching
Work Environment: Primarily indoors, Primarily multiple locations
Salary Range: $15,000 to $30,000 to $75,000+
Certification or Licensing: Required by certain states
Outlook: Faster than the average

The Job

Caterers plan, coordinate, and supervise food service at parties and other social functions. Working with their clients, they purchase appropriate supplies, plan menus, supervise food preparation, direct serving of food and refreshments, and ensure the overall smooth functioning of the event. The caterer must be in frequent contact with all parties involved in the affair, making sure, for example, that the food is delivered on time, the flowers are fresh, and the entertainment shows up and performs as promised.

As entrepreneurs, they are also responsible for budgeting, bookkeeping, and other administrative tasks.

Caterers need to be flexible in their approach to food preparation, that is, able to prepare food both on- and off-premises, as required by logistical considerations and the wishes of the client. The caterer and the client work together to establish a budget, develop a menu, and determine the desired atmosphere. Clients always want their affairs to be extra special, and the caterer's ability to meet or exceed the clients' expectations will ensure customer satisfaction and future business.

Professional and Personal Requirements

Most states require caterers to be licensed. As a measure of professional status, many caterers become certified through the National Association of Catering Executives.

A professional caterer should be well-versed in proper food preparation techniques and be able to manage a food service operation. Many people develop these skills through on-the-job training, beginning as a caterer's helper or a restaurant worker.

Starting Out

Some caterers enter the profession as a matter of chance after helping a friend or relative prepare a large banquet or volunteering to coordinate a group function. Most caterers, however, begin their careers after graduating from college with a degree in a program such as home economics or finishing a culinary training program at a vocational school or community college.

Qualified people may begin work as a manager for a large catering firm, hotel, country club, or banquet service. An individual will most likely start a catering business only with extensive experience and sufficient finances to purchase equipment and other start-up costs.

Earnings

Full-time caterers can earn between $15,000 and $60,000 per year, depending on skill, reputation, and experience. An extremely successful caterer can easily earn more than $75,000 annually. A part-time caterer may earn $7,000 to $15,000 per year, subject to the same variables as the full-time caterer. Because most caterers are self-employed, paid vacations and other benefits are usually not part of the wage structure.

A caterer who works as a manager for a company cafeteria or other industrial client may earn between $18,000 and $35,000 per year, with vacation, health insurance, and other benefits usually included.

Employment Outlook

Because of the strong food service industry in the United States, employment opportunities in catering should continue to grow through 2006. Opportunities will be good for firms that handle weddings, bar and bat mitzvahs, business functions, and other events.

Competition is keen as many hotels and restaurants branch out to offer catering services. Despite the competition and fluctuating economic conditions, highly skilled and motivated caterers should be in demand throughout the country, especially in and around large metropolitan areas.

For More Information

General career information is available from:

■ **International Food Service Executives Association**
1100 South State Road #7, Suite 103
Margate, FL 33068
Tel: 954-977-0767
Web: http://www.ifsea.org

This trade association offers information on certification and other career information.

■ **National Association of Catering Executives**
60 Revere Drive, Suite 500
Northbrook, IL 60062
Tel: 847-480-9080
Web: http://www.nacefoundation.org

For extensive information about the industry, and information about publications and training, visit the LCA Web site, or contact:

■ **Leading Caterers of America (LCA)**
2167 South Bayshore Drive
Miami, FL 33133
Tel: 800-743-6660
Web: http://www.leadingcaterers.com

Chemical Technicians

School Subjects: Chemistry, Mathematics
Personal Skills: Following instructions, Technical/scientific
Work Environment: Primarily indoors, Primarily one location
Salary Range: $21,000 to $31,000 to $42,000+
Certification or Licensing: None available
Outlook: About as fast as the average

The Job

Most *chemical technicians* who work in the chemical industry are involved in the development, testing, and manufacturing of plastics, paints, detergents, synthetic fibers, industrial chemicals, and pharmaceuticals. Others work in the petroleum, aerospace, metals, electronics, automotive, and construction industries. Some chemical technicians work in universities and government laboratories.

Chemical technicians may work in any of the fields of chemistry, including analytical, inorganic, organic, physical, or biochemistry. Within these subfields, chemical technicians work in research and development, design and production, or quality control. Technicians often determine the chemical composition, concentration, stability, and level of purity on a wide range of materials. They assist chemists with experiments, perform analyses, and report test results.

Other subspecialties in this field include fuel technicians, pilot plant operators, and applied research technicians.

Professional and Personal Requirements

There is no certification or licensing available in this field.

Chemical technicians must be capable of precise, detailed work. They also need excellent organizational and communications skills, mechanical aptitude, and the ability to follow directions closely. In addition, technicians should have good eyesight, color perception, and eye-hand coordination.

Starting Out

Graduates of chemical technology programs often find jobs during the last term of their two-year programs. A number of programs offer co-op/internship programs, which are highly regarded by employers. Some companies work with local community colleges and technical schools to maintain a supply of trained chemical technicians. Recruiters regularly visit most colleges where chemical technology programs are offered.

More and more companies are using contract workers to perform technicians' jobs, and this is another way to enter the field. There are local agencies that place technicians with companies for special projects or temporary assignments that last anywhere from a month to a year or more. Many of these contract workers are later hired on a full-time basis.

Earnings

The median salary in 1997 for all chemical technicians and technologists was $31,000 according to the Bureau of Labor Statistics. Ten percent earned less than $21,000 and 10 percent earned over $42,000. Salaries are highest in private industry and lowest in colleges and universities. The greatest variation in salary is from region to region. Starting salaries are highest in the Middle Atlantic region and lowest in the East South Central region.

Benefits depend on the employer, but they usually include paid vacations and holidays, insurance, and tuition reimbursement plans.

Employment Outlook

Employment levels for chemical technicians are expected to grow about as fast as the average of all occupations through 2006, according to the U.S. Department of Labor. Employment prospects are particularly bright in specialty chemicals and parts of the industry that sell directly to consumers, such as pharmaceutical firms. Technologies expected to grow include biotechnology, environment, catalysis, materials science, communication and computer technology, and energy. Business areas with the most potential for growth include environmental services and "earth-friendly" products, analytical development and services, custom or niche products and services, and quality control.

For More Information

A list of chemical technology programs and single copies of other career materials are free. A directory of opportunities listing internships, summer jobs, and co-op programs is available for a fee. Contact:

■ **American Chemical Society**
Career Education
1155 16th Street, NW
Washington, DC 20036
Tel: 202-452-2113
Web: http://www.acs.org

Civil Engineering Technicians

School Subjects: Mathematics, Physics
Personal Skills: Following instructions, Technical/scientific
Work Environment: Indoors and outdoors, Primarily multiple locations
Salary Range: $17,700 to $32,700 to $54,800
Certification or Licensing: Recommended
Outlook: About as fast as the average

The Job

Civil engineering technicians help civil engineers design, plan, and build public as well as private works to meet the community's needs. They are employed in a wide range of projects, such as highways, drainage systems, water and sewage facilities, railroads, subways, airports, dams, bridges, and tunnels. State highway departments use their services to collect data, to design and draw plans, and to supervise the construction and maintenance of roadways. Railroad and airport facilities require similar services. Cities and counties need to have transportation systems, drainage systems, and water and sewage facilities planned, built, and maintained with the help of civil engineering technicians.

Some technicians specialize in certain types of construction projects, such as highway technicians, rail and waterway technicians, and assistant city engineers. Other technicians specialize in certain phases of the construction process, such as construction materials testing technicians, photogrammetric technicians, and party chiefs. There are other specialized positions for civil engineering technicians, such as research engineering technicians, sales engineering technicians, and water resources technicians.

Professional and Personal Requirements

To advance in professional standing, civil engineering technicians need to become certified. The National Institute for Certification in

Engineering Technologies and the American Society of Certified Engineering Technicians offer voluntary certification program for engineering technicians.

Civil engineering projects are often complex and long term, requiring a variety of specialized skills. Civil engineering technicians need the ability to think and plan ahead, as well as patience and great attention to detail.

Starting Out

Most schools maintain placement offices, which many prospective employers contact when they have job openings. The placement offices, in turn, help the student or graduate prepare a resume of relevant school and work experiences, and usually arrange personal interviews with prospective employers. Many schools also have cooperative work-study programs with particular companies and government agencies. With such a program, the company or government agency often becomes the new technician's place of full-time employment after graduation.

Earnings

According to the *Occupational Outlook Handbook,* civil engineering technicians usually begin their first jobs at a salary range of $17,700 to $22,800 a year, with the higher paying jobs going to those with advanced education. Most experienced technicians earn an average of $32,700. Some senior technicians with management duties earn as much as $54,800 a year or more.

Paid vacations, pension plans, and insurance are among the typical benefits civil engineering technicians receive. Many companies pay a bonus if a job is completed ahead of schedule or for less than the estimated cost.

Employment Outlook

The outlook for civil engineering technicians is generally favorable. As in most industries, those with certification and the most education will have the best opportunities. Construction is, however, one of the industries most likely to feel the effects of economic recessions, so civil engineering technicians must be prepared for slow-downs in business.

For More Information

For information on scholarships, contact:

- **American Congress on Surveying and Mapping**
  5410 Grosvenor Lane
  Bethesda, MD 20814-2122
  Tel: 301-493-0200
  Web: http://www.survmap.org/

This organization offers the brochure Engineering: Your Future *online:*

- **American Society for Engineering Education**
  11 Dupont Circle, Suite 200
  Washington, DC 20036
  Tel: 202-331-3500
  Web: http://www.asee.org

For information on educational programs and society membership, contact:

- **American Society of Civil Engineers**
  1801 Alexander Bell Drive
  Reston, VA 20191-4400
  Tel: 703-295-6000
  Web: http://www.asce.org

For information on certification, contact the following organizations:

- **National Institute for Certification in Engineering Technologies**
  1420 King Street
  Alexandria, VA 22314-2794
  Web: http://www.nicet.org/
- **American Society of Certified Engineering Technicians**
  PO Box 1348
  Flowery Branch, GA 30542
  Tel: 404-967-9173
  Web: http://www.nmsu.edu/~ascet/ASCET

Computer and Office Machine Service Technicians

School Subjects: Computer science, Technical/Shop
Personal Skills: Mechanical/manipulative, Technical/scientific
Work Environment: Primarily indoors, Primarily multiple locations
Salary Range: $15,000 to $30,264 to $40,000
Certification or Licensing: Required
Outlook: Much faster than the average

The Job

Computer and office machine service technicians install, calibrate, maintain, troubleshoot, and repair equipment such as computers and their peripherals, office equipment, and specialized electronic equipment used in many factories, hospitals, airplanes, and numerous other businesses. A large part of their work is the maintenance, diagnostic, and repair of computer equipment. They may also be responsible for training employees on the equipment. Other duties may include presenting company products and services to potential clients and bidding for maintenance contracts. Many computer and office machine service technicians are required to carry pagers and be prepared to respond to unexpected situations 24 hours a day. Traveling is also a common requirement of employees in this field, sometimes amounting to 80 percent of a technician's work hours.

Professional and Personal Requirements

Most employers require certification, which is considered by many as a measure of industry knowledge. A variety of certification programs are available from the International Society of Certified Electronics Technicians, and the Institute for Certification of Computing Professionals, among other organizations.

Computer and office machine service technicians need a strong technical background, manual dexterity, and an aptitude for learning about new technologies. They should be task oriented, organized, and personable, and able to convey technical terms in writing and orally.

Starting Out

Many times, school placements and counseling centers are privy to job openings that are filled before being advertised in the newspaper. There are also other avenues to take when searching for a job in this industry. Many jobs are advertised in the Jobs section of your local newspaper. Look under "Computers" or "Electronics." Also, graduates should inquire directly with the personnel department of companies that appeal to them and fill out an application. Trade association Web sites are good sources of job leads; many will post employment opportunities as well as allow applicants to post their resumes.

Earnings

According to the *Occupational Outlook Handbook,* in 1996, service technicians specializing in communications and industrial electronic equipment earned an average annual salary of $31,304; computer equipment service technicians earned an average of $30,264 a year. Technicians with extensive work experience and certification earn more.

Standard work benefits include health and life insurance, paid vacation and sick time, and often a retirement plan. Most technicians are given travel stipends; some receive company cars.

Employment Outlook

According to the *Occupational Outlook Handbook,* employment opportunities for service technicians working with computer and office equipment are expected to grow much faster than the average through the year 2006—about 37 percent faster than the average for all other occupations. Demand for service technicians specializing in commercial and industrial electronic equipment is expected to grow about 12 percent. As corporations, the government, hospitals, and universities worldwide continue their reliance on computers to help manage their daily business, demand for qualified and skilled technicians will increase.

Modern office equipment is better designed and can run longer without needing maintenance or repair. As a result, demand for service technicians specializing in office equipment repair is expected to grow only as fast as the average.

For More Information

For certification information, contact:

- **Institute for Certification of Computing Professionals**
  2200 East Devon Avenue, Suite 247
  Des Plaines, IL 60018-4503
  Tel: 800-843-8422
  Web: http://www.iccp.org

For information on certification, contact:

- **International Society of Certified Electronics Technicians**
  2708 West Berry Street
  Fort Worth, TX 76109-2356
  Tel: 817-921-9101
  Web: http://www.iscet.org

Contact ACM for information on internships, student membership, and the ACM magazine, Crossroads. ACM also offers a student Web site at http://www.acm.org/membership/student/.

- **Association for Computing Machinery (ACM)**
  1515 Broadway, 17th Floor
  New York, NY 10036-5701
  Tel: 212-869-7440
  Email: SIGS@acm.org
  Web: http://www.acm.org

For certification, career, and placement information, contact:

- **Electronics Technicians Association and Satellite Dealers Association**
  602 North Jackson
  Greencastle, IN 46135
  Tel: 765-653-4301
  Web: http://www.eta-sda.com

Computer Programmers

School Subjects: Computer science, Mathematics
Personal Skills: Communication/ideas, Technical/scientific
Work Environment: Primarily indoors, Primarily one location
Salary Range: $19,520 to $40,100 to $65,200+
Certification or Licensing: Voluntary
Outlook: Faster than the average

The Job

Computer programmers work in the field of electronic data processing. They write instructions that tell computers what to do in a computer language, or code, that the computer understands.

Broadly speaking, there are two types of computer programmers: *systems programmers* and *applications programmers*. Systems programmers maintain the instructions, called programs or software, that control the entire computer system, including both the central processing unit and the equipment with which it communicates, such as terminals, printers, and disk drives. Applications programmers write the software to handle specific jobs and may specialize as engineering and scientific programmers or as business programmers. Some of the latter specialists may be designated *chief business programmers,* who supervise the work of other business programmers.

Other specific positions in the field include programmer-analysts, information system programmers, process control programmers, and numerical control tool programmers.

Professional and Personal Requirements

Certification, which is voluntary, is offered by the Institute for Certification of Computing Professionals.

Personal qualifications such as a high degree of reasoning ability, patience, and persistence, as well as aptitude for mathematics, are important for computer programmers. Some employers whose work is highly technical require that programmers be qualified in the area in which the firm or agency operates.

Starting Out

Individuals with the necessary qualifications should apply directly to companies, agencies, or industries that have announced job openings through a school placement office, an employment agency, or the classified ads. Students in two- or four-year degree programs should work closely with their schools' placement offices.

If the market for programmers is particularly tight, new graduates may want to obtain an entry-level job with a large corporation or computer software firm, even if the job does not include programming. As jobs in the programming department open up, current employees in other departments are often the first to know, and are often favored over nonemployees during the interviewing process.

Earnings

According to the National Association of Colleges and Employers, the average 1997 starting salary for college graduates employed in the private sector was about $35,167. Salaries for experienced programmers averaged $40,100 a year; some earned more than $65,200. Programmers employed by the federal government were paid between $19,520 and $24,180, depending on their academic record.

Most programmers receive the customary paid vacation and sick leave and are included in such company benefits as group insurance and retirement benefit plans.

Employment Outlook

Employment opportunities for computer programmers should increase faster than the average through 2006, according to the U.S. Department of Labor. Job applicants with the best chances of employment will be college graduates with a knowledge of several programming languages, especially newer ones used for computer networking and database management. In addition, the best applicants will have some training or experience in an applied field, such as accounting, science, engineering, or management. Competition for jobs will be heavier among graduates of two-year data processing programs and among people with equivalent experience or with less training.

For More Information

For more information about careers in computer programming, contact:

■ **Association for Computing Machinery**
1515 Broadway, 17th Floor
New York, NY 10036
Tel: 212-869-7440
Email: ACMHELP@acm.org
Web: http://www.acm.org

For information on certification programs, contact:

■ **Institute for Certification of Computing Professionals**
2200 East Devon Avenue, Suite 247
Des Plaines, IL 60018
Tel: 800-843-8422
Email: 74040.3722@compuserve.com
Web: http://www.iccp.org

Computer Support Service Owners

School Subjects: Business, Computer science, Technical/Shop
Personal Skills: Helping/teaching, Technical/scientific
Work Environment: Primarily indoors, Primarily multiple locations
Salary Range: $20,000 to $60,000 to $150,000+
Certification or Licensing: Voluntary
Outlook: Much faster than the average

The Job

The owners of computer support services help businesses and individuals install and maintain computer hardware and software. They also teach the computer operators, either one on one or in group training sessions, how to use the new systems. They may advise in the purchase of hardware and software and prepare backup methods. Many computer consultants also offer their expertise in Web design and multimedia for uploading a Web page, preparing a presentation, and offering desktop publishing services. They also help to create computer databases. Some computer consultants are involved in issues of programming. Though some of their assistance is offered over the phone, much of their work is performed on-site.

In addition to the technical work, the owners of computer support services must handle all the details of running their businesses. They handle phone calls, bookkeeping, and client records. They must also research new technologies and keep up to date on advanced technical skills.

Professional and Personal Requirements

There are many different kinds of certifications available to people working in computer support and consulting. No one certification, however, serves all the varying needs of computer professionals. The Institute for Certification of Computer Professionals offers a Certified

Computer Professional exam. Around 50,000 computer professionals hold the certification, having passed an exam that tests knowledge of business information systems, data resource management, software engineering, and other subjects.

Computer support service owners should have good business and money management skills. Though computer skills are very important, computer support service owners can't be computer "geeks"—they need good people skills to maintain customer relations. Teaching skills are also important, as training people in how to use their systems is part of the job.

Starting Out

Before starting their own business, computer support workers should work for a large corporation to learn about human resources, compensation packages, and benefits. Computer knowledge isn't enough; they need to develop a good business sense to succeed on their own. It is recommended that aspiring computer support service owners decide on a niche, such as networking, or package customization, then promote those specific services.

Earnings

The estimated median annual earnings for computer consultants is $55,000 to $65,000. In the first few years of a business, a consultant will make about $40,000 or less, depending on location. Those working in large cities like New York and Los Angeles average more than those in the Midwest, the Southwest, and the Northwest. Some very experienced, business-minded consultants can make $150,000 a year or more.

Employment Outlook

The industry is expected to grow quickly as computer systems become more important to more businesses. Lower prices on computer hardware and software will inspire businesses to expand their systems and to invest in the services needed to keep them up and running. Computers will also become more sophisticated and will be able to perform more complex operations; consultants will be needed to help people understand these new, complicated computer programs. With companies relying more on complex computer systems, they'll be less likely to take risks in the installation of hardware and software. *Working at Home* magazine lists computer consulting as the best high-tech home business.

For More Information

To subscribe to a free electronic newsletter, and to check out an extensive list of related Web links, visit the ACSS Web page. You can also write to them to learn more about membership and their career training courses.

- **Association of Computer Support Specialists (ACSS)**
  218 Huntington Road
  Bridgeport, CT 06608
  Tel: 203-332-1524
  Web: http://www.acss.org

To learn about membership benefits of the ICCA, contact:

- **Independent Computer Consultants Association (ICCA)**
  11131 South Towne Square, Suite F
  St. Louis, MO 63123
  Tel: 800-774-4222
  Web: http://www.icca.org

For more information on certification, contact:

- **Institute for Certification of Computing Professionals**
  2200 East Devon Avenue, Suite 247
  Des Plaines, IL 60018
  Tel: 800-843-8422
  Email: 74040.3722@compuserve.com
  Web: http://www.iccp.org

Computer-Aided Design Drafters and Technicians

School Subjects: Computer science, Mathematics, Technical/Shop

Personal Skills: Mechanical/manipulative, Technical/scientific

Work Environment: Primarily indoors, Primarily one location

Salary Range: $17,316 to $33,410 to $49,504

Certification or Licensing: Voluntary

Outlook: About as fast as the average

The Job

Computer-aided design drafters and technicians, sometimes called *CAD technicians* or *CAD designers,* use computer-based systems to produce or revise technical illustrations needed in the design and development of machines, products, buildings, manufacturing processes, and other work. Using CAD machinery, they manipulate and create design concepts so that they are feasible to produce and use in the real world. The CAD workstation is equipped to allow technicians to perform calculations, develop simulations, and manipulate and modify the displayed material. Using typed commands at a keyboard, a stylus or light pen for touching the screen display, a mouse, joystick, or other electronic methods of interacting with the display, technicians can move, rotate, zoom in on any aspect of the drawing on the screen, and project three-dimensional images from two-dimensional sketches. Compared to traditional drafting and design techniques, CAD offers virtually unlimited freedom to explore alternatives, and in far less time.

CAD technicians work in any field where detailed drawings, diagrams, and layouts are important aspects of developing new product designs. Most CAD technicians specialize in a particular industry or on one part of a design.

Professional and Personal Requirements

Certification for CAD technicians is voluntary. Certification in drafting is available from the American Design and Drafting Association (ADDA).

CAD technicians and designers should be able to think logically, have good analytical skills, and be methodical, accurate, and detail-oriented in all their work. They should be able to work both independently and as part of a team.

Starting Out

Students in formal training programs often learn of jobs through their school's placement office. Graduates of a postsecondary programs can also conduct their own job search by contacting architects, building firms, manufacturers, high technology companies, and government agencies. State or private employment agencies may also be helpful, and classified ads in newspapers and professional journals may provide additional leads.

Earnings

According to the ADDA's 1996 salary survey, apprentice CAD drafters can expect to make an average of $17,316 per year. The most experienced CAD designers can expect an average of $49,504 per year, with a median salary of $33,410. Technicians with special skills, extensive experience, or added responsibilities may earn more.

Benefits usually include insurance, paid vacations and holidays, pension plans, and sometimes stock-purchase plans.

Employment Outlook

The U.S. Department of Labor predicts that the employment outlook for CAD technicians will be about as fast as average for all other occupations through 2006. Many companies in the near future will feel pressures to increase productivity in design and manufacturing activities, and CAD technology provides some of the best opportunities to improve that productivity. By some estimates, there will be as many as a million jobs available for technically trained personnel in the field of CAD/CAM technology in the next few years.

For More Information

For information about certification, student drafting contests, and job postings, contact:

- **American Design and Drafting Association**
  PO Box 11937
  Columbia, SC 29211
  Tel: 803-771-0008
  Email: national@adda.org
  Web: http://www.adda.org/

For information about the electrical field or to find the IEEE student branch nearest you, contact:

- **Institute of Electrical and Electronics Engineers (IEEE)**
  1828 L Street, NW, Suite 1202
  Washington, DC 20036-5104
  Tel: 202-785-0017
  Web: http://www.ieee.org/usab

For information about scholarships and grants as well as student membership, contact:

- **Society of Manufacturing Engineers**
  International Headquarters
  One SME Drive
  Dearborn, MI 48121
  Tel: 800-733-4763
  Web: http://www.sme.org/

Cooks, Chefs, and Bakers

School Subjects: Family and consumer science, Mathematics
Personal Skills: Artistic, Following instructions
Work Environment: Primarily indoors, Primarily one location
Salary Range: $13,520 to $38,000 to $50,000+
Certification or Licensing: Required by certain states
Outlook: About as fast as the average

The Job

Cooks, chefs, and bakers are primarily responsible for the preparation and cooking of foods. They order food from various suppliers and check it for quantity and quality when it arrives. They measure and mix ingredients and prepare foods for baking, roasting, broiling, and steaming. They may use blenders, mixers, grinders, slicers, or tenderizers to prepare the food and ovens, broilers, grills, roasters, or steam kettles to cook it. Cooks, chefs, and bakers rely on their judgment and experience to add seasonings; they constantly taste and smell food as they prepare it and must know when it is cooked and seasoned properly.

Specific jobs within this field include broiler cooks, prep cooks, cafeteria and mess cooks, pastry chefs, executive chefs, sous chefs, barbecue cooks, pizza bakers, and short order cooks.

Professional and Personal Requirements

To protect the public's health, chefs, cooks, and bakers are required by law in most states to possess a health certificate and to be examined by a physician periodically.

Immaculate personal cleanliness and good health are necessities in this trade. Applicants should possess physical stamina and a keen sense of taste and smell. Hand and finger agility, hand-eye coordination, and a good memory are helpful.

Starting Out

Apprenticeship programs are one method of entering the trade. In many cases, a cook begins as a kitchen helper or cook's helper and, through experience gained in on-the-job training, is able to move into the job of cook. Cooks are hired as chefs only after they have acquired a number of years of experience. Cooks who have been formally trained through public or private trade or vocational schools or in culinary institutes may be able to take advantage of school placement services.

Job opportunities may be located through employment bureaus, trade associations, unions, contacts with friends, newspaper want ads, or local offices of the state employment service. Another method is to apply directly to restaurants or hotels.

Earnings

As reported in the *Occupational Outlook Handbook,* the median salary for short-order cooks and bread and pastry bakers is about $6.50 an hour, or $13,520 a year. Fast food workers generally earn the minimum wage. Cooks and chefs in famous restaurants, of course, earn much more. The average, according to the National Restaurant Association, is about $38,000, although some renowned executive chefs are paid considerably more. Chefs and cooks usually receive free meals during working hours and are furnished with any necessary job uniforms.

Employment Outlook

In the late 1990s, approximately 3.4 million cooks, chefs, and bakers were employed in the United States. Most worked in hotels and restaurants, but many worked in schools, colleges, airports, and hospitals. Still others were employed by government agencies, factories, private clubs, and other organizations.

The employment of chefs, cooks, and bakers is expected to increase as fast as the average for all occupations through the year 2006, according to the U.S. Department of Labor. The demand will grow not only with the population, but with lifestyle changes as well. As people earn higher incomes and have more leisure time, they dine out more often and take more vacations. Working parents and their families will dine out frequently as a convenience.

For More Information

For information on careers in baking and cooking, contact these organizations:

- **American Culinary Federation, Inc.**
  10 San Bartola Drive
  St. Augustine, FL 32086
  Tel: 904-824-4468
  Web: http://www.acfchefs.org

- **American Institute of Baking**
  PO Box 3999
  Manhattan, KS 66502-3999
  Tel: 785-537-4758
  Web: http://www.aibonline.org

- **Culinary Institute of America**
  433 Albany Post Road
  Hyde Park, NY 12538-1499
  Tel: 800-285-4627 (CULINARY), 914-452-9600
  Web: http://www.ciachef.edu

- **Educational Foundation of the National Restaurant Association**
  250 South Wacker Drive, Suite 1400
  Chicago, IL 60606
  Tel: 312-715-1010
  Web: http://www.edfound.org

- **Educational Institute of the American Hotel and Motel Association**
  800 North Magnolia Avenue, Suite 1800
  Orlando, FL 32803
  Tel: 407-999-8100
  Email: info@ei-ahma.org
  Web: http://www.ei-ahma.org

Corrections Officers

The Job

Corrections officers guard people who have been arrested and are awaiting trial or who have been tried, convicted, and sentenced to serve time in a penal institution. They search prisoners and their cells for weapons, drugs, and other contraband; inspect windows, doors, locks, and gates for signs of tampering; observe the conduct and behavior of inmates to prevent disturbances or escapes; and make verbal or written reports to superior officers. Corrections officers assign work to inmates and supervise their activities. They guard prisoners who are being transported between jails, courthouses, mental institutions, or other destinations, and supervise prisoners receiving visitors. When necessary, these workers use weapons or force to maintain discipline and order. There are approximately 320,000 corrections officers employed in the United States.

Professional and Personal Requirements

A few states require passing a written examination. Corrections officers who work for the federal government and most state governments are covered by civil service systems or merit boards and may be required to pass a competitive exam for employment. Many states require random or comprehensive drug testing of their officers, either during hiring procedures or while employed at the facility.

Corrections officers need good health and physical strength, and many states have set minimum height, vision, and hearing standards. Sound judgment and the ability to think and act quickly are important qualities for this occupation. A candidate must have a clean police record. The ability to speak foreign languages is often a plus when applying for corrections jobs.

Starting Out

Aspiring corrections officers should contact federal or state civil service commissions, state departments of correction, or local correctional facilities and ask for information about entrance requirements, training, and job opportunities. Private contractors and other companies are also a growing source of employment opportunities. Many officers enter this field from social work areas and parole and probation positions.

Earnings

According to a 1996 national survey in *Correction Compendium,* beginning corrections officers received an average of $20,200. The average salary for all corrections officers was $33,540, but salaries range widely from one state to another.

Beginning corrections officers at the federal level are generally rated GS-6, with a salary range in 1999 of $22,948 to $29,833 depending on the location of service. Sergeants and other supervisors generally start at $41,000. The average for all federal corrections officers and sergeants is $30,000 per year, and supervisors average more than $50,000.

Benefits may include health, disability, and life insurance; uniforms or a cash allowance to buy their own uniforms; and sometimes meals and housing. Some corrections officers also receive retirement and pension plans, and retirement is often possible after 20 years of service.

Employment Outlook

Employment in this field is expected to increase much faster than the average for all jobs, according to the U.S. Department of Labor.

The prison population has more than doubled in the last 10 years, and this growth is expected to be sustained for the near future. It is estimated that another 120,000 jobs will be created through the year 2006. The ongoing war on illegal drugs, new tough-on-crime legislation, and increasing mandatory sentencing policies will create a need for more prison beds and more corrections officers. A greater number of officers will also be required as a result of the expansion or new construction of facilities.

For More Information

For information on training, conferences, and membership, contact:

- **American Correctional Association**
  4380 Forbes Boulevard
  Lanham, MD 20706-4322
  Tel: 800-222-5646
  Web: http://www.corrections.com/aca

The Corrections Connection Network bills itself as the "Largest Online Resource for News & Information in Corrections"

- **The Corrections Connection Network**
  Web: http://www.corrections.com/

For information on training, contact:

- **American Probation and Parole Association**
  c/o Council of State Governments
  PO Box 11910
  Lexington, KY 40578-1910
  Tel: 606-244-8203
  Web: http://www.appa-net.org

Contact the FBP for information on entrance requirements, training, and career opportunities for corrections officers at the federal level.

- **Federal Bureau of Prisons (FBP)**
  National Recruitment Office
  320 First Street, NW, Room 460
  Washington, DC 20534
  Email: cmahan@bop.gov
  Web: http://www.bop.gov

Court Reporters

School Subjects: English, Foreign language, Government
Personal Skills: Communication/ideas
Work Environment: Primarily indoors, Primarily multiple locations
Salary Range: $30,000 to $43,000 to $60,000+
Certification or Licensing: Required by certain states
Outlook: Faster than the average

The Job

Court reporters record every word at hearings, trials, depositions, and other legal proceedings by using a stenotype machine to take shorthand notes. In the courtroom, court reporters use symbols or shorthand forms of complete words to record what is said as quickly as it is spoken on a stenotype machine that looks like a miniature typewriter. The stenotype machine has 24 keys on its keyboard. Each key prints a single symbol, each of which represents a different sound, word, or phrase. Court reporters must record testimony word for word and quickly. Accuracy is imperative, as the reporter's record becomes the official transcript for the entire proceeding; if a court reporter misses a word or phrase, he or she must interrupt the proceedings to have the words repeated.

After the trial or hearing, the court reporter uses a CAT program to translate the stenotype notes into English. This rough translation is then edited, printed, and bound.

Professional and Personal Requirements

The National Court Reporters Association (NCRA) offers several levels of certification for its members. Also, 42 states grant licenses in either shorthand reporting or court reporting, although not all of these states require a license to work as a court reporter.

Court reporters need to be able to work well under pressure and meet deadlines with accuracy and attention to detail. They must be familiar with a wide range of medical and legal terms and must be assertive enough to ask for clarification when necessary.

Starting Out

Job placement counselors at community colleges can help students finding their first job. Court reporters usually work for a freelance reporting company that provides court reporters for business meetings and courtroom proceedings on a temporary basis. Occasionally a court reporter will be hired directly out of school as a courtroom official, but ordinarily only those with several years of experience are hired for full-time judiciary work.

Earnings

Beginning reporters may earn up to $30,000 a year. According to a 1997 salary survey conducted by the NCRA, experienced court reporters earned an average of $43,000 per year and higher according to skill level and length of service. Official court reporters not only earn a salary, but also a per-page fee for transcripts. According to that same NCRA survey, a court reporter earning the average $43,000 per year also makes about $17,000 in transcript fees.

Those working for the government or full-time for private companies usually receive health insurance and other benefits, such as paid vacations and retirement pensions. Freelancers may or may not receive health insurance or other benefits, depending on the policies of their agencies.

Employment Outlook

The opportunities for court reporters are plentiful and continue to evolve to meet the needs of the legal system, according to the NCRA. The U.S. Department of Labor predicts that employment of court reporters should remain stable. The rising number of criminal court cases and civil lawsuits will cause both state and federal court systems to expand. Job opportunities should be greatest in and around large metropolitan areas, but qualified court reporters should be able to find work in most parts of the country.

For More Information

Information on certification and court reporting careers is available from:

■ **National Court Reporters Association**
8224 Old Courthouse Road
Vienna, VA 22182-3808
Tel: 703-556-6272
Email: msic@ncrahq.org
Web: http://www.verbatimreporters.com

For tips on preparing for the certification exams, and for other career information, contact:

■ **National Verbatim Reporters Association**
2729 Drake Street, Suite 130
Fayetteville, AR 72703
Tel: 501-582-2200
Email: nvra@aol.com
Web: http://www.nvra.org

Dental Assistants

School Subjects: Health
Personal Skills: Following instructions, Technical/scientific
Work Environment: Primarily indoors, Primarily one location
Salary Range: $14,700 to $23,500 to $25,000
Certification or Licensing: Recommended
Outlook: Much faster than the average

The Job

Dental assistants perform a variety of duties in the dental office, including helping the dentist examine and treat patients and completing laboratory and office work. They assist the dentist by preparing patients for dental exams, handing the dentist the proper instruments, taking and processing X-rays, preparing materials for making impressions and restorations, and instructing patients in oral health care. They also perform administrative and clerical tasks so that the office runs smoothly and the dentist's time is available for working with patients.

Professional and Personal Requirements

Dental assistants may wish to obtain certification from the Dental Assisting National Board, but this is usually not required for employment. Certified Dental Assistant (CDA) accreditation shows that an assistant meets certain standards of professional competence. In 21 states dental assistants are allowed to take X rays (under a dentist's direction) only after completing a precise training program and passing a test. Completing the program for CDA certification fulfills this requirement. To keep their CDA credentials, however, assistants must either prove their skills through retesting or acquire further education.

Dental assistants need a clean, well-groomed appearance and a pleasant personality. Manual dexterity and the ability to follow directions are also important.

Starting Out

High school guidance counselors, family dentists, dental schools, dental placement agencies, and dental associations may provide applicants with leads about job openings. Students in formal training programs often learn of jobs through school placement services. Most dentists work in private practice, so that's where a dental assistant is most likely to find a job. Other places to work include dental schools, hospitals, public health departments, and U.S. Veterans and Public Health Service hospitals.

Earnings

According to the American Dental Association's 1996 Survey of Dental Practice, the average earnings of full-time dental assistants working for general dentists were between $14,700 and $23,500 a year. Dental assistants working for specialists, such as orthodontists or pediatric dentists, earn slightly more. Some offices offer benefits packages such as paid vacations and insurance coverage.

Employment Outlook

According to the U.S. Department of Labor, employment for dental assistants is expected to grow much faster than average for all occupations through 2006, with about 50 percent more jobs expected to open in the field. Advances in dental care now allow the general population to maintain better dental health as well as keep their natural teeth longer. Thus, more people will seek dental services for preventative care and cosmetic improvements.

In addition, dentists who earned their dental degrees since the 1970s are more likely then other dentists to hire one or more assistants. Also, as dentists increase their knowledge of innovative techniques such as implantology and periodontal therapy, they generally delegate more routine tasks to assistants so they can make the best use of their time and increase profits.

Job openings will also be created through attrition as other assistants leave the field or change jobs.

For More Information

For career and scholarship information, and a list of dental schools, contact:

■ **American Association of Dental Schools**
1625 Massachusetts Avenue, NW, Suite 600
Washington, DC 20036
Tel: 202-667-9433
Email: aada@aads.jhu.edu
Web: http://www.aads.jhu.edu

For information on dental assisting careers and scholarships, contact:

■ **American Dental Assistants Association**
203 North LaSalle Street, Suite 1320
Chicago, IL 60601
Tel: 312-541-1320
Web: http://member.aol.com/adaa1/index.html

For information on certification, contact:

■ **Dental Assisting National Board**
216 East Ontario Street
Chicago, IL 60611

Dental Hygienists

School Subjects: Biology, Health
Personal Skills: Helping/teaching, Mechanical/manipulative
Work Environment: Primarily indoors, Primarily one location
Salary Range: $15,200 to $31,000 to $39,500
Certification or Licensing: Required
Outlook: Much faster than the average

The Job

In clinical settings, *dental hygienists* help prevent gum diseases and cavities by removing deposits from teeth and applying sealants and fluoride to prevent tooth decay. They remove tartar, stains, and plaque from teeth; take X rays and other diagnostic tests; place and remove temporary fillings; take health histories; remove sutures; polish amalgam restorations; and examine head, neck, and oral regions for disease.

Their tools include hand and rotary instruments to clean teeth; syringes with needles to administer local anesthetic (such as Novocain); teeth models to demonstrate home care procedures; and X-ray machines to take pictures of the oral cavity that the dentist uses to detect signs of decay or oral disease.

A hygienist also provides nutritional counseling and screens patients for oral cancer and high blood pressure. More extensive dental procedures are done by dentists. The hygienist is also trained and licensed to take and develop X rays. Other responsibilities depend on the employer.

Professional and Personal Requirements

After graduation from accredited schools, dental hygienists must pass state licensing examinations, both written and clinical.

116

Aptitude tests sponsored by the American Dental Hygienists' Association are frequently required by dental hygiene schools to help applicants determine whether they will succeed in this field. Skill in handling delicate instruments, a sensitive touch, and depth perception are important attributes that are tested. The hygienist should be neat, clean, and personable.

Starting Out

Once dental hygienists have passed the National Board exams and a licensing exam in a particular state, they must decide on an area of work. Most dental hygiene schools maintain placement services for their graduates, and finding a satisfactory position usually is not difficult.

Earnings

According to the U.S. Department of Labor, in 1996 the average earnings of full-time hygienists ranged between $24,000 and $39,500 a year. The average hourly wage for full-time hygienists was $20.40; the average for part-time hygienists was $24.50. Beginning hygienists earned an average of $15,200 to $17,500 a year. Salaries in large metropolitan areas are generally somewhat higher than those in small cities and towns. Dental hygienists in research, education, or administration may earn higher salaries.

A salaried dental hygienist in a private office typically receives a paid two- or three-week vacation. Part-time or commissioned dental hygienists in private offices usually have no paid vacation.

Employment Outlook

The U.S. Department of Labor projects the career of dental hygienist to be among the 20 fastest growing occupations. About 50 percent more dental hygiene positions are expected to be created between 1996 and 2006. The demand for dental hygienists is expected to grow as younger generations that grew up receiving better dental care keep their teeth longer. Other factors contributing to growth in this field include population growth, increased public awareness of proper oral home care, and the availability of dental insurance. Moreover, as the population ages, there will be a special demand for hygienists to work with older people, especially those who live in nursing homes.

For More Information

For publications, information on dental schools, and scholarship information, contact:

■ **American Association of Dental Schools**
1625 Massachusetts Avenue, NW, Suite 600
Washington, DC 20036
Tel: 202-667-9433
Email: aada@aads.jhu.edu
Web: http://www.aads.jhu.edu

For education information, contact:

■ **American Dental Association**
211 East Chicago Avenue
Chicago, IL 60611
Tel: 312-440-2500
Web: http://www.ada.org/prac/careers/apl-03.html

For career information and tips for dental hygiene students on finding a job, contact:

■ **American Dental Hygienists' Association**
444 North Michigan Avenue, Suite 3400
Chicago, IL 60611
Tel: 312-440-8900
Email: mail@adha.net
Web: http://www.adha.org

Desktop Publishing Specialists

School Subjects: Art, Computer science, English
Personal Skills: Artistic, Communication/ideas
Work Environment: Primarily indoors, Primarily one location
Salary Range: $18,000 to $30,000 to $83,000
Certification or Licensing: Voluntary
Outlook: Much faster than the average

The Job

Desktop publishing specialists prepare reports, brochures, books, cards, and other documents for printing. They create computer files of text, graphics, and page layout. They work with files others have created, or they compose original text and graphics for their clients. There are approximately 50,000 desktop publishing specialists working in the printing industry, either as freelancers or for corporations, service bureaus, and advertising agencies.

Desktop publishing specialists work on computers, converting and preparing files for printing presses and other media, such as the Internet and CD-ROM. Much of desktop publishing fits into the prepress category, and desktop publishing specialists typeset, or arrange and transform, text and graphics. Once they have created the file to be printed, they either submit it to a commercial printer, or they print the pieces themselves. Commercial printing involves catalogs, brochures, and reports, while business printing encompasses products used by businesses, such as sales receipts and forms.

Professional and Personal Requirements

Certification is not mandatory, and currently there is only one certification program offered in desktop publishing. The Association of Graphic Communications has an Electronic Publishing Certificate designed to set industry standards and measure the competency levels of desktop publishing specialists

Desktop publishing specialists are detail-oriented, possess problem-solving skills, and have a sense of design and artistic skills. Other helpful qualities include patience, flexibility, an aptitude for computers, and the ability to type quickly and accurately.

Starting Out

To start their own businesses, desktop publishing specialists must have a great deal of experience with design and page layout, and a solid understanding of the computer design programs they'll be using. Most desktop publishing specialists enter the field through the production side or the editorial side of the industry. Those with training as a designer or artist can easily master the finer techniques of production. Working within the industry, they can make connections and build up a clientele.

Earnings

The average wage of desktop publishing specialists in the prepress department ranged from $11.72 to $14.65 an hour, with the highest rate at $40 an hour. Entry-level desktop publishing specialists with little or no experience generally earn minimum wage. Electronic page makeup system operators earned an average of $13.62 to $16.96, and scanner operators ranged from $14.89 to $17.91 per hour.

According to the *Occupational Outlook Handbook,* full-time prepress workers in typesetting and composition earned a median wage of $421 a week, or $21,892 annually.

Employment Outlook

According to the U.S. Department of Labor, the field of desktop publishing is projected to be one of the fastest growing occupations, increasing about 75 percent through the year 2006.

A survey conducted by Printing Industries of America (PIA) in 1997 also indicates the printing industry is growing; this can be attributed partly to the growth experienced by the North American economy.

The electronic prepress segment of the printing market enjoyed the most growth, with an average change from 1996 of 9.3 percent. Traditional prepress, on the other hand, suffered a decline of 5.7 percent. PIA's survey also indicates that printing firms have been experiencing difficulties finding new, qualified employees. This is a good sign for desktop publishing specialists with skills and experience.

For More Information

For career information, and information about scholarships and education, contact:

- **Association for Suppliers of Printing, Publishing, and Converting Technologies**
  1899 Preston White Drive
  Reston, VA 20191-4367
  Tel: 703-264-7200
  Web: http://www.npes.org

For scholarship information, contact:

- **National Scholarship Trust Fund of the Graphic Arts**
  200 Deer Run Road
  Sewickley, PA 15143-2600
  Tel: 800-900-GATF
  Web: http://www.gatf.org

For career brochures and information about grants and scholarships, contact:

- **Society for Technical Communication**
  901 North Stuart Street, Suite 904
  Arlington, VA 22203-1854
  Tel: 703-522-4114
  Web: http://www.stc-va.org

For information on membership, contact:

- **Independent Computer Consultants Association**
  11131 South Towne Square, Suite F
  St. Louis, MO 63123
  Tel: 800-774-4222
  Web: http://www.icca.org

Diagnostic Medical Sonographers

School Subjects: Biology, Chemistry
Personal Skills: Helping/teaching, Technical/scientific
Work Environment: Primarily indoors, Primarily one location
Salary Range: $23,500 to $30,500 to $41,600
Certification or Licensing: Recommended
Outlook: Faster than the average

The Job

Diagnostic medical sonographers, or *sonographers,* use advanced technology in the form of high-frequency sound waves similar to sonar to produce two-dimensional, gray-scale images of the internal body for analysis by radiologists and other physicians.

Sonographers work on the orders of a physician or radiologist. They are responsible for the proper set up and selection of the ultrasound equipment for each specific exam. They explain the procedure to patients, recording any additional information that may be of later use to the physician.

When the patient is properly positioned, the sonographer applies a gel to the skin that improves the diagnostic image. He or she selects the transducer, a microphone-shaped device that directs high-frequency sound waves into the area to be imaged, and adjusts equipment controls. Sonographers must master the location and visualization of human anatomy to be able to clearly differentiate between healthy and pathological areas.

When a clear image is obtained, the sonographer activates equipment that records individual photographic views or sequences as real-time images of the affected area. The sonographer removes the film after recording and prepares it for analysis by the physician.

Professional and Personal Requirements

Although certification is not mandatory in this field, it is required by many employers. The American Registry of Diagnostic Medical Sonographers offers certification to sonographers.

Sonographers should be technically adept and detail and precision minded. They need both a professional demeanor and an ability to express empathy, patience, and understanding in order to reassure patients.

Starting Out

Those interested in becoming diagnostic medical sonographers must complete an accredited sonographic educational program such as one offered by teaching hospitals, colleges and universities, technical schools, and the armed forces.

Voluntary registration with the American Registry of Diagnostic Medical Sonographers (ARDMS) is key to gaining employment. Most employers require registration with ARDMS. Other methods of entering the field include responding to job listings in sonography publications, registering with employment agencies specializing in the health care field, contacting headhunters, or applying to the personnel officers of health care employers.

Earnings

According to the American Society of Radiologic Technologists, starting sonographers can expect to earn from $23,500 to $28,400 per year. Those with experience will earn between $30,500 and $34,000 per year. Senior diagnostic medical sonographers with superior expertise, experience, and managerial duties can earn up to $41,600 yearly. Beyond base salaries, sonographers can expect to enjoy many fringe benefits, including paid vacation, sick and personal days, and health and dental insurance.

Employment Outlook

The use of diagnostic medical sonography, like many other imaging fields, will continue to grow because of its safe, nonradioactive imaging and its success in detecting life-threatening diseases and in analyzing previously nonimageable internal organs. Sonography will play an increasing role in the fields of obstetrics/gynecology and cardiology. Furthermore, the aging population will create high demand for qualified technologists. Currently, the demand for qualified diagnostic medical sonographers exceeds the supply in some areas of the country, especially rural communities, small towns, and some retirement areas. Those flexible about location and compensation will enjoy the best opportunities in current and future job markets.

For More Information

For information about their job service and certification, contact:

- **American Registry of Diagnostic Medical Sonographers**
  2368 Victory Parkway, Suite 510
  Cincinnati, OH 45206-2810
  Tel: 800-541-9754
  Web: http://www.ardms.org

For information regarding a career in sonography or to subscribe to the Journal of Diagnostic Medical Sonography, *contact:*

- **Society of Diagnostic Medical Sonographers**
  12770 Coit Road, Suite 508
  Dallas, TX 75251
  Tel: 214-239-7367
  Web: http://www.sdms.org

For information regarding certified programs of sonography, contact:

- **American Medical Association**
  515 North State Street
  Chicago, IL 60610
  Tel: 312-464-5000
  Web: http://www.ama-assn.org

Dialysis Technicians

School Subjects: Biology, Chemistry
Personal Skills: Helping/teaching, Technical/scientific
Work Environment: Primarily indoors, Primarily one location
Salary Range: $14,000 to $25,000 to $40,000
Certification or Licensing: Required by certain states
Outlook: About as fast as the average

The Job

Dialysis technicians, also called *nephrology technicians* or *renal dialysis technicians,* set up and operate hemodialysis artificial kidney machines for patients with chronic renal (kidney) failure.

The National Association of Nephrology Technicians/Technologists recognizes three types of dialysis technicians: the *patient-care technician,* the *biomedical equipment technician,* and the *dialyzer reprocessing (reuse) technician.* Dialysis patient-care technicians are responsible for preparing the patient for dialysis, monitoring the procedure, and responding to any emergencies that occur during the treatment. Biomedical equipment technicians maintain and repair the dialysis machines. Dialyzer reuse technicians care for the dialyzers—the apparatus through which the blood is filtered. In many dialysis facilities, the technicians' duties as described above may overlap. This depends on the size, staff, and structure of each facility.

Professional and Personal Requirements

Certification is required only in California and New Mexico; in the rest of the states, certification is voluntary. The Board of Nephrology Examiners-Nursing and Technology (BONENT) and the National Nephrology Technology Certification Board (NNTCB) offer a voluntary program of certification for technicians.

Because the slightest mistake can have deadly consequences, a technician must be thorough and detail oriented, able to respond to stressful situations calmly, and capable of quick thinking in an emergency. An understanding of mathematics and the metric system is necessary. Technicians need to have good interpersonal skills and sensitivity in order to help patients deal with both the physical and the emotional effects of their condition.

Starting Out

The best way to enter this field is through a formal training program in a hospital or other training facility. You may also contact your local hospital and dialysis center to determine the possibility of on-the-job training.

Other ways to enter this field are through schools of nurse assisting, practical nursing, or nursing programs for emergency medical technicians. The length of time required to progress through the dialysis training program and advance to higher levels of responsibility should be shorter if you first complete a related training program. Most dialysis centers offer a regular program of in-service training for their employees. A few community colleges also offer training programs for dialysis technicians.

Earnings

Dialysis technicians can earn between $14,000 and $35,000 per year, depending on their job performance, responsibilities, locality, and length of service. Some employers pay higher wages to technicians who are certified. Technicians who rise to management positions can earn from $35,000 to $40,000.

Technicians receive the customary benefits of vacation, sick leave or personal time, and health insurance. Many hospitals or health care centers not only provide in-service training but offer tuition reimbursement as well as an incentive to further self-development and career advancement.

Employment Outlook

There should continue to be a need for dialysis technicians in the future. The number of patients receiving dialysis in the United States doubled in the ten years from 1978 to 1988, and it continues to grow.

Technicians make up the largest proportion of the dialysis team, since they can care for only a limited number of patients at a time. The turnover rate in this field is high, and there is a shortage of trained dialysis technicians.

A factor that may decrease employment demand is the further development of procedures that may remove the need for dialysis treatments in health care facilities, such as home dialysis and kidney transplants.

For More Information

The following are organizations that provide information on careers in renal technology, training programs, certification, and employers:

- **American Nephrology Nurses Association**
  East Holly Avenue, Box 56
  Pitman, NJ 08071
  Tel: 609-256-2320
  Web: http://anna.nurse.com/

- **Board of Nephrology Examiners-Nursing and Technology**
  PO Box 15945-282
  Lenexa, KS 66285
  Tel: 913-541-9077
  Web: http://www.applmeapro.com/bonent/

- **National Association of Nephrology Technicians/Technologists**
  11 West Monument Avenue, Suite 510
  Dayton, OH 45402
  Tel: 513-223-9765

- **National Nephrology Technology Certification Board**
  PO Box 2307
  Dayton, OH 45401-2307
  Tel: 513-223-9765

Dietetic Technicians

School Subjects: Biology, Chemistry
Personal Skills: Helping/teaching, Technical/scientific
Work Environment: Primarily indoors, Primarily one location
Salary Range: $15,000 to $25,000 to $35,000
Certification or Licensing: Voluntary
Outlook: About as fast as the average

The Job

Dietetic technicians usually work under the direction of a dietician. They serve in two basic areas: as service personnel in food-service administration and as assistants in the nutrition care of individuals. In food-service management, dietetic technicians often supervise other food-service employees and oversee the food production operation on a day-to-day basis. They may act as administrative assistants to dietitians. They may also be responsible for planning menus and modifying existing recipes to meet specific requirements.

Dietetic technicians who specialize in nutrition care and counseling work under the direction of a clinical or community dietitian. They often work in a health care facility, where they may observe and interview patients about their eating habits and food preferences. Dietetic technicians then report diet histories to the dietitians, along with the patients' progress reports. They may also supervise the serving of food to ensure that meals are nutritionally adequate and in conformance with the physicians' prescriptions.

Professional and Personal Requirements

The American Dietetic Association offers certification, which is voluntary. Those who successfully complete the certification exam are designated Dietetic Technicians, Registered.

Dietetic technicians should have an interest in nutrition and a desire to serve people. They should be should be patient and understanding, since they may have to deal with people who are ill or uncooperative. Communication skills also are vital since the job often involves working closely with patients and co-workers.

Starting Out

Contacts gained during the clinical experience part of their training program are often good sources of first jobs for dietetic technicians. Applying to the personnel offices of potential employers can be another productive approach. Other good places to check are school placement offices, job listings in health care journals, newspaper classified ads, and private and public employment agencies.

Earnings

Entry-level technicians earn $15,000 to $20,000 per year; with 10 to 15 years' experience, they earn between $20,000 to $25,000; and those at the top of the pay scale earn between $30,000 to $35,000. Those who work in food-production administration tend to earn slightly more than those in clinical nutrition. The median salary for food-production technicians is $25,255; the median salary for technicians in clinical settings $22,350.

Fringe benefits usually include paid vacations and holidays, health insurance plans, and meals during working hours.

Employment Outlook

The outlook is good for dietetic technicians for the near future. This is partly because of the strong emphasis on nutrition and health in this country and the fact that more health services will be used in future years. The population is growing, and the percentage of older people, who need the most health services, is increasing even faster.

Another reason for the positive outlook for technicians is that health care organizations now realize the advantages of utilizing them for many jobs. Many of the tasks dietitians used to perform can be done well by dietetic technicians, leaving dietitians to do more specialized work. In addition, dietetic technicians are less expensive to hire and are therefore more cost-efficient for the employer. Job opportunities will most likely be best for those technicians who have received their certification.

For More Information

For information on career development, continuing education, and scholarships, contact:

- **American Dietetic Association**
  216 West Jackson Boulevard, Suite 800
  Chicago, IL 60606
  Tel: 800-877-1600
  Web: http://www.eatright.org

Dispensing Opticians

School Subjects: Biology, Mathematics
Personal Skills: Helping/teaching, Technical/scientific
Work Environment: Primarily indoors, Primarily one location
Salary Range: $15,000 to $27,432 to $35,000
Certification or Licensing: Required by certain states
Outlook: About as fast as the average

The Job

Dispensing opticians measure and fit clients with prescription eyeglasses, contact lenses, other low-vision aids, and sometimes artificial eyes. They help clients select appropriate frames and order all necessary ophthalmic laboratory work. Their tasks include ensuring that eyeglasses are made according to the optometrist's prescription, determining exactly where the lenses should be placed in relation to the pupils of the eyes, assisting the customer in selecting appropriate frames, preparing work orders for the optical laboratory mechanic, and sometimes selling optical goods.

Opticians record lens prescriptions, lens size, and the style and color of the frames to submit to the ophthalmic laboratory so the technicians can grind the lenses and insert them into the frames. After the lenses return from the lab, the optician makes sure the glasses are made according to the prescription and that they fit the customer correctly. Opticians use small hand tools and precision instruments to make minor adjustments to the frames. Most dispensing opticians work with prescription eyeglasses, but some work with contact lenses. They measure the curvature of the cornea, and, following the prescription, prepare complete specifications for the optical mechanic who manufactures the lens. They must teach the customer how to remove, adjust to, and care for the lenses, a process that can take several weeks.

Professional and Personal Requirements

More than 20 states currently require licensing of dispensing opticians. Licensing requires meeting certain educational standards and passing a written examination. Some states require a practical, hands-on examination.

Professional credentials may also include voluntary certification. Certification is offered by the American Board of Opticianry and the National Contact Lens Examiners.

Opticians should be good at dealing with people and with handling administrative tasks. They must exercise great precision, skill, and patience in fitting contact lenses.

Starting Out

Since the usual ways of entering the field are either through completion of a two-year associate degree or through completion of an apprenticeship program, students can use the services of their school's placement office or they can apply directly to optical stores.

Earnings

Beginning salaries average between $15,000 and $20,000 per year for dispensing opticians just entering the field. Experienced workers can make between $18,000 and $35,000; the average is $27,432 per year, according to survey published in the April 1997 issue of *Eyecare Business* magazine. Supervisors earn about 20 percent more than skilled workers, depending on experience, skill, and responsibility. Dispensing opticians who own their own stores can earn much more.

Employment Outlook

Currently, there are more than 67,000 dispensing opticians in the U.S., and the demand for them is expected to grow at an average rate through 2006, according to the U.S. Department of Labor. One reason is an increase in the number of people who need corrective eyeglasses. Educational programs such as vision screening have made the public more aware of eye problems, therefore increasing the need for dispensing opticians. Insurance programs cover more optical needs, which means more clients can afford optical care. The wide variety of fashionable frames also has increased demand for eyeglasses.

Employment opportunities should be especially good in larger urban areas because of the greater number of retail optical stores. Those with an associate's degree in opticianry should be most successful in their job search.

For More Information

For general information on the career of dispensing optician, contact:

■ National Academy of Opticianry
8401 Corporate Drive, #605
Landover, MD 20785
Tel: 800-229-4828
Web: http://www.nao.org/

■ Opticians Association of America
10341 Democracy Lane
Fairfax, VA 22030-2521
Tel: 703-691-8355
Web: http://www.opticians.org

For information on certification, contact:

■ American Board of Opticianry
National Contact Lens Examiners
10337 Democracy Lane
Fairfax, VA 22030-2521

For a list of accredited training programs, contact:

■ Commission on Opticianry Accreditation
10111 Martin Luther King, Jr. Highway, #100
Bowie,, MD 20720-4299
Tel: 301-459-8075

Drafters

School Subjects: Mathematics, Technical/Shop
Personal Skills: Artistic, Technical/scientific
Work Environment: Primarily indoors, Primarily one location
Salary Range: $21,000 to $40,000 to $55,000
Certification or Licensing: Recommended
Outlook: Faster than the average

The Job

Drafters prepare working plans and detail drawings of products or structures from the rough sketches, specifications, and calculations of engineers, architects, and designers. These drawings are used in engineering or manufacturing processes to reproduce exactly the product or structure desired, according to the specified dimensions. The drafter uses knowledge of various machines, engineering practices, mathematics, and building materials, along with other physical sciences and fairly extensive computer skills, to complete the drawings. The drawings, which usually provide a number of different views of the object, must be exact and accurate.

Drafters often are classified according to the type of work they do (chief drafters, detailers, checkers, and tracers). Drafters also may specialize in a particular field of work, such as mechanical, electrical, electronic, plumbing, landscaping, automotive, aeronautical, structural, or architectural drafting.

Professional and Personal Requirements

Certification is not presently required but is recommended in this field. More and more, employers are looking for graduates whose skills have been vetted by a reliable industry source. The American Design Drafting Association (ADDA) offers student certification services; recent graduates who take advantage of these services not only will enhance their professional credibility but also gain an edge in the job market.

Students interested in drafting should have a good sense of both spatial and formal perception. Good hand-eye coordination is also necessary for the fine detail work involved in drafting.

Starting Out

Beginning drafters generally have graduated from a postsecondary program at a technical institute or junior college. Skill certification through the American Design Drafting Association may be advantageous. Applicants for government positions may need to take a civil service examination. Beginning or inexperienced drafters often start as tracers. Students with some formal postsecondary technical training often qualify for positions as junior drafters who revise detail drawings and then gradually assume drawing assignments of a more complex nature.

Earnings

According to the ADDA, junior college graduates may begin at around $21,000, while graduates of four-year technical schools may make as much as $40,000 to start. Senior drafters can make upwards of $55,000. Salaries also are affected by regional demands in specific specialties.

Employers generally offer drafters a range of benefit options, including health insurance, retirement plans, and so on.

Employment Outlook

Opportunities for drafters are becoming available at a faster pace than the average, and that is expected to continue for the next several years, according to the American Design Drafting Association. Economic conditions contributing to such trends as a boom in both residential and commercial construction suggest that the demand for well-educated drafters will continue to be high for some time.

While in the past the increased use of CAD systems was expected to offset some of the demand, particularly for lower-level drafters who do routine work, this same technology is creating new opportunities for drafters who have a thorough familiarity with it.

For More Information

The ADDA is an excellent resource for information on careers in drafting. It is best contacted via email or at its helpful Web site.

- **American Design Drafting Association (ADDA)**
  PO Box 11937
  Columbia, SC 29211
  Email: national@adda.org
  Web: http://www.adda.org

The IFPTE is the union associated with the drafting community. It can tell you about such things as legislative changes affecting the field.

- **International Federation of Professional and Technical Engineers (IFPTE)**
  8630 Fenton Street, Suite 400
  Silver Spring, MD 20910
  Tel: 301-565-9016
  Web: http://www.ifpte.org

Electricians

School Subjects: Mathematics, Physics
Personal Skills: Mechanical/manipulative, Technical/scientific
Work Environment: Primarily indoors, Primarily multiple locations
Salary Range: $16,000 to $41,000 to $80,000+
Certification or Licensing: Required by certain states
Outlook: Much faster than the average

The Job

Electricians design, lay out, assemble, install, test, and repair electrical fixtures, apparatus, and wiring used in a wide range of electrical, telecommunications, and data communications systems that provide light, heat, refrigeration, air-conditioning, power, and communications.

Many electricians specialize in either construction or maintenance work, although some work in both fields. Electricians in construction are usually employed by electrical contractors. Other *construction electricians* work for building contractors or industrial plants, public utilities, state highway commissions, or other large organizations that employ workers directly to build or remodel their properties. A few are self-employed.

Maintenance electricians, also known as *electrical repairers,* do many of the same kinds of tasks as construction electricians, but their activities are usually aimed at preventing trouble before it occurs.

Professional and Personal Requirements

Some states and municipalities require that electricians be licensed. To obtain a license, electricians usually must pass a written examination on electrical theory, National Electrical Code requirements, and local building and electrical codes. Electronics specialists receive certification training and testing through the International Society of Certified Electronic Technicians.

Good color vision is necessary, because electricians need to be able to distinguish color-coded wires. Agility and manual dexterity are also desirable characteristics, as are a sense of teamwork, an interest in working outdoors, and a love of working with one's hands.

Starting Out

People seeking to enter this field may either begin working as helpers or they may enter an apprenticeship program. Leads for helper jobs may be located by contacting electrical contractors directly or by checking with the local offices of the state employment service or in newspaper classified advertising sections. Students in trade and vocational programs may be able to find job openings through the placement office of their school.

Those interested in an apprenticeship may start by contacting the union local of the International Brotherhood of Electrical Workers (IBEW), the local chapter of Independent Electrical Contractors, Inc., or the local apprenticeship training committee. Information on apprenticeship possibilities also can be obtained through state employment services.

Earnings

Most established, full-time electricians working for contractors average earnings about $21 per hour, or $41,000 per year, according to the National Joint Apprenticeship Training Committee—and it is possible to make much more. Beginning apprentices earn 40 percent of the base electrician's wage and receive periodic increases each year of their apprenticeship.

Electricians who are members of the IBEW, the industry's labor union, are entitled to benefits including paid vacation days and holidays, health insurance, pensions to help with retirement savings, supplemental unemployment compensation plans, and so forth.

Employment Outlook

The next three to five years will show a much faster than average increase in job availability for electrical workers, according to the National Joint Apprenticeship Training Committee. The growth in this field principally will be related to the overall increase in both residential and commercial construction. In addition, growth will be driven by the ever-expanding use of electrical and electronic devices and equipment. In particular, the growing use of sophisticated telecommunications and data-processing equipment and automated manufacturing systems is expected to lead to many job opportunities for electricians.

For More Information

IECI is the industry association for nonunion, or independent, electrical contractors.

■ **Independent Electrical Contractors, Inc. (IECI)**
  2010-A Eisenhower Avenue
  Alexandria, VA 22314
  Web: http://www.ieci.org

The IBEW is the national labor union for the electrical industry. It can provide more information about union rules, benefits, and so forth.

■ **International Brotherhood of Electrical Workers (IBEW)**
  1125 15th Street, NW
  Washington, DC 20005
  Web: http://www.ibew.org

For information on certification, contact:

■ **International Society of Certified Electronics Technicians**
  2708 West Berry Street
  Fort Worth, TX 76109-2356
  Web: http://www.iscet.org/

The NJATC is a good beginning resource for background on apprenticeship and training programs for union workers.

■ **National Joint Apprenticeship Training Committee (NJATC)**
  301 Prince George's Boulevard, Suite F
  Upper Marlboro, MD 20774
  Web: http://www.njatc.org

Electroneurodiagnostic Technologists

School Subjects: Mathematics, Physics
Personal Skills: Mechanical/manipulative, Technical/scientific
Work Environment: Primarily indoors, Primarily one location
Salary Range: $16,000 to $26,800 to $46,000
Certification or Licensing: Voluntary
Outlook: Faster than the average

The Job

Electroneurodiagnostic technologists, sometimes called *EEG technologists* or *END technologists*, operate electronic instruments called electroencephalographs. These instruments measure and record the brain's electrical activity.

The EEG technologist's first task with a new patient is to take a simplified medical history. This entails asking questions and recording answers about his or her past health status and present illness.

The technologist then applies electrodes to the patient's head, which are connected to the recording equipment. Here, a bank of sensitive electronic amplifiers transmits information. Tracings from each electrode are made on a moving strip of paper or recorded on optical disks in response to the amplified impulses coming from the brain. The resulting graph is a recording of the patient's brain waves.

EEG technologists are not responsible for interpreting the tracings (that is the job of the neurologist); however, they must be able to recognize abnormal brain activity and any readings on the tracing that are coming from somewhere other than the brain, such as readings of eye movement or nearby electrical equipment.

Professional and Personal Requirements

The American Board of Registration of Electroencephalographic and Evoked Potential Technologists registers technologists at one level of experience and education—that is, as a registered electroencephalographic technologist. Technicians who have been in the field for at least one year can earn this registration by passing an exam.

EEG technologists need good vision and manual dexterity, an aptitude for working with mechanical and electronic equipment, and the ability to get along well with patients, their families, and members of the hospital staff.

Starting Out

Technologists often obtain permanent employment in the hospital where they received their on-the-job or work-study training.

Prospective technologists can also find employment through classified ads in newspapers and by contacting the personnel offices of hospitals, medical centers, clinics, and government agencies that employ EEG technologists.

Earnings

Starting salaries are approximately $16,000 a year. Experienced EEG technologists averaged approximately $26,800 in January 1997, according to a Hay Group survey. Some technologists may earn as much as $35,000 to $46,000 a year. Salaries for registered EEG technologists tend to be $6,000 to $10,000 a year higher than nonregistered technologists with equivalent experience.

The highest salaries for EEG technologists tend to go to those who work as laboratory supervisors, teachers in training programs, and program directors in schools of electroencephalographic technology.

Electroencephalographic technicians working in hospitals receive the same fringe benefits as other hospital workers, including hospitalization insurance, paid vacations, and sick leave.

Employment Outlook

The U.S. Department of Labor predicts that employment for electroneurodiagnostic technologists will grow faster than the average for other occupations through the year 2006. This growth will be caused by a number of factors, most notably the increased use of electroencephalographs in surgery, diagnosing and monitoring patients, and research on the human brain.

For More Information

For information and an application to start the EEG or Evoked Potential examination process, contact:

■ **American Society of Electroneurodiagnostic Technologists**
204 West 7th
Carroll, IA 51401
Tel: 712-792-2978
Email: aset@netins.net
Web: http://www.aset.org

For information on becoming a registered electroneurodiagnostic technologist, contact:

■ **The American Board of Registration of Electroencephalographic and Evoked Potential Technologists**
PO Box 916633
Longwood, FL 32791-6633
Web: http://www.graphicinsight.com/ABRETmirror/

Electronics Engineering Technicians

School Subjects: Computer science, Mathematics, Physics
Personal Skills: Mechanical/manipulative, Technical/scientific
Work Environment: Primarily indoors, Primarily one location
Salary Range: $17,700 to $32,700 to $54,800+
Certification or Licensing: Voluntary
Outlook: Faster than the average

The Job

Electronics engineering technicians work with electronics engineers to design, develop, and manufacture industrial and consumer electronic equipment, including sonar, radar, and navigational equipment and computers, radios, televisions, stereos, and calculators. They are involved in fabricating, operating, testing, troubleshooting, repairing, and maintaining equipment. Those involved in the development of new electronic equipment help make changes or modifications in circuitry or other design elements.

Other electronics technicians inspect newly installed equipment or instruct and supervise lower-grade technicians' installation, assembly, or repair activities.

As part of their normal duties, all electronics engineering technicians set up testing equipment, conduct tests, and analyze the results; they also prepare reports, sketches, graphs, and schematic drawings to describe electronics systems and their characteristics. Their work involves the use of a variety of hand and machine tools, including such equipment as bench lathes and drills.

Professional and Personal Requirements

Certification, which is voluntary, is offered by the International Society of Certified Electronics Technicians, the Electronics Technicians Association, and the American Society of Certified Engineering Technicians.

Prospective electronics technicians should have an interest in and an aptitude for mathematics and science and should enjoy using tools and scientific equipment; on the personal side, they should be patient, methodical, persistent, and able to get along with different kinds of people. They should be quick learners who are willing to keep themselves informed of new developments in the industry.

Starting Out

Students may find their first full-time positions through their schools' job placement offices. Another way to obtain employment is through direct contact with a particular company. There are also many excellent public and commercial employment organizations that can help graduates obtain jobs appropriate to their training and experience. In addition, the classified ads in most metropolitan Sunday newspapers list a number of job openings, and professional associations compile information on job openings and publish job lists.

Earnings

Engineering technicians who have completed a two-year postsecondary training program and are working in private industry earn starting salaries of approximately $17,700 to $22,800 a year, according to the *Occupational Outlook Handbook*. Average yearly earnings of all engineering technicians are approximately $32,700. At the very top pay levels, technicians in supervisory positions or with considerable experience can earn $54,800 or higher.

Most employers offer benefit packages that include paid holidays, paid vacations, sick days, and health insurance.

Employment Outlook

The U.S. Department of Labor estimates that opportunities for electronics engineering technicians will grow slightly faster than the average through 2006. Consumer products such as large screen and high-definition televisions, videocassette recorders, compact disc players, personal computers, and home appliances with solid-state controls are constantly evolving and in high demand. Two areas showing high growth are computers and telecommunications products. Foreign competition, general economic conditions, and levels of government spending may affect certain areas of the field to some degree, but it is unlikely that any single factor could substantially curb its growth and its need for specially trained personnel.

For More Information

For information on careers and educational programs, contact:

■ **Institute of Electrical and Electronics Engineers**
1828 L Street, NW, Suite 1202
Washington, DC 20036-5104
Web: http://www.ieee.org

For information on student chapters and certification, contact:

■ **International Society of Certified Electronics Technicians**
2708 West Berry Street
Fort Worth, TX 76109
Web: http://www.iscet.org

For information on educational programs and certification, contact:

■ **Electronics Technicians Association**
602 North Jackson
Greencastle, IN 46135
Web: http://www.eta-sda.com

■ **American Society of Certified Engineering Technicians**
PO Box 1348
Flowery Branch, GA 30542
Web: http://www.nmsu.edu/~ascet/ASCET

For information on student clubs and educational programs, contact:

■ **Junior Engineering Technical Society, Inc.**
1420 King Street, Suite 405
Alexandria, VA 22314
Tel: 703-548-5387
Web: http://www.asee.org/jets

Emergency Medical Technicians

School Subjects: Biology, Health
Personal Skills: Helping/teaching, Technical/scientific
Work Environment: Indoors and outdoors, Primarily multiple locations
Salary Range: $18,617 to $30,407 to $32,000+
Certification or Licensing: Required
Outlook: Faster than the average

The Job

Emergency medical technicians, or *EMTs,* provide on-site emergency care, with the goal of rapidly identifying the nature of the emergency, stabilizing the patient's condition, and initiating proper medical procedures at the scene and en route to a hospital. Once at the scene, they may find victims who are burned, trapped under fallen objects, lacerated, in childbirth, poisoned, emotionally disturbed, or appear to have had heart attacks. After evaluating the situation and the victim's condition, EMTs establish the priorities of required care. They administer emergency treatment, continue to monitor the patients, and provide care while transporting victims to the hospital. Once at the hospital, EMTs help the staff bring the victims into the emergency department and may assist with the first steps of in-hospital care. EMTs then check in with their dispatchers and then prepare the vehicle for another emergency call.

Professional and Personal Requirements

All 50 states have some certification requirements. The National Registry of Emergency Medical Technicians offers registration to qualified EMTs.

EMTs should have a desire to serve people and be emotionally stable, clearheaded, and in good physical condition. They need good manual dexterity and motor coordination, the ability to lift and carry up to 125 pounds, good vision and judgment, and competence in giving and receiving verbal and written communication.

Starting Out

A good source of employment leads for a recent graduate of the basic EMT training program is the school or agency that provided the training. You can also apply directly to local ambulance services, fire departments, and employment agencies.

In some areas, you may face stiff competition if you are seeking full-time paid employment immediately upon graduation, and you are generally more likely to be successful in pursuing positions with private companies.

Volunteer work is an option and can be advantageous to new, inexperienced EMTs who hope to find full-time employment.

Earnings

EMTs working for police and fire departments usually receive a higher wage than those working for ambulance companies and hospitals. According to a 1996 *Journal of Emergency Medical Services* survey, the average salary is $25,051 for those classified as EMT-Basic and $30,407 for EMT-Paramedic. To show the disparity in pay between employers, the average pay for an experienced EMT-Basic at a private ambulance service is $18,617; at a fire department, it is $29,859.

Benefits vary widely, but generally include paid holidays and vacations, health insurance, and pension plans.

Employment Outlook

The employment outlook for paid EMTs depends partly on the community in which they are seeking employment. Maintaining a high-quality emergency medical services system can be expensive, and financial strains on some local governments could inhibit the growth of these services. The employment outlook should remain favorable in larger communities whose tax dollars can support these services.

Another important factor affecting the outlook is that the proportion of older people is growing in many communities, placing more demands on the emergency medical services delivery system and increasing the need for EMTs.

For More Information

This organization represents companies that provide emergency and nonemergency medical transportation services:

- **American Ambulance Association**
  1255 23rd Street, NW
  Washington, DC 20037-1174
  Tel: 202-452-8888
  Email: aaa911@the-aaa.org
  Web: http://www.the-aaa.org

For membership information, contact:

- **National Association of Emergency Medical Technicians**
  102 West Leake Street
  Clinton, MS 39056
  Tel: 800-346-2368
  Web: http://www.naemt.org/

For information on testing for EMT certification, contact:

- **National Registry of Emergency Medical Technicians**
  Box 29233
  6610 Busch Boulevard
  Columbus, OH 43229
  Tel: 614-888-4484
  Web: http://www.nremt.org

Farm Crop Production Technicians

School Subjects: Business, Earth science
Personal Skills: Leadership/management, Technical/scientific
Work Environment: Indoors and outdoors, Primarily multiple locations
Salary Range: $18,000 to $23,467 to $30,000
Certification or Licensing: Required by certain states
Outlook: About as fast as the average

The Job

Farm crop production technicians are involved with farmers and agricultural businesses in all aspects of planting, growing, and marketing crops. With backgrounds in agriculture and scientific research, they advise farmers on how best to produce crops, increase yields, and market their products. The work can involve grading and handling, pest and disease control, finding new uses for crops, and similar tasks. They may also work for companies that produce agricultural products such as fertilizer and equipment to make sure they are meeting the needs of farmers.

Specific positions within this field include processing and distributing technicians; laboratory technicians; field technicians; seed production field supervisors; agricultural inspectors; biological aides; disease and insect control field inspectors; spray equipment operators; and aircraft crop dusters.

Professional and Personal Requirements

The majority of technicians in the field are not required to have a license or certification. However, technicians involved in grading or inspecting for local, state, or federal government units must pass examinations to be qualified. Some other government jobs, such as that of research assistant, may also require a competitive examination.

Farm crop production technicians need manual skills and mechanical ability to operate various kinds of equipment and machinery. They must also be able to apply scientific principles to the processing procedures, materials, and measuring and control devices found at the modern laboratory or farm. Technicians must be able to communicate what needs to be done and interpret the orders they're given.

Starting Out

Students in postsecondary programs are encouraged to decide as early as possible which phase of crop technology they prefer to enter, because contacts made while in school can be helpful in obtaining a job after the program's completion. Most faculty members in a technical program have contact with prospective employers and can help place qualified students. Students are often hired by the same firm they worked for during a work-study program. If that firm does not have a position open, a recommendation from the employer will help with other firms.

Earnings

According to a 1998 salary survey conducted by AGRIcareers, Inc., crop assistants made an average of $23,467 a year. Those on the low end of the wage scale received $18,000 annually; those on the high end earned $30,000. Technicians employed in off-the-farm jobs often receive higher salaries than technicians working on farms. Technicians working on farms, however, often receive food and housing benefits that can be the equivalent of several thousand dollars a year. Health coverage and other benefits also depend on the position and employer.

Employment Outlook

Although the part of the population living on farms has decreased over the last century from 85 percent to just a few percent, farming has not decreased in importance. Agribusiness, the processing and production end of agriculture, employs 21 percent of the U.S. labor force. There may be fewer farmers today, but they farm more acres, are more mechanized, and are outproducing the farmers of 100 years ago. In addition to jobs within the United States, the Peace Corps and other organizations can use large numbers of agricultural technicians in the underdeveloped nations of the world.

Because of all these factors, food production in all of its manifestations should continue to provide good employment opportunities through the coming years.

For More Information

For a career resources booklet, contact:

■ **American Society of Agronomy (Crop Science Society of America)**
677 South Segoe Road
Madison, WI 53711
Tel: 608-273-8095
Web: http://www.agronomy.org

To read about research projects concerning crop production, visit the USDA Web site, or contact:

■ **U.S. Department of Agriculture (USDA)**
14th Street and Independence, SW
Washington, DC 20250
Tel: 202-720-2791
Web: http://www.usda.gov

Fashion Designers

School Subjects: Art, Family and consumer science
Personal Skills: Artistic, Communication/ideas
Work Environment: Primarily indoors, One location with some travel
Salary Range: $11,960 to $32,480 to $140,000
Certification or Licensing: None available
Outlook: About as fast as the average

The Job

Fashion designers create or adapt original designs for clothing for men, women, and children. Most specialize in one particular type of clothing, such as ladies' dresses or men's suits. Most designers work for textile, apparel, and pattern manufacturers. Some designers are self-employed and develop a clientele of individual customers or manufacturers. Others work for fashion salons, high-fashion department stores, and specialty shops. A few work in the entertainment industry, designing costumes.

An interesting specialty in fashion designing is theatrical design, a relatively limited field but challenging to those who are interested in combining an interest in theater with a talent for clothing design.

Professional and Personal Requirements

There is no certification or licensing available in this field.

Fashion designers must be artistic and imaginative with a flair for color and clothing coordination. They need a working knowledge of clothing construction and an eye for trends. They must possess technical aptitudes, problem-solving skills, and the ability to conceptualize in two- and three-dimensions. Personal qualifications include self-motivation, team spirit, and the ability to handle pressure, deadlines, and long hours. This career also demands energy and a good head for business.

Starting Out

Few people begin their careers as fashion designers. Well-trained college graduates often begin as assistant designers; they must prove their ability before being entrusted with the responsible job of the designer. Many young people find that assistant designer jobs are difficult to locate, so they accept beginning jobs in the workroom where they spend time cutting or constructing garments.

Fashion design school graduates may receive placement information from their school or college placement office. Approaching stores and manufacturers directly is another way to secure a beginning position.

Earnings

Designers in all fields other than interior design earned an average annual salary of $32,480 in 1997. The median hourly wage was $13.31. The lowest annual wage was $11,960. A few highly skilled and well-known designers in top firms earn annual incomes of $50,000 to $140,000. Top fashion designers who have successful lines of clothing can earn bonuses that bring their annual incomes into the millions of dollars.

The annual incomes for theatrical designers usually are not as great as those of fashion designers, although while they are working they may be making more than $1,000 per week.

Employment Outlook

Good designers always will be needed, although not in great numbers. Even though increasing populations and growing personal incomes are expected to spur the demand for fashion designers, there always will be more people hoping to break into the field than there are available jobs. It takes a great deal of talent and perseverance to achieve success as a high-fashion designer. The employment outlook may be better in specialized areas, such as children's clothing. Openings are more readily available for assistant designers.

For More Information

For referrals to design schools, contact:

- **International Association of Clothing Designers**
  475 Park Avenue, South, 17th Floor
  New York, NY 10016
  Tel: 212-685-6602

For a list of accredited schools, contact:

- **National Association of Schools of Art and Design**
  11250 Roger Bacon Drive, Suite 21
  Reston, VA 22090
  Tel: 703-437-0700
  Web: http://www.arts-accredit.org

For information about the school and an application, contact:

- **Fashion Institute of Technology**
  Admissions Office
  Seventh Avenue at 27th Street
  New York, New York 10001-5992
  Tel: 800-468-6348

Fiber Optics Technicians

School Subjects: Technical/Shop
Personal Skills: Mechanical/manipulative, Technical/scientific
Work Environment: Indoors and outdoors, Primarily multiple locations
Salary Range: $26,779 to $29,902 to $36,857
Certification or Licensing: Voluntary
Outlook: Faster than the average

The Job

Fiber optics technicians prepare, install, and test fiber optics transmission systems. These systems are composed of fiber optic cables and allow for data communication between computers, phones, and faxes. When working for a telecommunications company, fiber optics technicians are often required to install lines for local area networks—these data networks serve small areas of linked computers, such as in an office.

Fiber optics technicians work for telecommunications companies which contract with a company to create a communications system. A salesman first evaluates the customer's needs, then orders the materials for the installation. Fiber optics technicians take these materials to the job site.

After fiber optics technicians ready the area for cable, they run the cable from the computer's main frame to individual work stations. Then they test the cable, using power meters and other devices, to measure the amount of time it takes for the laser to go through and to determine if there are any faults in the fiber link or signal loss.

Professional and Personal Requirements

Certification isn't required of fiber optics technicians, but may be available from local community colleges and training programs. The Fiber Optic Association offers national certification.

Because of the fine nature of the fibers, fiber optics technicians need to have a steady hand and good eyesight in assembling fiber optic cables. They also need good math skills for working with detailed plans and designs. Some companies may require technicians to have their own special fiber optic tools.

Starting Out

There are many sources of information about developments in fiber optics and the telecommunications industry, including *Fiber Optic Product News* online (http://www.fpnmag.com), which features employment opportunities. When you complete a fiber optics technology program, your school will be able to direct you to local job opportunities. Information Gatekeepers publishes a fiber optics career directory listing over 1,000 companies. You can contact Information Gatekeepers at 800-323-1088.

Earnings

The Women in Cable and Telecommunications Foundation and *Cablevision Magazine* conducted a survey in 1998 to examine salary parities between men and women in the telecommunications industry. In entry level professional/technical positions, men had average annual salaries of $26,779 and women had salaries of $26,034. At the associate level, men made $29,902 a year, while women made $31,133. At the senior level, men averaged $36,857 and women averaged $36,803. At all levels, women represented a very small percentage of technicians.

Benefits can include any of the following: paid holidays, vacations, and sick days; personal days; medical, dental, and life insurance; profit-sharing plans; 401(k) plans; retirement and pension plans; and educational assistance programs.

Employment Outlook

Digital transmissions will soon be the norm for telecommunications—not only do modern offices require data communications systems, but cable companies are investing in fiber optics to offer digital TV, as well as quality phone service. Also, the cost of fiber is dropping, which means more companies will invest in fiber optics. As a result, experienced fiber optics assemblers and installers will find plenty of job opportunities.

For More Information

To learn about telecommunications technology and the number of uses for fiber optics, visit the OSA Web site:

■ **Optical Society of America**
2010 Massachusetts Avenue, NW
Washington, DC 20036
Tel: 202-223-8130
Web: http://www.osa.org/

To learn about certification and training opportunities, contact:

■ **The Fiber Optic Association**
Box 230851
Boston, MA 02123-0851
Tel: 617-469-2362
Web: http://world.std.com/~foa/

Fire Safety Technicians

School Subjects: Chemistry, Mathematics
Personal Skills: Following instructions, Technical/scientific
Work Environment: Indoors and outdoors, One location with some travel
Salary Range: $20,500 to $33,000 to $60,000+
Certification or Licensing: Required for certain positions
Outlook: Faster than the average

The Job

Fire safety technicians work to prevent fires. Typical duties include conducting safety inspections and planning fire protection systems. In the course of their job, fire safety technicians recognize fire hazards, apply technical knowledge, and perform services to control and prevent fires. Fire safety technicians are employed by local fire departments, fire insurance companies, industrial organizations, government agencies, and businesses dealing with fire protection equipment and consulting services.

Public education is an important area of activity for fire control and safety technicians. By working with the public through schools, businesses, and service clubs and organizations, they can expand the level of understanding about the dangers of fire and teach people about methods of fire protection and fire prevention.

Specific positions in this field include fire science specialists; fire extinguisher servicers; fire insurance inspectors; fire insurance underwriters; fire insurance adjusters; fire protection engineering technicians; fire inspectors; plant protection inspectors; fire alarm superintendents; and fire service field instructors.

Professional and Personal Requirements

Certification is required for certain fire safety careers. For example, fire protection engineering technicians and fire alarm superintendents

158

can obtain certification from the National Institute for Certification in Engineering Technologies.

Fire science technicians must have excellent oral and written communication skills. They must be willing to study to keep abreast of new developments in the field, including improvements in fire detection instruments, equipment, and methods for fireproofing materials.

Starting Out

Graduates of two-year programs in technical colleges, community colleges, or technical institutes usually secure jobs before they graduate. They are hired by company recruiters sent to the school placement offices, which arrange interviews for graduating students.

Some schools have cooperative work-study programs where students study part-time and work part-time for pay. Often students in such programs are hired permanently by the cooperating employer.

Some students may find jobs in fire departments that are large enough to need special technicians outside the ranks of regular firefighters. Others may choose to become firefighters and advance to technical positions.

Earnings

Starting salaries for fire safety technicians are approximately $20,500 to $22,000. Experienced technicians earn salaries that average between $33,000 to $44,000 per year. Those who advance to positions of great responsibility may earn $60,000 per year or more.

Benefits for these employees usually include compensatory time off or overtime pay for hours worked beyond the regular work schedule. Other benefits include liberal pension plans, disability benefits, and early retirement options, in addition to paid vacations, paid sick leave, and paid holidays.

Employment Outlook

Technical careers in fire prevention and control are predicted to grow more rapidly than the average for all other occupations. In the future, these technicians will probably be needed in more places than ever before. The greatest increase in employment will be in industry. More industries are finding that the cost of replacing buildings and property destroyed by fire is greater than the yearly cost of fire protection and the expertise and equipment of these specialists.

New fire prevention and control techniques must be developed as technology continues to change. Skilled and ambitious fire safety technicians will be needed to address and monitor this changing technology.

For More Information

For information on fire prevention careers, contact:

- **National Fire Protection Association**
  One Batterymarch Park
  Quincy, MA 02269-9101
  Tel: 617-770-3000
  Web: http://www.nfpa.org

For information on student chapters, a list of universities that offer programs in fire protection engineering, and to obtain a copy of Careers in Fire Protection Engineering, *contact:*

- **Society of Fire Protection Engineers**
  7315 Wisconsin Avenue, Suite 1225W
  Bethesda, MD 20814
  Tel: 301-718-2910
  Web: http://www.sfpe.org/

For information on training programs, contact:

- **National Fire Sprinkler Association**
  PO Box 1000
  40 Jon Barrett Road
  Patterson, NY 12563
  Tel: 914-878-4200
  Web: http://www.nfsa.org

For information on certification, contact:

- **National Institute for Certification in Engineering Technologies**
  1420 King Street
  Alexandria, VA 22314-2794
  Web: http://www.nicet.org

Firefighters

School Subjects: Biology, Chemistry
Personal Skills: Leadership/management, Mechanical/manipulative
Work Environment: Indoors and outdoors, Primarily multiple locations
Salary Range: $26,064 to $38,000 to $80,000+
Certification or Licensing: None available
Outlook: Little change or more slowly than the average

The Job

Firefighters are responsible for protecting people's lives and property from the hazards of fire and other emergencies. They provide this protection by fighting fires to prevent property damage and by rescuing people trapped or injured by fires or other accidents. Through inspections and safety education, firefighters also work to prevent fires and unsafe conditions that could result in dangerous, life-threatening situations. They assist in many types of emergencies and disasters in everyday life. Firefighters often answer calls requesting emergency medical care, such as help in giving artificial respiration to drowning victims or emergency aid for heart attack victims on public streets. They may also administer emergency medical care. Many fire departments operate emergency medical services. Most firefighters are cross-trained to participate in both fire and emergency activities.

Professional and Personal Requirements

There is no certification or licensing available in this field.

Firefighters must meet a wide array of criteria in such areas as age, size, vision, physical fitness, stamina, and intelligence. A mechanical aptitude is an asset to a person in this career. Firefighters need sound judgment, mental alertness, and the ability to reason and think logically in situations demanding courage and bravery. The ability to remain calm and compassionate is a valuable asset.

Starting Out

After completing an associate degree, many people enter this occupation by applying to take the local civil service examinations. If they successfully pass all of the required tests and receive a job appointment, new firefighters may serve a probationary period during which they receive intensive training. After the completion of this training, they may be assigned to a fire department or engine company for specific duties.

In some small towns and communities, applicants may enter this occupation through on-the-job training as volunteer firefighters or by applying directly to the local government for the position.

Earnings

The average starting salary for a full-time firefighter was $26,064 in 1996, according to the International City/County Management Association. Experienced firefighters earned an average of $38,000 a year. Many firefighters receive longevity pay for each year they remain in service, which may add as much as $1,000 per year of service to their salaries. Average annual earnings (with longevity pay) range from about $35,310 in the smaller cities to $48,538 in the largest cities. Firefighters also earn overtime pay and shift differentials. Benefits, which often include early retirement options, typically include health, life, and disability insurance.

Fire lieutenants, captains, and fire chiefs average between $47,000 and $55,000, although fire chiefs in larger cities may earn as much as $80,000 per year or more. Inspectors and fire protection engineers earn an average of $34,000 per year.

Employment Outlook

Fire fighting is forecasted to remain a very competitive field, and the number of people interested in becoming firefighters will outweigh the number of available positions in most areas.

Most new jobs will be created as small communities grow and augment their volunteer staffs with career firefighters. There are also growing numbers of "call" firefighters, who are paid only when responding to fires. Little growth is expected in large, urban fire departments. Some local governments are expected to contract for fire-fighting services with private companies.

For More Information

The following organizations have information on careers in the fire service.

- **International Association of Fire Chiefs**
  4025 Fair Ridge Drive
  Fairfax, VA 22033-2868
  Tel: 703-273-0911
  Web: http://www.iafc.org

- **National Fire Protection Association**
  1 Batterymarch Park
  Quincy, MA 02269-9101
  Tel: 617-770-3000
  Email: library@nfpa.org
  Web: http://www.nfpa.org

For information on scholarships, contact:

- **International Association of Firefighters**
  1750 New York Avenue, NW
  Washington, DC 20006
  Tel: 202-737-8484
  Web: http://www.iaff.org

Fluid Power Technicians

School Subjects: Mathematics, Technical/Shop
Personal Skills: Mechanical/manipulative, Technical/scientific
Work Environment: Primarily indoors, Primarily multiple locations
Salary Range: $22,000 to $33,000 to $40,000+
Certification or Licensing: Voluntary
Outlook: Faster than the average

The Job

Fluid power technicians deal with equipment that utilizes the pressure of a liquid or gas in a closed container to transmit, multiply, or control power. Working under the supervision of an engineer or engineering staff, they assemble, install, maintain, and test fluid power equipment, which is found in almost every facet of American daily life. Many different machines use some kind of fluid power system, including equipment used in industries such as agriculture, manufacturing, defense, and mining. Fluid power machines can be either hydraulic (activated by liquid) or pneumatic (activated by gas).

In their work, fluid power technicians analyze blueprints, drawings, and specifications; set up various milling, shaping, grinding, and drilling machines and make precision parts; use sensitive measuring instruments to make sure the parts are exactly the required size; and use hand and power tools to put together components of the fluid power system they are assembling or repairing.

Some technicians work on research and development teams; others work as sales and service representatives for companies that make and sell fluid power equipment to industrial plants. Some technicians repair and maintain fluid power components of heavy equipment used in construction, on farms, or in mining. Many technicians are also employed in the aircraft industry.

Professional and Personal Requirements

Certification for fluid power technicians, which is voluntary, is offered through the Fluid Power Certification Board.

Technicians must be able to understand and analyze mechanical systems. They should have both mechanical aptitude and an analytical mindset, as well as the ability to communicate easily with others. Finally, a successful technician should enjoy challenges and the troubleshooting of problems.

Starting Out

Most fluid power technicians obtain their jobs through their community and technical college placement offices. In addition, organizations such as the Fluid Power Society and the Fluid Power Educational Foundation have lists of their corporate members that can be used to start a job search. Some openings might be listed in the employment sections of newspapers.

Earnings

The average starting salary for fluid power technicians varies according to geographic location and industry, but technical colleges estimate $22,000 per year. An estimated national average wage for technicians might be in the low to mid-$30,000s. Those who move into consulting or other advanced positions can earn even more. Most workers in this field receive a full benefits package, often including vacation days, sick leave, medical and life insurance, and a retirement plan.

Employment Outlook

Because fluid power is used in so many different industries, the need for technicians is growing rapidly. Currently, in fact, the demand for these trained workers exceeds the supply. In the '90s, electrohydraulic and electropneumatic technologies opened up new markets such as active suspensions on automobiles and reestablished older markets such as robotics. Therefore, the fluid power industry is expected to continue growing and the outlook for technicians should remain excellent through the year 2006.

For More Information

For information about certification, contact:

- **The Fluid Power Society**
  Fluid Power Certification Board
  2433 North Mayfair Road, Suite 111
  Milwaukee, WI 53226
  Tel: 414-257-0910
  Web: http://www.ifps.org/certific.html

For a list of schools offering courses in fluid power technology and information about available scholarships, contact:

- **Fluid Power Educational Foundation**
  3333 North Mayfair Road, Suite 311
  Milwaukee, WI 53222
  Tel: 414-778-3364
  Web: http://www.fpef.org

For information about the fluid power industry, contact:

- **National Fluid Power Association**
  3333 North Mayfair Road
  Milwaukee, WI 53222
  Tel: 414-778-3344
  Web: http://www.nfpa.com

Funeral Home Workers

School Subjects: Biology, Psychology
Personal Skills: Leadership/management, Technical/scientific
Work Environment: Primarily indoors, Primarily one location
Salary Range: $25,000 to $50,000 to $150,000+
Certification or Licensing: Required
Outlook: About as fast as the average

The Job

The *funeral director,* also called a *mortician* or *undertaker,* makes arrangements with the families of the deceased for removal of the body to the funeral home, secures information for and files the death certificate, and makes complete arrangements for the burial plans and funeral service, in accordance with the family's wishes. The director also supervises the personnel who prepare bodies for burial. An *embalmer* uses chemical solutions to disinfect, preserve, and restore the body and employs cosmetic aids to simulate a lifelike appearance. A *mortuary science technician* works under the direction of a mortician or funeral director to perform embalming and related funeral service tasks. Most are trainees working to become licensed embalmers and funeral directors.

People who work in the funeral services industry are employed throughout the world in small communities as well as large metropolitan areas. Because societies vary worldwide regarding the rites of passage, some areas of the world may have different legal and traditional requirements regarding death and burial procedures.

Professional and Personal Requirements

All states require embalmers to be licensed, and most states require licenses for funeral directors as well.

Funeral service workers must always be compassionate, courteous, and sympathetic, as well as confident, knowledgeable, and stable. The work sometimes requires lifting the deceased or their caskets, which may require physical strength.

Starting Out

Almost the only way to enter a funeral service career is to attend an accredited school of mortuary science after obtaining a high school diploma and then to enter the field as a mortuary science technician.

Most mortuary science schools maintain close contact with funeral homes in the area and provide a free placement service for graduates. Additionally, since many schools conduct internship programs that place students in funeral homes as part of their formal education, students are often able to obtain permanent jobs where they have interned.

Earnings

The average starting salary for entry-level licensed funeral directors and embalmers in the 1990s is in the mid-twenties range. Many owners of funeral homes earn more than $50,000 annually. Some owners of funeral homes in large metropolitan areas may earn over $150,000 a year.

In some metropolitan areas, many funeral-home employees are unionized; in these cases, salaries are determined by union contracts and are generally higher.

Benefits may vary depending on the position and the employer.

Employment Outlook

Growth in this field is expected to be about as fast as the average through the year 2006. The demand for funeral services will rise as the population grows and deaths increase; however, most funeral homes will be able to meet the demand without adding new employees. The average funeral home conducts only one or two funerals each week and is usually capable of handling several more without hiring additional professional personnel.

Job security in the funeral service industry is relatively unaffected by economic downturns. Despite the flux and movement in the population, funeral homes are a stable institution. The average firm has been in its community for more than 40 years and funeral homes with a history of over 100 years are not uncommon.

For More Information

For information on scholarships and a list of accredited funeral service and mortuary science college programs, contact:

■ **American Board of Funeral Service Education**
PO Box 1305
Brunswick, ME 04011
Tel: 207-798-5801
Email: abfse@clinic.net
Web: http://www.abfse.org

For information on funeral service careers and home-study, contact:

■ **National Funeral Directors Association**
13625 Bishops Drive
Brookfield, WI 53005
Tel: 414-789-1880
Web: http://www.nfda.org

Graphic Designers

School Subjects: Art, Computer science
Personal Skills: Artistic, Communication/ideas
Work Environment: Primarily indoors, Primarily one location
Salary Range: $23,000 to $50,000 to $85,000+
Certification or Licensing: None available
Outlook: Faster than the average

The Job

Graphic designers are practical artists whose creations are intended to express ideas, convey information, or draw attention to a product. They design a wide variety of materials including advertisements; displays; packaging; signs; computer graphics and games; book and magazine covers and interiors; animated characters; and company logos to fit the needs and preferences of their various clients.

Most designs commissioned to graphic designers involve both artwork and copy (that is, words). Thus, designers must not only be familiar with the wide range of art media (photography, drawing, painting, collage, etc.) and styles, but they must also be familiar with a wide range of typefaces and know how to manipulate them for the right effect. When a design has been approved by the client, the designer prepares the design for printing, which requires a good understanding of the printing process, including color separation, paper properties, and halftone (i.e., photograph) reproduction.

Professional and Personal Requirements

There is no certification or licensing available in this field.

As with all artists, graphic designers need a degree of artistic talent, creativity, and imagination. They must be sensitive to beauty and have an eye for detail and a strong sense of color, balance, and proportion. More and more graphic designers need solid computer

170

skills and working knowledge of several of the common drawing, image editing, and page layout programs.

Starting Out

The best way to enter the field of graphic design is to have a strong portfolio. Potential employers rely on portfolios to evaluate talent and how that talent might be used to fit the company's special needs. Beginning graphic designers can assemble a portfolio from work completed at school, in art classes, and in part-time or freelance jobs.

Job interviews may be obtained by applying directly to companies that employ designers. Many colleges and professional schools have placement services to help their graduates find positions, and sometimes it is possible to get a referral from a previous part-time employer.

Earnings

The Society of Publication Designers has estimated that entry-level graphic designers earned between $23,000 and $27,000 annually in 1997. In general, computer graphics designers earn wages on the higher end of the range. Design managers or directors earn about $60,000 a year and corporate vice-presidents make $70,000 and up. The owner of a consulting firm can make $85,000 or more.

Graphic designers who work for large corporations receive full benefits, including health insurance, paid vacation, and sick leave. Self-employed designers should expect inconsistency in their earnings, and they also must provide their own insurance and benefits.

Employment Outlook

The U.S. Department of Labor predicts that employment for qualified graphic designers will be very good through the year 2006, especially for those involved with computer graphics. The design field in general is expected to grow at a faster than average rate, according to the U.S. Department of Labor. As computer graphic technology continues to advance, there will be a need for well-trained computer graphic designers. Companies that have always used graphics will expect their designers to perform work on computers. Companies for which graphic design was once too time consuming or costly are now sprucing up company newsletters and magazines, among other things, and need graphic designers to do it.

For More Information

For more information about careers in graphic design, contact the following organizations:

- **American Institute of Graphic Arts**
  164 Fifth Avenue
  New York, NY 10160-1652
  Tel: 800-548-1634
  Email: aiganatl@aol.com
  Web: http://www.aiga.org

- **American Center for Design**
  325 West Huron, Suite 711
  Chicago, Illinois 60610
  Tel: 312.787.2018
  Web: http://www.ac4d.org/

For information on accredited schools, contact:

- **National Association of Schools of Art and Design**
  11250 Roger Bacon Drive, Suite 21
  Reston, VA 22090
  Tel: 703-437-0700

Heating and Cooling Technicians

School Subjects: Mathematics, Technical/Shop

Personal Skills: Following instructions, Mechanical/manipulative

Work Environment: Indoors and outdoors, Primarily multiple locations

Salary Range: $15,000 to $33,000 to $42,000

Certification or Licensing: Required for certain positions

Outlook: About as fast as the average

The Job

Heating and cooling technicians work on systems that control the temperature, humidity, and air quality of enclosed environments. They help design, manufacture, install, and maintain climate-control equipment. They provide people with heating and air-conditioning in such structures as shops, hospitals, malls, theaters, factories, restaurants, offices, and apartment buildings, and private homes. They may work to provide climate-controlled environments for temperature-sensitive products such as computers, foods, medicines, and precision instruments. They may also provide comfortable environments or refrigeration in such modes of transportation as ships, trucks, planes, and trains.

Professional and Personal Requirements

For the most part, no special licensing or certification is required for heating and cooling technicians. However, all technicians who handle refrigerants must receive approved refrigerant recovery certification, which is a recent requirement of the Environmental Protection Agency.

Voluntary certification through professional associations, such as the Air Conditioning Contractors of America, is also available. In some areas of the field, certification is increasingly the norm and viewed as a basic indicator of competence.

Heating and cooling technicians need an aptitude for working with tools, manual dexterity and manipulation, and the desire to perform challenging work that requires a high level of competence and quality.

Starting Out

Many students in two-year educational programs work at a job related to their area of training during the summer between their first and second years. At some schools, work experience is part of the curriculum, particularly during the latter part of their program. It is not unusual for graduates of two-year programs to receive several offers of employment, either from contacts they have made themselves or from companies that routinely recruit new graduates.

In addition to using their schools' job placement services, students can independently explore other leads by applying directly to local heating and cooling contractors; sales, installation, and service shops; or manufacturers of air-conditioning, refrigeration, and heating equipment.

Earnings

In private industry, the average beginning salary for heating and cooling technicians who have completed a two-year postsecondary school program is approximately $15,000. Salaries for nonsupervisory heating and cooling technicians, including those with several years' experience, usually fall between $24,000 and $42,000 and average around $33,000 a year.

Many employers offer medical insurance and paid vacation days, holidays, and sick days, although the actual benefits vary from employer to employer.

Employment Outlook

Employment in the heating and cooling field is expected to increase about as fast as the average for all occupations through the year 2006, according to the U.S. Department of Labor. Some openings will occur because experienced workers retire or transfer to other work.

Other openings will be generated because of a demand for new climate-control systems for residences and industrial and commercial users. In addition, many existing systems are being upgraded to provide more efficient use of energy and to provide benefits not originally built into the system. There is a growing emphasis on improving indoor air. There is an increasing awareness on making equipment more environmentally friendly, and with the implementation of the Clean Air Act Amendment of 1990, systems that use CFCs need to be retrofitted or replaced with new equipment.

For More Information

For information on careers, educational programs, and certification, contact:

- **Air-Conditioning and Refrigeration Institute**
  4301 North Fairfax Drive, Suite 425
  Arlington, VA 22203
  Tel: 703-524-8800

For information on certification, contact:

- **Air Conditioning Contractors of America**
  1712 New Hampshire Avenue, NW
  Washington, DC 20009
  Tel: 202-483-9370

For general career information, contact the following organizations:

- **National Association of Plumbing-Heating-Cooling Contractors**
  PO Box 6808
  180 South Washington Street
  Falls Church, VA 22040
  Tel: 703-237-8100

- **Refrigerating Engineers and Technicians Association**
  401 North Michigan Avenue
  Chicago, IL 60611-4267
  Tel: 312-644-6610

Hotel and Motel Managers

School Subjects: Business, Mathematics, Speech
Personal Skills: Helping/teaching, Leadership/management
Work Environment: Primarily indoors, Primarily one location
Salary Range: $39,000 to $54,000 to $84,000+
Certification or Licensing: Voluntary
Outlook: About as fast as the average

The Job

A *hotel general manager* is responsible for the overall supervision of the hotel, the different departments, and their staff. They follow operating guidelines set by the hotel's owners, or, if part of a chain, by the hotel's main headquarters and executive board. A general manager, also known as the GM, allocates funds to all departments of the hotel, approves expenditures, sets room rates, and establishes standards for food and beverage service, hotel decor, and all guest services. GMs tour the hotel property every day, usually with the head of the housekeeping department, to make certain the hotel is kept clean and orderly. GMs are responsible for keeping the hotel's accounting books in order; advertising and marketing the hotel; maintaining and ordering supplies; and interviewing and training new employees. However, in larger hotels, the GM is usually supported by one or more assistants.

Specific positions within this field include resident managers, front office managers, executive housekeepers, personal managers, restaurant managers, food and beverage managers, and convention services managers.

Professional and Personal Requirements

Certification, though not required, is widely recognized as a measurement of industry knowledge and job experience. Programs are offered by industry trade associations, such as the Educational Institute of the American Hotel and Motel Association.

Hotel managers are strong leaders who have a flair for organization and communication. They need outstanding people skills and calm demeanors when dealing with difficult situations.

Starting Out

The position of general manager is among the top rungs of the hotel career ladder. It is unlikely this would be anyones first industry job. In today's highly technical age, experience, though still important, is not enough for job advancement. Most candidates have some postsecondary education; many have at least an associate degree in hotel and restaurant management. Graduates entering the hotel industry usually pay their dues by working as assistant hotel managers, assistant departmental managers, or shift managers.

College career centers, the local library, and the Internet can all be helpful when researching college programs or specific businesses.

Earnings

According to a 1997 salary review conducted by Roth Young Personnel Service, general managers earned an average annual low of $39,000, median $54,000, and high of $84,000 or more. Assistant managers' salaries averaged a low of $27,000, median $39,000, and a high of $58,000. Managers can also boost their annual income with company year-end bonuses—up to 25 percent of their base salary.

All managers receive paid holidays and vacations, sick leave, and other benefits, such as medical and life insurance, pension or profit-sharing plans, and educational assistance.

Employment Outlook

The job-growth outlook for hotel managers is about as fast as the average through the year 2006, according to the U.S. Department of Labor. However, the number of jobs for hotel managers is not expected to grow as rapidly as in the past due largely to hotel consolidation and the rise of less expensive lodging properties. Also, some managerial duties have been reassigned to front desk employees.

Candidates with the best opportunities will be college graduates with degrees in hotel or restaurant management or business and managers with excellent work experience. Certification in hotel management will also be a good drawing card.

For More Information

For information on careers in hotel management, contact:

- **American Hotel and Motel Association**
  1201 New York Avenue, NW, Suite 600
  Washington, DC 20005-3931
  Tel: 202-289-3100
  Web: http://www.ahma.org/

For information on careers, education, and certification, contact:

- **International Executive Housekeepers Association**
  1001 Eastwood Drive, Suite 301
  Westerville, OH 43081
  Tel: 614-895-7166
  Email: excel@ieha.org
  Web: http://www.ieha.org

For information on internships, scholarships, or certification requirements, contact:

- **Educational Institute of the American Hotel & Motel Association**
  800 North Magnolia
  Orlando, FL 32803
  Tel: 800-752-4567
  Web: http://www.ei-ahma.org

For education information and a list of available school programs, contact:

- **Council on Hotel, Restaurant, and Institutional Education**
  1200 17th Street, NW
  Washington, DC 20036-3097
  Tel: 202-331-5990
  Web: http://chrie.org/

Human Services Workers

School Subjects: Health, Sociology
Personal Skills: Communication/ideas, Helping/teaching
Work Environment: Primarily indoors, Primarily one location
Salary Range: $15,000 to $25,000 to $30,000
Certification or Licensing: None available
Outlook: Much faster than the average

The Job

Under the supervision of social workers, psychologists, sociologists, and other professionals, *human services workers* offer support to families, the elderly, the poor, and others in need. They teach life and communication skills to people in mental health facilities or substance abuse programs. Employed by agencies, shelters, halfway houses, and hospitals, they work individually with clients or in group counseling. They also direct clients to social services and benefits.

Professional and Personal Requirements

There is no certification or licensing available in this field.

A genuine interest in the lives and concerns of others and a sensitivity to their situations are important qualities for a human services worker. Their responsibilities can be difficult and their work can be very stressful. The workload for a human services worker can also be overwhelming; since staff are often overworked due to funding limitations, employee burnout is a common problem.

Starting Out

Students may find jobs through their high school counselors or local and state human services agencies. Sometimes summer jobs and volunteer work can develop into full-time employment upon graduation. Employers try to be selective in their hiring because many human services jobs involve direct contact with people who are impaired and therefore vulnerable to exploitation. Evidence of helping others is a definite advantage.

Earnings

Salaries of human services workers depend in part on their employer and amount of experience. According to the *Occupational Outlook Handbook,* starting salaries for human services workers range from $15,000 to $24,000 a year. Experienced workers can earn from $20,000 to $30,000 annually.

Employment Outlook

Employment for human services workers will grow much faster than the average through 2006, according to the U.S. Department of Labor. Much of this growth is expected to occur in homes for the mentally impaired and developmentally disabled. Also, the life expectancy for people in the United States continues to rise, requiring more assistance for the elderly, such as adult day care and meal delivery. Correctional facilities are also expected to employ many more human services workers. Because counseling inmates and offenders can be undesirable work, there are a number of high-paying jobs available in that area.

New ideas in treating disabled or mentally ill people also influence employment growth in group homes and residential care facilities. Public concern for the homeless—many of whom are former mental patients who were released under service reductions in the 1980s—as well as troubled teenagers and those with substance abuse problems, will likely bring about new community-based programs and group residences.

Job prospects in public agencies are not as bright as they once were because of fiscal policies that tighten eligibility requirements for federal welfare and other payments. State and local governments are expected to remain major employers, however, as the burden of providing social services such as welfare, child support, and nutrition programs is shifted from the federal government to the state and local level.

For More Information

■ **American Association for Counseling and Development**
5999 Stevenson Avenue
Alexandria, VA 22304
Tel: 800-545-2223

For education information, contact:
■ **Council for Standards in Human Service Education**
Northern Essex Community College
Haverhill, MA 01830

This organization offers student memberships.
■ **National Organization for Human Service Education**
5326 Avery Road
New Port Richey, FL 34652
Tel: 727-847-7533
Email: wipertn66@aol.com
Web: http://www.nohse.org

Industrial Engineering Technicians

School Subjects: Computer science, Mathematics
Personal Skills: Following instructions, Technical/scientific
Work Environment: Primarily indoors, Primarily one location
Salary Range: $22,000 to $38,360 to $59,000+
Certification or Licensing: Voluntary
Outlook: About as fast as the average

The Job

Industrial engineering technicians assist industrial engineers in their duties: they collect and analyze data and make recommendations for the efficient use of personnel, materials, and machines to produce goods or to provide services. They may study the time, movements, and methods a worker uses to accomplish daily tasks in production, maintenance, or clerical areas.

Industrial engineering technicians prepare charts to illustrate workflow, floor layouts, materials handling, and machine utilization. They make statistical studies, analyze production costs, prepare layouts of machinery and equipment, help plan work flow and work assignments, and recommend revisions to revamp production methods or improve standards. As part of their job, industrial engineering technicians often use equipment such as computers, timers, and camcorders.

Specific positions in this field include work measurement technicians; time study technicians; production control technicians; inventory control technicians; quality control technicians; cost control technicians; budget technicians; and plant layout technicians.

Professional and Personal Requirements

The National Institute for Certification in Engineering Technologies has established a certification program that some technicians may wish to participate in. Although certification is not generally required by employers, those with certification often have a competitive advantage when it comes to hiring and promotions.

Industrial engineering technicians should be adept at compiling and organizing data and be able to express themselves clearly and persuasively both orally and in writing. They should be detail oriented and enjoy solving problems.

Starting Out

Many industrial engineering technicians find their first jobs through interviews with company recruiters who visit campuses. In many cases, students are invited to visit the prospective employer's plant for further consultation and to become better acquainted with the area, product, and facilities. For many students, the job placement office of their college or technical school is the best source of possible jobs. Local manufacturers or companies are in constant contact with these facilities, so they have the most current, up-to-date job listings.

Earnings

According to the U.S. Bureau of Labor Statistics, the average annual salary for industrial engineering technicians in 1997 was $38,360. Some technicians, however, especially those at the very beginning of their careers, earn about $22,000 a year, while some senior technicians with special skills and experience earn over $59,000 a year. In addition to salary, most employers offer paid vacation time, holidays, insurance and retirement plans, and tuition assistance for work-related courses.

Employment Outlook

As products become more technically demanding to produce, competitive pressures will force companies to improve and update manufacturing facilities and product designs. Thus, the demand for well-trained industrial engineering technicians will stay about average through 2006, according to the U.S. Department of Labor. Opportunities will be best for individuals who have up-to-date skills. As technology becomes more sophisticated, employers will continue to seek technicians who require the least amount of additional job training.

Prospective technicians should keep in mind that advances in technology and management techniques make industrial engineering a constantly changing field. Technicians will be able to take advantage of new opportunities only if they are willing to continue their training and education throughout their careers.

For More Information

For information about membership in a professional society specifically created for engineering technicians, contact:

- **American Society of Certified Engineering Technicians**
  PO Box 1348
  Flowery Branch, GA 30542
  Tel: 770-967-9173

For more information on careers and training as an industrial engineering technician, contact:

- **IEEE Industry Applications Society**
  c/o Institute of Electrical and Electronics Engineers
  3 Park Avenue, 17th floor
  New York, NY 10017
  Tel: 212-419-7900
  Web: http://www.ieee.org/eab/

- **Institute of Industrial Engineers**
  25 Technology Park/Atlanta
  Norcross, GA 30092
  Tel: 404-449-0460
  Web: http://www.iienet.org

For information about obtaining certification, please contact:

- **National Institute for Certification in Engineering Technologies**
  1420 King Street
  Alexandria, VA 22314-2715
  Tel: 888-476-4238
  Web: http://www.nicet.org

Interior Designers and Decorators

School Subjects: Art, Business
Personal Skills: Artistic, Communication/ideas
Work Environment: Primarily indoors, Primarily multiple locations
Salary Range: $19,296 to $39,967 to $250,000
Certification or Licensing: Required by certain states
Outlook: Much faster than the average

The Job

Interior designers and *interior decorators* evaluate, plan, and design the interior areas of residential, commercial, and industrial structures. The terms "interior designer" and "interior decorator" are sometimes used interchangeably. However, there is an important distinction between the two. Interior designers plan and create the overall design for interior spaces, while interior decorators focus on the decorative aspects of the design and furnishing of interiors.

Interior designers and decorators perform a wide variety of services, depending on the type of project and the clients' requirements. A job may range from designing a single room in a private residence to coordinating the entire interior arrangement of a huge building complex. Typical responsibilities include helping clients select equipment and fixtures, supervising the coordination of colors and materials, obtaining estimates and costs within the client's budget, and overseeing the execution and installation of the project. They often advise clients on architectural requirements and space planning.

Professional and Personal Requirements

Over 20 states and jurisdictions in the United States require licensing for interior designers. When licensing is not required, accreditation programs are often recommended.

Interior designers and decorators need to have artistic talent, including an eye for color, proportion, balance, and detail, as well as patience, enthusiasm, and attention to detail. Designers should be creative, analytical, and ethical. They need to be able to work well with a variety of other people, including clients and suppliers.

Starting Out

Most large department stores and design firms with established reputations hire only trained interior designers with four-year degrees and experience. Students with associate degrees may be able to locate entry-level positions with smaller firms. Many schools offer apprenticeship or internship programs which make it possible for students to apply their academic training in an actual work environment prior to graduation.

After graduating, a beginning designer must be prepared to spend one to three years as an assistant to an experienced interior designer before achieving full professional status.

Earnings

A report issued by the Economic Research Institute indicates that, as of October 1997, interior designers with one year of experience earn $19,296 to $28,149 per year. Those with five years of experience make $23,825 to $34,757 annually, while designers with 10 years of experience earn $27,397 to $39,967 a year. Established designers can earn $60,000 to $100,000 a year, and some nationally known professionals enjoy salaries of up to $250,000 annually. Overall, compensation is strong and salaries are increasing.

Benefits may include bonuses, paid vacations, health and life insurance, and paid sick or personal days.

Employment Outlook

Employment opportunities are expected to be very good for interior designers and decorators well into the next decade. Although the job outlook is heavily dependent on the economy, the U.S. economy is predicted to remain strong well into the new millennium, so interior designers and decorators with formal training and talent should find plenty of career opportunities.

While competition for good designing and decorating positions is expected to be fierce, especially for those lacking experience, there is currently a great need for industrial interior designers in housing developments, hospital complexes, hotels, and other large building projects. In addition, as construction of houses increases, there will be many projects available for residential designers.

For More Information

ASID is the oldest and largest organization of professional interior designers in the world.

- **American Society of Interior Designers (ASID)**
  608 Massachusetts Avenue, NE
  Washington, DC 20002-6006
  Tel: 202-546-3480
  Web: http://www.asid.org

FIDER promotes excellence in interior design education through research and the accreditation of academic programs.

- **Foundation for Interior Design Education Research (FIDER)**
  60 Monroe Center, NW, Suite 300
  Grand Rapids, MI 49503-2920
  Tel: 616-458-0400
  Web: http://www.fider.org

NCIDQ is an independent organization created to establish minimum standards and to develop and administer a minimum competency examination for the qualification of professional interior designers.

- **National Council for Interior Design Qualification (NCIDQ)**
  1200 18th Street, NW, Suite 1001
  Washington, DC 20036
  Tel: 202-721-0220
  Web: http://www.ncidq.org/

Laboratory Testing Technicians

School Subjects: Chemistry, Physics
Personal Skills: Following instructions, Technical/scientific
Work Environment: Primarily indoors, Primarily one location
Salary Range: $17,500 to $25,000 to $32,000
Certification or Licensing: Voluntary
Outlook: Faster than the average

The Job

Laboratory testing technicians conduct tests on countless substances and products. Their laboratory duties include measuring and evaluating materials and running quality control tests. They work in a variety of unrelated fields such as medicine, metallurgy, manufacturing, geology, and meteorology. Specific positions in this field include quality control technicians; assayers; medical technicians; geology technicians; and pharmaceutical technicians.

Regardless of the specific nature of the tests conducted by technicians, they must always keep detailed records of every step. Laboratory technicians often do a great deal of writing and must make charts, graphs, and other displays to illustrate results. They may be called on to interpret test results, to draw overall conclusions, and to make recommendations. Occasionally, laboratory testing technicians are asked to appear as witnesses in court to explain why a product failed and who may be at fault.

Professional and Personal Requirements

Licensing or registration is required by certain states. Voluntary certification is also available from such associations as the American Society for Clinical Laboratory Science and the American Medical Technologists.

Laboratory technicians should be detail oriented and enjoy figuring out how things work. They should like problem solving and trouble shooting. Laboratory technicians must have the patience to repeat a test many times, perhaps even on the same material. They should be independent and motivated to work on their own until their assigned tasks are completed.

Starting Out

Technical schools often help place graduating technicians. Many laboratories contact these schools directly looking for student employees or interns. Students can also contact local manufacturing companies and laboratories to find out about job openings in their area.

Earnings

Beginning, full-time laboratory testing technicians usually earn between $17,500 and $19,000 annually. Medium-range salaries for laboratory testing technicians range from about $24,000 to $26,000. The highest paid technicians earn about $32,000 per year. Salaries increase as technicians gain experience and as they take on supervisory responsibility. Most companies that employ laboratory testing technicians offer medical benefits, sick leave, and vacation time. However, these benefits will depend on the individual employer.

Employment Outlook

Job opportunities for laboratory technicians are expected to be good in the next decade. Laboratory technicians will be needed to test new production procedures as well as prototypes of new products. This growth will be especially high for metallurgical technicians.

Employment possibilities at testing laboratories will also grow, as many plants and companies come to rely on outside instead of in-house quality control. Also, as machinery grows increasingly complex, trained technicians will be needed not only to operate the equipment, but to test and evaluate it as well. The medical field, too, will need laboratory technicians who are well-versed in the latest medical and pharmaceutical technology and procedures.

Growth will be slower in industries focused on such materials as stone, clay, glass, fabricated metal products, and transportation equipment.

For More Information

For general career information, contact:

■ **American Chemical Society**
Career Education
1155 16th Street, NW
Washington, DC 20036
Tel: 202-872-4600
Web: http://www.acs.org

For information on student membership, contact:

■ **The Minerals, Metals, and Materials Society**
184 Thorn Hill Road
Warrendale, PA 15086
Tel: 724-776-9000
Web: http://www.tms.org

For information on certification, contact the following organizations:

■ **American Medical Technologists**
710 Higgins Road
Park Ridge, IL 60068
Tel: 708-823-5169
Web: http://www.amt1.com

■ **American Society for Clinical Laboratory Science**
7910 Woodmont Avenue, Suite 530
Bethesda, MD 20814
Tel: 301-657-2768
Web: http://www.ascls.org

Landscapers and Grounds Managers

School Subjects: Biology, Chemistry
Personal Skills: Following instructions, Mechanical/manipulative
Work Environment: Primarily outdoors, Primarily multiple locations
Salary Range: $11,440 to $29,120 to $50,000+
Certification or Licensing: Required for certain positions
Outlook: About as fast as the average

The Job

Landscapers and grounds managers plan, design, and maintain gardens, parks, lawns, and other landscaped areas and supervise the care of the trees, plants, and shrubs that are part of these areas. Specific job responsibilities depend on the type of area involved. Landscapers and grounds managers direct projects at private homes, parks, schools, arboretums, office parks, shopping malls, government offices, and botanical gardens. They are responsible for purchasing material and supplies and for training, directing, and supervising employees. Grounds managers maintain the land after the landscaping designs have been implemented. They may work alone or supervise a grounds staff. They may have their own business or be employed by a landscaping firm.

Specific jobs in this field include greenskeepers, greens superintendents, arboriculture technicians, tree surgeons, tree-trimming supervisors, pest management scouts, lawn-service workers, horticulturists, and turf grass consultants.

Professional and Personal Requirements

Licensing and certification differ by state and vary according to specific job responsibilities. For example, in most states landscapers and grounds managers need a certificate to spray insecticides or other chemicals.

Aspiring landscapers and grounds managers should have "green thumbs" and an interest in preserving and maintaining natural areas. They should be reasonably physically fit, have an aptitude for working with machines, and display good manual dexterity.

Starting Out

Summer or part-time jobs often lead to full-time employment with the same employer. If you enroll in a college or other training program you can receive help in finding work from the school's job placement office. In addition, directly applying to botanical gardens, nurseries, or golf courses is common practice. Jobs may also be listed in newspaper want ads. Most landscaping and related companies provide on-the-job training for entry-level personnel.

Earnings

According to the *Occupational Outlook Handbook,* the median starting salary for landscapers and groundskeepers in 1996 was $15,600 a year. Fifty percent earned from $11,440 to $21,320 a year. Top landscape workers earned about $29,120 a year. Landscape contractors and others who run their own businesses earn between $23,000 and $50,000 per year, and in some cases even more.

A readership salary survey conducted by the *Grounds Maintenance Magazine* found the average golf course superintendent earned $38,600 a year; company grounds manager, $38,900; and lawn care contractor, $32,500.

Fringe benefits vary from employer to employer but generally include medical insurance and paid vacation.

Employment Outlook

Job growth for this field is expected to grow as fast as the average for all occupations through the year 2006, according to the U.S. Department of Labor. Landscapers and their services will be in strong demand due to increased construction of buildings, shopping malls, homes, and other structures. Upkeep and renovation of existing landscapes will create jobs as well. There is also a high degree of turnover in this field.

Another factor for job growth is the increase in amount of disposable income. In order to have more leisure time, people are beginning to contract out for lawn care and maintenance. The popularity of home gardening will create jobs with local nurseries and garden centers. Jobs should be available with governmental agencies as well as in the private sector.

For More Information

For information on career opportunities and education, contact the following organizations:

- **American Society for Horticultural Sciences**
  113 South West Street, Suite 400
  Alexandria, VA 22314-2824
  Tel: 703-836-4606
  Web: http://www.ashs.org

- **Associated Landscape Contractors of America**
  12200 Sunrise Valley Drive, Suite 150
  Reston, VA 22091
  Tel: 703-620-6363
  Web: http://www.alca.org

- **American Nursery and Landscape Association**
  1250 I Street, NW, Suite 500
  Washington, DC 20005
  Tel: 202-789-2900
  Web: http://www.anla.org

- **Professional Grounds Management Society**
  120 Cockeysville Road, Suite 104
  Hunt Valley, MD 21031
  Tel: 410-584-9754
  Web: http://www.pgms.org

Laser Technicians

School Subjects: Computer science, Mathematics, Physics
Personal Skills: Mechanical/manipulative, Technical/scientific
Work Environment: Primarily indoors, Primarily one location
Salary Range: $21,000 to $30,000 to $38,000
Certification or Licensing: None available
Outlook: Faster than the average

The Job

Laser technicians produce, install, operate, service, and test laser systems and fiber optics equipment in industrial, medical, or research settings. They work under the direction of engineers or physicists who conduct laboratory activities in laser research and development or design. Depending upon the type of laser system—gas or solid state—a technician generally works either with information systems or with robotics, manufacturing, or medical equipment.

Laser technicians working with semiconductor systems are involved mainly with computer and telephone systems. In addition to helping to test, install, and maintain these systems, technicians work with engineers in their design and improvement. Technicians who work with gas-type systems usually assist scientists, engineers, or doctors. These systems are used primarily in the fields of robotics, manufacturing, and medical procedures.

In general, most technicians are employed in one of five areas: materials processing, communications, military, medical, and research. Technicians' duties include taking measurements, cleaning, aligning, inspecting, and operating lasers, and collecting data.

Professional and Personal Requirements

There is no certification or licensing available in this field.

Technicians should have an interest in instruments, laboratory apparatus, and how devices and systems work. Written and spoken communications are very important since technicians often have to work closely with people of varied technological backgrounds.

Good manual dexterity and coordination are important. Because lasers can be extremely dangerous and the work is very detailed, technicians must be able to work carefully, efficiently, and patiently.

Starting Out

Colleges that offer associate's degrees in laser technology usually work closely with industry, providing their graduating students with placement services and lists of potential employers. Most laser technicians graduating from a two-year program, in fact, are interviewed and recruited while still in school by representatives of companies who need laser technicians. If hired, they begin working soon after graduation.

Another way to enter the career is to join a branch of the U.S. Armed Forces under a technical training program for laser technicians. Military laser training is not always compatible to civilian training, however, and further study of theory and applications may be needed to enter the field as a civilian.

Earnings

According to a survey done by the Laser Institute of America, the overall average starting salary for laser technicians is between $21,000 and $25,000 per year. Salaries for technicians with at least five years of experience average approximately $30,000 per year, depending on background, experience, and the industry in which they are employed.

In addition to salary, technicians usually receive benefits such as insurance, paid holidays and vacations, and retirement plans.

Employment Outlook

Employment opportunities for laser technicians are expected to be very good through the year 2006. Rapid changes in technology and continued growth in the industry will almost certainly lead to an increase in the number of technicians employed.

Fiber optics is one of the fastest-growing areas for laser technicians. Optical fiber is replacing wire cables in communication lines and in many electronic products. This trend is expected to continue, so the demand for technicians in the fiber optics field should be especially strong. Growth is also expected to be strong in production, defense, medicine, construction, and entertainment.

For More Information

For information on laser technology and fellowships, contact:

■ **Institute of Electrical and Electronics Engineers, Lasers and Electro-Optical Society**
445 Hoes Lane
Piscataway, NJ 08854
Tel: 732-562-3892
Web: http://www.ieee.org/leos

For information on becoming a laser technician, contact:

■ **Laser Institute of America**
12424 Research Parkway, Suite 125
Orlando, FL 32826
Tel: 407-380-1553
Web: http://www.laserinstitute.org

Legal Secretaries

School Subjects: English, Government, Journalism
Personal Skills: Communication/ideas, Following instructions
Work Environment: Primarily indoors, Primarily one location
Salary Range: $22,204 to $30,000 to $39,450+
Certification or Licensing: Recommended
Outlook: About as fast as the average

The Job

Legal secretaries, sometimes called *litigation secretaries* or *trial secretaries,* assist lawyers by performing the administrative and clerical duties in a law office or firm.

They may type letters and legal documents, such as subpoenas, appeals, and motions; handle incoming and outgoing mail; maintain a detailed filing system; and deliver legal documents to the court. Besides these duties, legal secretaries spend much of their time making appointments with clients and dealing with client questions. The legal secretary is a sort of personal assistant to one or more lawyers as well, and must maintain the calendars and schedules for the office.

Legal secretaries are often called upon to conduct legal research for the cases that are current within the office. They may research and write legal briefs on a topic or case that is relevant to the lawyer's current cases. They also help lawyers find information such as employment, medical, and criminal records.

Professional and Personal Requirements

Two general legal secretary certifications are offered by the National Association of Legal Secretaries: the ALS (Accredited Legal Secretary) certification is for legal secretaries with education but no experience.

The PLS (Professional Legal Secretary) certification designates a legal secretary with exceptional skills and experience.

Legal secretaries must learn a great deal about court structures and practices and legal terminology. They must be able to grasp the inner workings of the law. Legal secretaries must also be able to quickly learn computer programs, especially word processing and database programs, and be able to use them skillfully.

Starting Out

Many legal secretaries get their first jobs through the career placement offices of their college or vocational school. Still other legal secretaries take the part-time job route to get their first full-time position. New graduates should contact the local law offices in their area and let them know they are available; often direct contact now can lead to a job later.

Earnings

As reported by Abbott, Langer & Associates, experienced legal secretaries averaged an annual salary of over $30,000. Ten percent earned a low average of $22,204; 10 percent averaged over $39,450. Certified legal secretaries and those who work for high-ranking attorneys (such as partners in a firm) receive higher pay.

Most law firms provide employees with sick days, vacation days, and holidays. Health insurance, 401(k) programs, and profit sharing may be offered as well.

Employment Outlook

According to the U.S. Department of Labor, the legal secretary field will continue to grow about as fast as the average. Because the legal services industry as a whole is growing, legal secretaries will be in high demand. Qualified legal secretaries will have plentiful job opportunities, especially in the larger metropolitan areas. There will be more than 440,000 legal secretaries employed in the United States by 2006, according to the U.S. Bureau of Labor Statistics.

For More Information

For information about certification, contact:

- **Legal Secretaries International, Inc.**
  8902 Sunnywood Drive
  Houston, TX 77088-3729
  Tel: 281-847-9754
  Email: phampton@stites.com
  Web: http://www.compassnet.com/legalsec

For information on certification, job openings, and more, contact:

- **National Association of Legal Secretaries**
  314 East 3rd Street, Suite 210
  Tulsa, OK 74120-2409
  Tel: 918-582-5188
  Email: yvonneb@nals.org
  Web: http://www.nals.org

Library Technicians

School Subjects: Computer science, English
Personal Skills: Helping/teaching, Technical/scientific
Work Environment: Primarily indoors, Primarily one location
Salary Range: $24,100 to $26,500 to $33,000
Certification or Licensing: None available
Outlook: Faster than the average

The Job

Library technicians, sometimes called *library technical assistants,* work in all areas of library services, supporting professional librarians or working independently to help people access information. They order and catalog books, help library patrons locate materials, and make the library's services and facilities readily available. Technicians verify bibliographic information on orders, and perform basic cataloging of materials received. They answer routine questions about library services and refer questions requiring professional help to librarians. Technicians also help with circulation desk operations and oversee the work of stack workers and catalog-card typists. They circulate audiovisual equipment and materials and inspect items upon return.

Work in libraries falls into three general categories: technical services, user services, and administrative services. Library technicians may be involved with the responsibilities of any of these areas. Specific positions within this field include catalogers, circulation counter attendants, media technicians, reference library technicians, school library technicians, automated system technicians, and information technicians.

Professional and Personal Requirements

There is no certification or licensing available in this field.

200

Library technicians should demonstrate aptitude for careful, detailed, analytical work. They should enjoy problem solving and working with people as well as with books and other library materials. Good interpersonal skills are invaluable, as are patience and flexibility. Good time management skills and judgment are also important qualities in a library technician.

Starting Out

Currently, most libraries are requiring their library technicians to be graduates of at least a two-year associate's degree program, so job applicants who have earned or are close to earning this degree will have the best employment opportunities.

In most cases, graduates of training programs for library technicians may seek employment through the placement offices of their community colleges. Job applicants may also approach libraries directly, usually by contacting the personnel officer of the library or the human resources administrator of the organization.

Many state library agencies maintain job hotlines listing openings for prospective library technicians. State departments of education also may keep lists of openings available for library technicians.

Earnings

Salaries for library technicians in the federal government averaged approximately $26,500 per year in 1997, according to the *Occupational Outlook Handbook*. Salaries in specialized libraries averaged $24,100 in 1996. Also in 1996, salaries for library technicians working at two-year colleges averaged $27,200, whereas technicians employed by four-year colleges and universities earned $30,200. Library technicians employed in public libraries earned an average of $33,000 in 1996.

Benefits vary according to employer, but most full time library technicians receive the same benefits as other employees, which may include the following: health insurance, dental insurance, paid vacations, paid holidays, compensated sick time, and retirement savings plans.

Employment Outlook

Currently there is a greater demand for library technicians than for librarians. Since the government is decreasing funding for public and school libraries, budgets will have to be cut. Because of the substantial savings an organization can have by employing a technician instead of a librarian, the U.S. Department of Labor predicts that the profession of library technician is expected to grow at a rate that is faster than the average through the year 2006. The continued growth of special libraries in medical, business, and law organizations will lead to growing opportunities for technicians who develop specialized skills.

For More Information

For career information, a list of accredited schools, information on scholarships and grants, and college student membership, contact:

- **American Library Association**
  Career Information
  50 East Huron Street
  Chicago, IL 60611
  Tel: 800-545-2433
  Web: http://www.ala.org/

For information on library technician careers, contact:

- **Association for Educational Communications and Technology**
  1025 Vermont Avenue, NW, Suite 820
  Washington, DC 20005-3516
  Tel: 202-347-7834
  Web: http://www.aect.org/

Licensed Practical Nurses

School Subjects: Biology, Chemistry
Personal Skills: Helping/teaching, Technical/scientific
Work Environment: Primarily indoors, Primarily multiple locations
Salary Range: $20,176 to $24,336 to $34,996+
Certification or Licensing: Required
Outlook: Faster than the average

The Job

Licensed practical nurses (LPNs), a specialty of the nursing profession, are sometimes called *licensed vocational nurses*. LPNs are trained to assist in the care and treatment of patients. They are responsible for many general duties of nursing such as administering prescribed drugs and medical treatments to patients; taking patients' temperatures and blood pressures; assisting patients with daily hygiene tasks; assisting in the preparation of medical examination and surgery; supervising nurse assistants; and performing routine laboratory tests. LPNs help with therapeutic and rehabilitation sessions; they may also participate in the planning, practice and evaluation of a patient's nursing care.

LPNs working in nursing homes have duties similar to those employed by hospitals. Those working in doctors' offices and clinics are sometimes required to perform clerical duties such as keeping records, maintaining files and paperwork, as well as answering phones and tending the appointment book. *Home health LPNs,* in addition to their nursing duties, may sometimes prepare and serve meals to their patients.

Professional and Personal Requirements

After graduating from a state-approved practical nursing program, a licensing examination is required by all 50 states. LPNs may also take the Certification Exam for Practical and Vocational Nurses in Long-Term Care (CEPN-LTC). Contact the National Council of State Boards of Nursing, Inc., for more information.

LPNs should be patient and nurturing and capable of following orders and working under close supervision. Stamina, both physical and mental, is a must for this occupation.

Starting Out

After licensing requirements are fulfilled, LPNs should check with human resource departments of hospitals, nursing homes, and clinics for openings. Employment agencies that specialize in health professions, and state employment agencies are other ways to find employment, as are school placement centers. Newspaper classified ads, nurses associations, and professional journals are great sources of job opportunities.

Earnings

According to the *Occupational Outlook Handbook,* LPNs earned an average of $24,336 annually in 1996. Fifty percent earned between $20,176 and $29,276; the top 10 percent earned over $34,996. A recent Buck Survey listed average earnings for LPNs employed at national chain nursing homes in 1996 at $12 an hour, or $480 weekly. Many LPNs are able to supplement their salaries with overtime pay and shift differentials. One-third of all LPNs work part time.

Employment Outlook

Employment prospects for LPNs are expected to grow faster than the average for all occupations through the year 2006, according to the U.S. Department of Labor. A growing elderly population requiring long term health care is the primary factor for the demand for qualified LPNs. Traditionally, hospitals provide the most job opportunities for LPNs. However, this source will only provide a moderate number of openings in the future. Inpatient population is not expected to increase significantly. Also, in many hospitals, certified nursing attendants are increasingly taking over many of the duties of LPNs.

Demand for LPNs will be greatest in nursing home settings and home health care agencies. Due to advanced medical technology, people are able to live longer, though many will require medical assistance. Private medical practices will also be good job sources since many medical procedures are now being performed on an outpatient basis in doctors' offices.

For More Information

For information on careers in nursing, a financial aid fact sheet, and a listing of AACN-member schools, contact:

- **American Association of Colleges of Nursing (AACN)**
  1 Dupont Circle, Suite 530
  Washington, DC 20036
  Tel: 202-463-6930
  Web: http://www.aacn.nche.edu

For information about state-approved programs and careers in nursing, contact:

- **National Association for Practical Nurse Education and Service, Inc.**
  1400 Spring Street, Suite 330
  Silver Spring, MD 20910
  Tel: 301-588-2491
  Email: napnes@aol.com

For information on certification, contact:

- **National Council of State Boards of Nursing, Inc.**
  676 North St. Clair Street, Suite 550
  Chicago, IL 60611-2921
  Tel: 312-787-6555
  Web: http://www.ncsbn.org

For career information and to subscribe to Practical Nursing Today, *a magazine geared toward the practicing practical nurse, contact:*

- **National Federation of Licensed Practical Nurses, Inc.**
  893 US Highway 70 West, Suite 202
  Garner, NC 27529
  Tel: 919-779-0046
  Web: http://www.nflpn.org/

Marine Services Technicians

School Subjects: Mathematics, Technical/Shop
Personal Skills: Following instructions, Mechanical/manipulative
Work Environment: Indoors and outdoors, One location with some travel
Salary Range: $11,648 to $21,424 to $35,152
Certification or Licensing: None available
Outlook: About as fast as the average

The Job

Marine services technicians work on the more than 16 million boats and other watercraft owned by people in the United States. They test and repair boat engines, transmissions, and propellers; rigging, masts, and sails; and navigational equipment and steering gear. They repair or replace defective parts and sometimes make new parts to meet special needs. They may also inspect and replace internal cabinets, refrigeration systems, electrical systems and equipment, sanitation facilities, hardware, and trim. Marine services technicians may work at boat dealerships, boat repair shops, boat engine manufacturers, or marinas. Naturally, jobs are concentrated near large bodies of water and coastal areas.

Specific positions within this field include motorboat mechanics; marine electronics technicians; field repairers; bench repairers; and fiberglass repairers.

Professional and Personal Requirements

There is no certification or licensing available in this field.

Motorboat technicians' work can sometimes be physically demanding, requiring them to lift heavy outboard motors or other components. Electronics technicians, on the other hand, must be able to work with delicate parts, such as wires and circuit boards; they should have good eyesight, color vision, and good hearing (to listen for malfunctions revealed by sound).

Technicians need to be able to adapt to the cyclical nature of this business. They typically are under a lot of pressure in the summer months, then have gaps in their work during the winter; some workers earn unemployment compensation at this time.

Starting Out

A large percentage of technicians get their start by working as general boatyard laborers—cleaning boats, cutting grass, painting, and so on. After showing interest and ability, they can begin to work with experienced technicians and learn skills on the job. Others attend vocational schools or technical colleges for training in skills such as engine repair and fiberglass work. Some professional organizations, such as International Women in Boating, Marine Trades Association of New Jersey, and Michigan Boating Industries Association, offer scholarships for those interested in marine technician training.

Earnings

According to the *Occupational Outlook Handbook,* a summary of earnings, which includes motorcycle and small-engine mechanics as well as boat mechanics, reflects that full-time workers had median earnings of $412 in 1996. The lowest 10 percent earned $224 a week, while the highest 10 percent earned $676 a week. The middle 50 percent earned between $289 and $549 a week.

Technicians in small shops tend to receive few fringe benefits, but larger employers often offer paid vacations, sick leave, and health insurance.

Employment Outlook

The marine services technician's job can be considered secure for the near future. Although marine services technology is a small field, it is expected to grow. Employment opportunities are expected to increase at an average rate through the year 2006. As boat design and construction become more complicated, the outlook will be best for well-trained technicians.

For More Information

The following professional organization awards scholarships to women in the marine industry. Write for information on eligibility, application requirements, and deadlines:

- **International Women in Boating**
  401 North Michigan Avenue
  Chicago, IL 60611
  Tel: 312-836-4747

To find out whether there is a marine association in your area, contact:

- **Marine Retail Association of America**
  150 East Huron Street, Suite 802
  Chicago, IL 60611
  Tel: 312-944-5080

Massage Therapists

School Subjects: Health, Physical education
Personal Skills: Helping/teaching, Mechanical/manipulative
Work Environment: Primarily indoors, Primarily one location
Salary Range: $12,710 to $40,000 to $72,800+
Certification or Licensing: Required by certain states
Outlook: Faster than the average

The Job

Massage therapy is a broad term referring to a number of health-related practices, including Swedish massage, sports massage, Rolfing, Shiatsu and acupressure, trigger point therapy, and reflexology. *Massage therapists* work to produce physical, mental, and emotional benefits through the manipulation of the body's soft tissue. Auxiliary methods, such as the movement of joints and the application of dry and steam heat, are also used. Although the techniques vary, most massage therapists (or *massotherapists*) press and rub the skin and muscles. Relaxed muscles, improved blood circulation and joint mobility, reduced stress and anxiety, and decreased recovery time for sprains and injured muscles are just a few of the potential benefits of massage therapy. Massage therapists are sometimes called *bodyworkers*. The titles *masseur* and *masseuse,* once common, are now rare among those who use massage for therapy and rehabilitation.

Professional and Personal Requirements

In about one-fourth of the states, massage therapists must have a license to practice. Certification—offered by the National Certification Board for Therapeutic Massage and Bodywork—is voluntary, although legislation is currently being considered to regulate certification across the country.

A person interested in becoming a massage therapist should be flexible, sensitive, and nurturing. Listening well and responding to the client is vital, as is focusing all attention on the task at hand. Manual dexterity is usually required to administer the treatments, as is the ability to stand for at least an hour at a time.

Starting Out

The American Massage Therapy Association (AMTA) offers job placement information to certified massage therapists who belong to the organization. Massage therapy schools have job placement offices, and newspapers often list jobs. Some graduates are able to enter the field as self-employed massage therapists, scheduling their own appointments and managing their own offices.

Networking is a valuable tool in maintaining a successful massage therapy enterprise. Many massage therapists get clients through referrals, and often rely on word of mouth to build a solid customer base.

Earnings

Some entry-level massage therapists earn as little as minimum wage (around $12,710 per year), but with experience, a massage therapist can charge from $10 to $70 for a one-hour session (the average rate in the United States is $50). Assuming 20 hours per week with clients is typical, a highly compensated massage therapist could make $72,800 or more per year. Additional earnings are made from tips.

Massage therapists are not, however, paid for the time spent on administrative and other business tasks. Those who are self-employed—more than two-thirds of all massage therapists—must also pay a self-employment tax and provide their own benefits. With membership in some national organizations, self-employed massage therapists may be eligible for group life, health, liability, and renter's insurance through the organization's insurance agency.

Employment Outlook

The employment outlook for massage therapists is good through the year 2006. For a 10-year period beginning in the early 1980s, the AMTA had a tenfold increase in the number of new members and a fourfold increase in the number of accredited or approved schools. The growing acceptance of massage therapy as an important health care discipline has led to the creation of additional jobs for massage therapists in many sectors.

For More Information

For more information about massage therapy, contact the following organizations:

■ **American Massage Therapy Association**
820 Davis Street, Suite 100
Evanston, IL 60201-4444
Tel: 847-864-0123
Web: http://www.amtamassage.org/

■ **Associated Bodywork and Massage Professionals**
28677 Buffalo Park Road
Evergreen, CO 80439-7347
Tel: 800-458-2267
Web: http://www.abmp.com/

For information about certification and education requirements for the state in which you plan to work, contact:

■ **National Certification Board for Therapeutic Massage and Bodywork**
8201 Greensboro Drive, Suite 300
McLean, VA 22102
Tel: 800-296-0664 or 703-610-9015
Web: http://www.ncbtmb.com/

Mechanical Engineering Technicians

School Subjects: English, Mathematics, Physics
Personal Skills: Mechanical/manipulative, Technical/scientific
Work Environment: Primarily indoors, Primarily one location
Salary Range: $23,000 to $39,000 to $64,000+
Certification or Licensing: Voluntary
Outlook: About as fast as the average

The Job

Mechanical engineering technicians work under the direction of mechanical engineers to design, build, maintain, and modify many kinds of machines, mechanical devices, and tools. They are employed in a broad range of industries. Technicians may specialize in any one of many areas including biomedical equipment; measurement and control; products manufacturing; solar energy; turbo machinery; energy resource technology; and engineering materials and technology.

Within each application, there are various aspects of the work with which the technician may be involved. One phase is research and development. In this area, the mechanical technician may assist an engineer or scientist in the design and development of anything from a ballpoint pen to a sophisticated measuring device. These technicians prepare rough sketches and layouts of the project being developed.

A second common type of work for mechanical engineering technicians is testing. For products such as engines, motors, or other moving devices, technicians may set up prototypes of the equipment to be tested and run performance tests. Technicians collect and compile all necessary data from the testing procedures and prepare reports for the engineer or scientist.

Professional and Personal Requirements

Certification, which is voluntary, is offered through the National Institute for Certification in Engineering Technologies.

Technicians need mathematical and mechanical aptitude and the ability to carry out detailed work. They must understand abstract concepts and apply scientific principles to problems in the shop or laboratory in both the design and the manufacturing process. They need the ability to analyze sketches and drawings and must possess patience, perseverance, and resourcefulness.

Starting Out

Schools offering associate's degrees in mechanical engineering technology and two-year technician programs usually help graduates find employment. At most colleges, in fact, company recruiters interview prospective graduates during their final semester of school. As a result, many students receive job offers before graduation. Other graduates may prefer to apply directly to employers, use newspaper classified ads, or apply through public or private employment services.

Earnings

In general, mechanical engineering technicians who develop and test machinery and equipment under the direction of an engineering staff earn between $28,000 and $50,000 a year. The average in 1997 was about $39,000, according to the U.S. Bureau of Labor Statistics. Some mechanical engineering technicians, especially those at the beginning of their careers, may make $23,000 a year or less, while some senior technicians with special skills and experience may make from $50,000 to $64,000 a year or more. Overtime or premium time pay may be earned for work beyond regular daytime hours or workweek. Benefits may include paid vacation days, insurance, retirement plans, profit sharing, and tuition-reimbursement plans.

Employment Outlook

Job opportunities for mechanical engineering technicians are expected to grow as fast as the average through the year 2006, according to the

U.S. Department of Labor. Manufacturing companies will be looking for more ways to apply the advances in mechanical technology to their operations. Opportunities will be best for technicians who are skilled in new manufacturing concepts, materials, and designs.

However, the employment outlook for engineering technicians is influenced by the economy. Hiring will fluctuate with the ups and downs of the nation's overall economic situation.

For More Information

For information on colleges and universities offering accredited programs in engineering technology, contact:

- **Accreditation Board for Engineering and Technology, Inc.**
  111 Market Place, Suite 1050
  Baltimore, MD 21202
  Tel: 410-347-7700
  Web: http://www.abet.org

For information about membership in a professional society for engineering technicians, contact:

- **American Society of Certified Engineering Technicians**
  PO Box 1348
  Flowery Branch, GA 30542
  Tel: 770-967-9173

For information about the field of mechanical engineering, contact:

- **American Society of Mechanical Engineers**
  Three Park Avenue
  New York, NY 10016
  Tel: 212-591-7000
  Web: http://www.asme.org

For information on certification of mechanical engineering technicians, contact:

- **National Institute for Certification in Engineering Technologies**
  1420 King Street
  Alexandria, VA 22314-2715
  Tel: 888-476-4238
  Web: http://www.nicet.org

Medical Assistants

School Subjects: Biology, Mathematics
Personal Skills: Helping/teaching, Technical/scientific
Work Environment: Primarily indoors, Primarily one location
Salary Range: $14,500 to $18,000 to $21,000
Certification or Licensing: Voluntary
Outlook: Much faster than the average

The Job

Depending on the size of the office, *medical assistants* may perform clerical or clinical duties, or both. The larger the office, the greater the chance that the assistant will specialize in one type of work. In their clinical duties, medical assistants help physicians by preparing patients for examination or treatment. They may check and record patients' blood pressure, pulse, temperature, height, and weight.

Medical assistants often ask patients questions about their medical histories and record the answers in the patients' file. In the examining room, the medical assistant may be responsible for arranging medical instruments and handing them to the physician as requested during the examination. Medical assistants may prepare patients for X rays and laboratory examinations, as well as administer electrocardiograms. They may apply dressings, draw blood, and give injections. They also may give patients instructions about taking medications, watching their diet, or restricting their activities before laboratory tests or surgery. In addition, medical assistants may collect specimens such as throat cultures for laboratory tests and may be responsible for sterilizing examining room instruments and equipment.

Professional and Personal Requirements

Medical assistants generally do not need to be licensed. However, they may voluntarily take examinations for credentials awarded by professional organizations such as American Medical Technologists, the American Registry of Medical Assistants, and the American Association of Medical Assistants.

Medical assistants must be able to interact with patients and other medical personnel. They must be dependable and compassionate and have the desire to help people. They also must be able to carry out detailed instructions accurately. Medical assistants must also respect patients' privacy by keeping medical information confidential.

Starting Out

Students enrolled in college or other post-high school medical assistant programs may learn of available positions through their school placement offices. High school guidance counselors may have information about positions for students about to graduate. Newspaper want ads and state employment offices are other good places to look for leads. Graduates may also wish to call local physicians' offices to find out about unadvertised openings.

Earnings

The earnings of medical assistants vary widely, depending on experience, skill level, and location. According to a survey conducted by the Commission on Accreditation of Allied Health Education Programs, the average starting salary for graduates of the medical assistant programs they accredit is about $14,500. With experience, medical assistants may eventually earn around $21,000 a year.

Employment Outlook

The employment outlook for medical assistants is exceptionally good through the next decade. Most openings will occur to replace workers who leave their jobs, but many will be the result of a predicted surge in the number of physicians' offices and outpatient care facilities. The growing number of elderly Americans who need medical treatment is also a factor in this increased demand for health services. In addition, new and more complex paperwork for medical insurance, malpractice insurance, government programs, and other purposes will create a growing need for assistants in medical offices.

Experienced and formally trained medical assistants are preferred by many physicians, so these workers have the best employment outlook. Word-processing skills, other computer skills, and formal certification are all definite assets.

For More Information

For information on accreditation and testing, contact:

- **Accrediting Bureau of Health Education Schools**
  Oak Manor Office
  29089 US 20 West
  Elkhart, IN 46514
  Tel: 219-293-0124

For information on certification and a career packet, contact:

- **American Association of Medical Assistants**
  20 North Wacker Drive, Suite 1575
  Chicago, IL 60606
  Tel: 312-899-1500
  Web: http://www.aama-ntl.org

For information on certification, contact the following organizations:

- **American Registry of Medical Assistants**
  69 Southwick Road, Suite A
  Westfield, MA 01085-4729
  Tel: 413-562-7336

- **American Medical Technologists**
  710 Higgins Road
  Park Ridge, IL 60068
  Tel: 708-823-5169
  Web: http://www.amt1.com

Medical Laboratory Technicians

School Subjects: Biology, Chemistry
Personal Skills: Helping/teaching, Technical/scientific
Work Environment: Primarily indoors, Primarily one location
Salary Range: $19,344 to $26,500 to $35,100
Certification or Licensing: Required by certain states
Outlook: About as fast as the average

The Job

Medical laboratory technicians perform routine tests in medical laboratories. These tests help physicians and other professional medical personnel diagnose and treat disease. Technicians prepare samples of body tissue; perform laboratory tests, such as urinalysis and blood counts; and make chemical and biological analyses of cells, tissue, blood, or other body specimens. They usually work under the supervision of a medical technologist or a laboratory director. Medical laboratory technicians may work in many fields or specialize in one specific medical area, such as cytology (the study of cells), hematology (blood), or histology (body tissue).

In their work, medical laboratory technicians frequently handle test tubes and other glassware and use precision equipment, such as microscopes and automated blood analyzers. Technicians also are often responsible for making sure machines are functioning and supplies are adequately stocked.

Professional and Personal Requirements

Students who have earned an associate degree are eligible for certification from several different agencies. They may become certified Medical Laboratory Technicians by one of two sources: by the Board of Registry of the American Society of Clinical Pathologists, which allows them to use the designation MLT (ASCP), or by the American

Medical Technologists, designated MLT (AMT); or, they may become certified as a Clinical Laboratory Technician, by the National Certification Agency for Medical Laboratory Personnel. In some states, state licensure, in addition to certification, is required for employment.

Besides fulfilling the academic requirements, medical laboratory technicians must have good manual dexterity, normal color vision, the ability to follow orders, and a tolerance for working under pressure.

Starting Out

Graduates of medical laboratory technology schools usually receive assistance from faculty and school placement services to find their first jobs. Hospitals, laboratories, and other areas employing medical laboratory technicians may notify local schools of job openings. Often the hospital or laboratory at which they received their practical training will offer full-time employment after graduation. Positions may also be secured using the various registries of certified medical laboratory workers. Newspaper job advertisements and commercial placement agencies are other sources of help in locating employment.

Earnings

A 1995 survey by the American Society of Clinical Pathologists found that the median average beginning pay for medical laboratory technicians was $19,344 per year. Those with bachelors degrees and certification make more. According to a Hay Group survey of acute care hospitals, the median annual base salary of full time laboratory technicians was $26,500 in January 1997. The middle 50 percent earned between $23,700 and $29,500. Full time salaried staff medical laboratory technologists earned about $35,100.

Most medical laboratory technicians receive paid vacations and holidays, sick leave, hospitalization and accident insurance, and retirement benefits.

Employment Outlook

Because the number of new graduates entering this field has dropped considerably, shortages are occurring. This is good news for prospective laboratory technicians. The U.S. Department of Labor predicts that employment of medical laboratory workers will grow about as fast as the average for all other occupations through the year 2006.

The overall national effort to control health care costs and increased automation are two factors that may slow the growth of employment in this field. Despite these factors, the overall amount of medical laboratory testing will probably increase, as much of medical practice today relies on high-quality laboratory testing. Medical laboratory testing is an absolutely essential element in today's medicine. For well-trained technicians who are flexible in accepting responsibilities and willing to continue their education throughout their careers, employment opportunities should remain good.

For More Information

For information on certification, contact the following organizations:

- **American Medical Technologists**
  710 Higgins Road
  Park Ridge, IL 60068
  Tel: 708-823-5169
  Web: http://www.amt1.com

- **National Certification Agency for Medical Laboratory Personnel**
  PO Box 15945-489
  Lenexa, KS 66285
  Tel: 913-438-5110

- **American Society of Clinical Pathologists, Board of Registry**
  PO Box 12277
  Chicago, IL 60612

For career information, contact:

- **American Society for Clinical Laboratory Science**
  7910 Woodmont Avenue, Suite 530
  Bethesda, MD 20814
  Tel: 301-657-2768
  Web: http://www.ascls.org

Medical Record Technicians

School Subjects: Biology, English

Personal Skills: Following instructions, Technical/scientific

Work Environment: Primarily indoors, Primarily one location

Salary Range: $20,000 to $35,500 to $80,000+

Certification or Licensing: Recommended

Outlook: Much faster than the average

The Job

Medical record technicians compile, code, and maintain patient records. They also tabulate and analyze data from groups of records in order to assemble reports. They review records for completeness and accuracy; assign codes to diseases, operations, diagnoses, and treatments according to detailed standardized classification systems; and post the codes on the medical record, thus making the information on the record easier to retrieve and analyze. Medical record technicians transcribe medical reports; maintain indices of patients, diseases, operations, and other categories of information; compile patient census data; and file records or supervise others who do so. In addition, they may direct the day-to-day operations of the medical records department. They maintain the flow of records and reports to and from other departments, and sometimes assist medical staff in special studies or research that draws on information in the records.

Professional and Personal Requirements

Medical record technicians who have completed an accredited training program are eligible to take a national qualifying examination—offered by the American Health Information Management Association(AHIMA)—to earn the credential of Accredited Record Technician (ART).

Technicians must have the capacity to do consistently reliable and accurate routine work. Computer skills also are essential, and some experience in transcribing dictated reports may be useful. Technicians must also be discreet, as they deal with records that are private and sometimes sensitive.

Starting Out

Most successful medical record technicians are graduates of two-year accredited programs. Graduates of these programs should check with their schools' placement offices for job leads. For those who have taken the accrediting exam and become ARTs, the AHIMA offers a resume referral service.

Candidates may also apply directly to the personnel departments of hospitals, nursing homes, outpatient clinics, and surgery centers. Many job openings are also listed in the classified advertising sections of local newspapers and with private and public employment agencies.

Earnings

Beginning technicians who have earned their ART status can expect to earn between $20,000 and $25,000 a year. The average salary for all ARTs is between $35,000 and $36,000. With experience, technicians may earn as much as $47,000 annually. Technicians who are not accredited typically earn somewhat less.

Technicians who have bachelor's or other advanced degrees eventually can reach salary levels in the high $70,000s or the low $80,000s.

Employment Outlook

Employment prospects through the year 2006 are excellent, according to the U.S. Department of Labor. The demand for well-trained medical record technicians will grow rapidly and will continue to exceed the supply. This expectation is related to the health care needs of a population that is both growing and aging and the trend toward more technologically sophisticated medicine and greater use of diagnostic procedures. It is also related to the increased requirements of regulatory bodies that scrutinize both costs and quality of care of health care providers. Because of the fear of medical malpractice lawsuits, doctors and other health care providers are documenting their diagnoses and treatments in greater detail. Also, because of the high cost of health care, insurance companies, government agencies, and courts are examining medical records with a more critical eye. These factors combine to ensure a healthy job outlook for medical record technicians.

For More Information

For information on careers in health information management and ART accreditation, contact:

■ **American Health Information Management Association**
919 North Michigan Avenue, Suite 1400
Chicago, IL 60611
Tel: 312-787-2672
Web: http://www.ahima.org

For a list of schools offering accredited programs in health information management, contact:

■ **Commission on Accreditation of Allied Health Education Programs**
American Medical Association
35 East Wacker Drive, Suite 1970
Chicago, IL 60601-2200
Tel: 312-464-5000
Web: http://www.caahep.org

Medical Secretaries

School Subjects: English, Health, Speech
Personal Skills: Communication/ideas, Following instructions
Work Environment: Primarily indoors, Primarily one location
Salary Range: $24,065 to $29,899 to $35,476
Certification or Licensing: Voluntary
Outlook: Faster than the average

The Job

Medical secretaries are responsible for the administrative and clerical work in medical offices, hospitals, or private physicians' offices. They keep records, answer phone calls, order supplies, handle correspondence, bill patients, complete insurance forms, and transcribe dictation. Medical secretaries might also keep financial records and handle other bookkeeping. They greet patients, schedule appointments, obtain medical histories, arrange hospital admissions, and schedule surgeries.

Doctors rely on medical secretaries to keep administrative operations under control. They are often the information clearinghouses for the office. They schedule appointments, provide information to callers, organize and maintain paper and electronic files, and produce correspondence for themselves and others. They might also type letters and handle travel arrangements. Medical secretaries also operate facsimile machines, photocopiers, and telephone systems. They use computers to run spreadsheet, word-processing, database-management, or desktop publishing programs.

Professional and Personal Requirements

The International Association of Administrative Professionals offers the Certified Professional Secretary (CPS) designation, which is voluntary. To achieve CPS certification, candidates must pass a rigorous exam covering a number of general secretarial topics.

Medical secretaries must use good judgment and discretion in dealing with confidential medical records. The work requires confidence in dealing with the public, both in person and on the telephone. Medical secretaries should have pleasant personalities and desire to help others in a dependable and conscientious manner.

Starting Out

Job seekers should apply directly to hospitals, clinics, and physicians' offices. Potential positions might be listed with school or college placement centers. Private employment agencies can also have some medical secretary jobs on file. Many employers list job openings in newspaper want ads. Networking with medical secretaries who are already working often leads to jobs, because employers tend to trust employee recommendations.

Earnings

According to Wageweb, the lower level salary range for medical secretaries was $24,065 in 1999. Mid-level earnings are approximately $29,899. Upper-level compensation tops off at about $35,476. Most employers pay for vacation, sick leave, and medical insurance. Many also offer dental insurance and partial retirement benefits. Some have paid vision care and life insurance, and a few receive profit sharing.

Employment Outlook

Growth in health services industries will spur faster than average employment growth for medical secretaries through the year 2006, according to the U.S. Department of Labor. A recent survey commissioned by the specialized administrative staffing company, Office Team, found that nearly 60 percent of executives believe administrative assistants have a more established career track today versus just five years ago. Organizations are demanding more from their support personnel, according to the International Association of Administrative Professionals, and are increasing salary levels accordingly.

For More Information

For information on certification and on seminars and workshops, contact:

■ **International Association of Administrative Assistants**
10502 NW Ambassador Drive
PO Box 20404
Kansas City, MO 64195-0404
Tel: 816-891-6600
Web: http://www.iaap-hq.org

For information on training, contact:

■ **Arlington Career Institute**
901 Avenue K
Grand Prairie, Texas 75050
Tel: 800-394-5445
Email: ACRI1@swbell.net
Web: http://www.themetro.com/aci

The Mayo Clinic is a major employer of medical secretaries. Visit their Web site for more information:

■ **Mayo Clinic**
Web: http://www.mayo.edu

Microelectronics Technicians

School Subjects: English, Mathematics, Physics
Personal Skills: Mechanical/manipulative, Technical/scientific
Work Environment: Primarily indoors, Primarily one location
Salary Range: $28,000 to $33,000 to $50,000
Certification or Licensing: Voluntary
Outlook: Faster than the average

The Job

Microelectronics technicians work in research laboratories, assisting the engineering staff in developing and constructing prototype and custom-designed microchips. Microchips, often called simply "chips," are tiny but extremely complex electronic devices which control the operations of many kinds of communications equipment, consumer products, industrial controls, aerospace guidance systems, and medical electronics. The process of manufacturing chips is often called fabrication.

Microelectronics technicians work closely with electronics engineers, who design the components, build and test them, and prepare the component or product for large-scale manufacture. Such components usually require the integrated operation of several or many different types of chips.

Microelectronics technicians generally work from a schematic received from the design engineer. Following the schematic, the technician constructs the component and then uses a variety of sophisticated, highly sensitive equipment to test the component's performance. Test results are reported to the engineering staff. The technician may be required to help in evaluating the results, preparing reports based on these evaluations, and completing the technical writing of the component's specifications.

Professional and Personal Requirements

Certification is not mandatory in most areas of electronics (although technicians working with radio-transmitting devices are required to be licensed by the Federal Communications Commission). Technicians who complete voluntary certification, offered by the International Society of Certified Electronics Technicians, may receive higher pay and more job responsibilities.

Microelectronics technicians must be able to follow the design engineer's specifications and instructions exactly. Similar diligence and attention to detail are necessary when following the different procedures for testing the new components. An understanding of the underlying technology is important.

Starting Out

Most schools provide job placement services to students completing their degree program. Many offer on-the-job training as a part of the program. An internship or other "real-life" experience is desirable but not necessary. Many companies have extensive on-site training programs.

Newspapers and trade journals are full of openings for people working in electronics, and some companies recruit new hires directly on campus. Government employment offices are also good sources when looking for job leads.

Earnings

Microelectronics technicians earn an average starting salary of $28,000, according to the U.S. Department of Labor. Those in managerial or supervisory positions earn higher salaries, ranging between $33,000 and $50,000 per year. Wage rates vary greatly, according to skill-level, type of employer, and location. Most employers offer some fringe benefits, including paid holidays and vacations, sick leave, and life and health insurance.

Employment Outlook

Jobs in the electronics industry are expected to grow faster than the average through 2006, according to the U.S. Department of Labor. This is because of increasing competition within the industry and the rapid technological advances that characterize the electronics industry. Electronics is also a rapidly growing industry, and the use of electronic technology will become more and more important to every aspect of people's lives. This in turn will create a demand for workers with the skills and training to sustain the industry's growth. In addition, as more and more manufacturers adapt electronic technology to their products and manufacturing processes, the need for skilled personnel will also increase.

For More Information

For information on certification, contact:

■ **International Society of Certified Electronics Technicians**
2708 West Berry Street
Fort Worth, TX 76109-2356
Tel: 817-921-9101
Email: iscetFW@aol.com
Web: http://www.iscet.org/

Musicians

School Subjects: Music, Theater/Dance
Personal Skills: Artistic, Communication/ideas
Work Environment: Indoors and outdoors, Primary multiple locations
Salary Range: $7,000 to $25,000 to $1,000,000+
Certification or Licensing: Required for certain positions
Outlook: Faster than the average

The Job

Musicians perform, compose, conduct, arrange, and teach music. They may play before live audiences in clubs or auditoriums, or they may perform on television or radio, in motion pictures, or in a recording studio. Musicians may play in symphony orchestras, dance bands, jazz bands, rock bands, country bands, or other groups, or they might work as solo performers. Some classical musicians accompany singers and choirs, and they may also perform in churches and temples. Many musicians supplement their incomes through teaching, while others teach as their full-time occupation, perhaps playing jobs occasionally.

Professional and Personal Requirements

Musicians who want to teach in state elementary and high schools must be state certified. To obtain a state certificate, musicians must satisfactorily complete a degree-granting course in music education at an institution of higher learning. Music teachers may also obtain certification from the Music Teachers National Association.

Beyond training, education, and study, a strong love of music is necessary to endure the arduous training and working life of a musician. An uncommon degree of dedication, self-discipline, and drive is necessary to become an accomplished musician and to be recognized in the field.

230

Starting Out

Young musicians need to enter as many playing situations as they can in their school and community musical groups. They should audition as often as possible, because experience at auditioning is very important. Jazz musicians and musicians who want to perform with established groups, such as choirs and symphony orchestras, enter the field by auditioning. Popular musicians often begin playing at low-paying social functions and at small clubs or restaurants.

Earnings

Musicians in the major U.S. symphony orchestras earn minimum salaries of between $140 and $1,200 a week. The season for these major orchestras, generally located in the largest U.S. cities, ranges from 10 to 52 weeks. Popular musicians are usually paid from $30 to $300 or more per night. Studio musicians are paid a minimum of about $185 for a three-hour session of recording film and television background music; for record company recordings they receive a minimum of about $234 for three hours. Instrumentalists performing live earn anywhere from $30 to $300 per engagement. Church organists, choir directors, and soloists make an average of $40 to $100 each week.

Employment Outlook

The U.S. Department of Labor predicts faster than average growth for musicians through the year 2006. The demand for musicians will be greatest in theaters, bands, and restaurants as the public continues to spend more money on recreational activities. The increasing numbers of cable television networks and television programs point to an increase in employment for musicians. The number of record companies has grown dramatically over the last decade, particularly among small, independent houses. Digital recording technology has also made it easier and less expensive for musicians to produce and distribute their own recordings. However, few musicians will earn substantial incomes from these efforts. Popular musicians may receive many short-term engagements in nightclubs, restaurants, and theaters, but these engagements offer little job stability. The supply of musicians for virtually all types of music will continue to exceed the demand for the foreseeable future.

For More Information

For general information on careers in music, contact the following organizations:

- **American Federation of Musicians of the United States and Canada**
  Paramount Building
  1501 Broadway, Suite 600
  New York, NY 10036
  Tel: 212-869-1330
  Web: http://www.afm.org/

- **International Guild of Symphony, Opera, and Ballet Musicians**
  5802 16th Street, NE
  Seattle, WA 98105
  Tel: 206-524-7050

For information on union membership, contact:

- **American Guild of Musical Artists**
  1727 Broadway
  New York, NY 10019
  Tel: 212-265-3687
  Web: http://www.agmanatl.com/

For information on teaching careers and certification, contact:

- **Music Teachers National Association**
  Carew Tower
  441 Vine Street, Suite 505
  Cincinnati, OH 45202
  Tel: 513-421-1420
  Web: http://www.mtna.org/

For a list of accredited schools and information on grants and scholarships, contact:

- **National Association of Schools of Music**
  11250 Roger Bacon Drive, Suite 21
  Reston, VA 20190
  Tel: 703-437-0700
  Web: http://www.arts-accredit.org/nasm/nasm.htm

Occupational Therapy Assistants

School Subjects: Health, Psychology
Personal Skills: Helping/teaching, Mechanical/manipulative
Work Environment: Primarily indoors, Primarily one location
Salary Range: $13,520 to $27,442 to $32,000
Certification or Licensing: Required
Outlook: Much faster than the average

The Job

Occupational therapy assistants help people who have mental, physical, developmental, or emotional limitations by using a variety of activities to improve basic motor functions and reasoning abilities. They work under the direct supervision of an occupational therapist to help plan, implement, and evaluate rehabilitation programs designed to regain patients' self sufficiency and to restore their physical and mental functions.

Under the supervision of the therapist, assistants implement patient care plans and activities. They help patients improve mobility and productivity using a variety of activities and exercises. They may use adaptive techniques and equipment to help patients perform tasks many take for granted.

Assistants may also help therapists evaluate a patient's progress, change care plans as needed, make therapy appointments, and complete office paperwork.

Professional and Personal Requirements

Upon graduation from an accredited community college or technical school, occupational therapy assistants must pass a national certification examination administered by the American Occupational Therapy Certification Board.

Assistants must be in good physical shape since heavy lifting—of patients as well as equipment—is a part of the daily job. They should also have stamina, since they are on their feet much of the day. Assistants should be able to take directions. They should have a pleasant disposition, patience, responsibility, strong people skills, and a desire to help others. It is important for assistants and aides to work well as a team.

Starting Out

Community college or technical school placement centers can provide a listing of jobs available in the occupational therapy field. Job openings are usually posted in hospital human resource departments. Also, the American Occupational Therapy Association's Web site has an employment page.

Earnings

The average annual salary of occupational therapy assistants is about $27,442, according to a membership survey conducted by the American Occupational Therapy Association. Occupational therapy assistants with experience can earn considerably more. Starting pay for therapy aides is about $6.50 to $7.50 an hour, or $13,520 to $15,600 annually. Those working in day care programs in school systems earn less than those employed by nursing homes.

Benefits for full time assistants and aides include health and life insurance, paid sick and vacation time, holiday pay, and a retirement fund.

Employment Outlook

According to the *Occupational Outlook Handbook,* employment for occupational therapy assistants will increase about 70 percent through the year 2006. However, only a small number of new jobs will actually be available due to the size of this occupation—about 16,000 occupational therapy assistants were employed in 1996. Occupational growth will stem from an increased number of elderly people. Though more people are living well into their 70s, 80s, and even 90s, they often need the kind of services occupational therapy provides. Medical technology has greatly improved, saving many lives that would in the past be lost through accidents, stroke, or other illnesses. Such people need rehabilitation therapy as they recuperate. Hospitals and employers, to reduce costs, are hiring more therapy assistants to help with the work load.

For More Information

For career information and job listings, contact:

- **American Occupational Therapy Association**
  4720 Montgomery Lane
  PO Box 31220
  Bethesda, MD 20824
  Tel: 301-652-2682
  Web: http://www.aota.org

For information on certification requirements, contact:

- **American Occupational Therapy Certification Board**
  4 Research Place, Suite 160
  Rockville, MD 20850
  Tel: 301-990-7979

Office Administrators

School Subjects: English, Mathematics, Speech
Personal Skills: Communication/ideas, Leadership/management
Work Environment: Primarily indoors, Primarily one location
Salary Range: $21,500 to $30,200 to $50,600+
Certification or Licensing: None available
Outlook: About as fast as the average

The Job

Office administrators, also called *office managers,* direct and coordinate the work activities of office workers within an office. They are usually responsible for interviewing prospective employees and making recommendations on hiring. They train new workers, explain office policies and performance criteria, and delegate work responsibilities. They supervise office clerks and other workers in their tasks and confer with other supervisory personnel in planning department activities. They evaluate the progress of their clerks and work with upper management to ensure that the office staff meets productivity and quality goals. Office administrators often know how to do many of the tasks done by their subordinates and assist or relieve them whenever necessary. Office administrators may recommend increases in salaries, promote workers when approved, and occasionally fire them. They often meet with office personnel to discuss job-related issues or problems, and they are responsible for maintaining a positive office environment.

Professional and Personal Requirements

There is no certification or licensing available in this field.

Office administrators must constantly juggle the demands of their superiors with the capabilities of their subordinates. They need an even temperament and the ability to work well with others.

236

Additional important attributes include organizational ability, judgment, attention to detail, dependability, and trustworthiness.

Starting Out

Qualified persons should contact the personnel offices of individual firms directly. This is especially appropriate if the candidate already has previous clerical experience. College placement offices or other job placement offices may also know of openings. Jobs may also be located through newspaper advertisements. Another option is to sign up with a temporary employment service. Working as a "temp" provides the advantage of getting a firsthand look at a variety of office settings and making many contacts. Many times, office administrators are promoted from another position within an organization.

Earnings

According to the *Occupational Outlook Handbook,* office administrators earned an average of $28,900 a year in 1996. Fifty percent earned between $21,500 and $38,900 a year, with the top 10 percent earning over $50,600. Higher wages are paid to those who work for larger private companies located in and around major metropolitan areas. Full-time workers also receive paid vacations and health and life insurance. Some companies offer year-end bonuses and stock options.

Employment Outlook

Employment of office administrators is expected to grow about as fast as the average for all occupations through the year 2006, according to the U.S. Department of Labor. Since some clerical occupations will be affected by increased automation, some office administrators may have smaller staffs and be asked to perform more professional tasks. A large number of job openings will occur as administrators transfer to other industries or leave the workforce for other reasons.

The federal government should continue to be a good source for job opportunities. Private companies, particularly those with large clerical staffs, such as hospitals, banks, and telecommunications companies, should also have numerous openings. Employment opportunities will be especially good for those trained to operate computers and other types of modern office machinery.

For More Information

Visit the AMA Web site to access job listings and information on training programs:

- **American Management Association (AMA)**
  1601 Broadway
  New York, NY 10019-7420
  Tel: 212-586-8100
  Web: http://www.amanet.org

For information on home-study, seminars, and membership, contact:

- **National Association of Executive Secretaries and Administrative Assistants**
  900 South Washington Street, Suite G-13
  Falls Church, VA 22046
  Tel: 703-237-8616
  Web: http://www.naesaa.com

For a career brochure, contact:

- **National Management Association**
  2210 Arbor Boulevard
  Dayton, OH 45439-1580
  Tel: 937-294-0421
  Email: nma@nma1.org
  Web: http://www.nma1.org

Orthotic and Prosthetic Technicians

School Subjects: Biology, Technical/Shop
Personal Skills: Helping/teaching, Mechanical/manipulative
Work Environment: Primarily indoors, Primarily one location
Salary Range: $16,700 to $25,000 to $42,000
Certification or Licensing: Voluntary
Outlook: Faster than the average

The Job

Orthotic technicians and *prosthetic technicians* make, fit, repair, and maintain orthotic and prosthetic devices according to specifications and under the guidance of orthotists and prosthetists. Orthotic devices, sometimes also referred to as orthopedic appliances, are braces used to support weak or ineffective joints or muscles or to correct physical defects, such as spinal deformities. Prosthetic devices are artificial limbs and plastic cosmetic devices. These devices are designed and fitted to the patient by prosthetists or orthotists. Orthotic and prosthetic technicians read the specifications prepared by orthotists and prosthetists to determine the materials and tools required to make the device. Part of their work involves making models of patients' torsos, limbs, or amputated areas. Most of the technicians' efforts, however, go into the actual building of the devices. Some technicians specialize in either orthotic devices or prosthetic devices, while others are trained and able to work with both types.

A technician whose work is closely related to that of the orthotic and prosthetic technician is the arch-support technician. *Arch-support technicians* make steel arch supports to fit a patient's foot according to prescriptions supplied by podiatrists, prosthetists, or orthotists.

Professional and Personal Requirements

There is a program for voluntary registration conducted by the American Board for Certification in Orthotics and Prosthetics.

Orthotic and prosthetic technicians must be skilled at working with hand and power tools. Since they work in a workshop setting, technicians must be prepared to work in a sometimes cluttered, loud, hot, and dusty work atmosphere. Orthotic and prosthetic technicians do not interact with patients, but they do need to work well with orthotists and prosthetists and other co-workers.

Starting Out

Graduates of one- or two-year programs of formal instruction usually have the easiest time finding a first job. Teachers and placement offices will have valuable advice and information about local employers that they can share with students about to graduate. Trade publications for the orthotics and prosthetics industry often carry classified advertising with listings of job openings.

Students with no prior experience who want to enter a supervised training program should contact hospitals, private brace and limb companies, and rehabilitation centers to inquire about programs.

Earnings

Salaries for orthotic and prosthetic technicians vary widely, depending upon several factors. An overall average for all technicians at all levels of experience is about $12.00 per hour, or $25,000 annually. The inexperienced technician in an entry-level position might earn $8 to $9 per hour, while those with several years of experience and a proven track record can make as much as $15 to $20 hourly.

The most significant factor influencing salary level is certification. Technicians who have received their certification average $3 more per hour than those who are noncertified, which translates into a difference of more than $6,000 yearly.

Employment Outlook

The employment outlook for orthotic and prosthetic technicians is generally good. Among the factors contributing to the favorable prospects are the general growth of the population and the fact that an increasing number of people are receiving access to medical and rehabilitation care through private and public insurance programs. Also, continuing developments in this field will mean that more people with different kinds of disabilities will be candidates for new or improved orthotic and prosthetic devices.

For More Information

For information on becoming an accredited orthotic or prosthetic technician, contact:

■ **American Board for Certification in Orthotics and Prosthetics**
1650 King Street, Suite 500
Alexandria, VA 22314
Tel: 703-836-7114
Web: http://www.opoffice.org

For information on orthotic and prosthetic careers with the U.S. government, contact:

■ **Veterans Health Administration**
810 Vermont Avenue, NW
Washington, DC 20420
Tel: 202-565-4293

Packaging Machinery Technicians

School Subjects: Mathematics, Technical/Shop
Personal Skills: Mechanical/manipulative, Technical/scientific
Work Environment: Primarily indoors, Primarily multiple locations
Salary Range: $20,200 to $32,700 to $54,800
Certification or Licensing: Voluntary
Outlook: Faster than the average

The Job

Packaging machinery technicians work in packaging plants of various industries or in the plants of packaging machinery manufacturers. Their jobs entail building machines, installing and setting up equipment, training operators to use the equipment, maintaining equipment, troubleshooting, and repairing machines.

There are several subspecialties within this field. *Machinery builders,* also called *assemblers,* assist engineers in the development and modification of new and existing machinery designs. They build different types of packaging machinery following engineering blueprints, wiring schematics, pneumatic diagrams, and plant layouts. *Field service technicians,* also called *field service representatives,* are employed by packaging machinery manufacturers. They install new machinery at customers' plants and train in-plant machine operators and maintenance personnel on its operation and maintenance.

Automated packaging machine mechanics, also called *maintenance technicians,* perform scheduled preventive maintenance as well as diagnose machinery problems and make repairs.

Professional and Personal Requirements

A voluntary certification program is available for engineering technicians through the National Institute for Certification in Engineering

Technologies. Certification is available at various levels and in different specialty fields.

Persons interested in this field should have mechanical and electrical aptitudes, manual dexterity, and the ability to work under time pressure. In addition, they should have analytical and problem-solving skills, as well as good communication skills.

Starting Out

Students in a technical program may be able to get job leads through their schools' job placement services. Many jobs in packaging are unadvertised and are learned about through contacts with professionals in the industry. Students may learn about openings from teachers, school administrators, and industry contacts they acquired during training.

Applicants can also apply directly to machinery manufacturing companies or companies with manufacturing departments. Local employment offices may also list job openings. Sometimes companies hire part-time or summer help in other departments, such as the warehouse or shipping. These jobs may provide an opportunity to move into other areas of the company.

Earnings

In general, technicians earn approximately $20,000 a year to start, and with experience can increase their salaries to about $33,000. Seasoned workers with two-year degrees who work for large companies may earn between $50,000 and $70,000 a year, particularly those in field service jobs or in supervisory positions.

Benefits vary and depend upon company policy, but generally include paid holidays, vacations, sick days, and medical and dental insurance. Some companies also offer tuition assistance programs, pension plans, profit sharing, and 401(k) plans.

Employment Outlook

Packaging machinery technicians are in high demand both by companies that manufacture packaging machinery and by companies that use packaging machinery. With the growth of the packaging industry, a nationwide shortage of trained packaging technicians has developed. There are far more openings than there are qualified applicants.

The packaging machinery industry is expected to continue its growth into the 21st century. The use of computers in packaging machinery will continue to increase, as will the role of robotics, fiber optics, and electronics. To be prepared for the jobs of the future, packaging machinery students should seek training in the newest technologies.

For More Information

For career and industry information and educational programs, contact the following organizations.

- **Institute of Electrical and Electronics Engineers**
  1828 L Street, NW, Suite 1202
  Washington, DC 20036-5104
  Web: http://www.ieee.org/usab

- **Institute of Packaging Professionals**
  481 Carlisle Drive
  Herndon, VA 22070-4823
  Web: http://www.pakinfo-world.org

- **National Institute of Packaging, Handling, and Logistic Engineers**
  6902 Lyle Street
  Lanham, MD 20706
  Tel: 301-459-9105

- **Packaging Education Forum**
  481 Carlisle Drive
  Herndon, VA 22070-4823
  Tel: 703-318-8970
  Web: http://www.packagingeducation.org

- **Packaging Machinery Manufacturers Institute**
  4350 North Fairfax Drive, Suite 600
  Arlington, VA 22203
  Tel: 703-243-8555
  Web: http://www.packnet.com

Painters and Sculptors

School Subjects: Art, History
Personal Skills: Artistic, Communication/ideas
Work Environment: Indoors and outdoors, Primarily one location
Salary Range: $30 or less to $300 to $10,000+ per piece
Certification or Licensing: None
Outlook: About as fast as the average

The Job

Painters use watercolors, oils, acrylics, and other substances to paint pictures or designs onto flat surfaces. *Sculptors* design and construct three-dimensional artwork from various materials, such as stone, concrete, plaster, and wood. Painters and sculptors use their creative abilities to produce original works of art. They are generally classified as fine artists rather than commercial artists because they are responsible for selecting the theme, subject matter, and medium of their artwork.

Professional and Personal Requirements

There is no certification or licensing available in this field.

An important requirement for a career as a painter or sculptor is artistic ability. Of course, this is entirely subjective, and it is perhaps more important that artists believe in their own ability and potential. Apart from being creative and imaginative, painters and sculptors should exhibit such traits as patience, determination, independence, and sensitivity.

Painters and sculptors should have good business and marketing skills if they intend to support themselves through their art. As small-business people, they must be able to market and sell their products to wholesalers, retailers, and the general public.

Starting Out

Artists interested in exhibiting or selling their products should investigate potential markets. Local fairs and art shows often provide opportunities for new artists to display their work. Art councils are a good source of information on upcoming fairs in the area.

Some artists sell their work on consignment. When a painter or sculptor sells work this way, a store or gallery displays an item; when the item is sold, the artist gets the price of that item minus a commission that goes to the store or gallery.

Earnings

The amount of money earned by painters and sculptors varies greatly. Most are self-employed and set their own hours and prices. Artists often work long hours and earn little, especially when they are first starting out. The price they charge is up to them, but much depends on the value the public places on their work.

Some artists obtain grants that allow them to pursue their art; others win prizes and awards in competitions. Most artists, however, have to work on their projects part-time while holding down a regular, full-time job.

Employment Outlook

The employment outlook for painters and sculptors is difficult to predict. Because they are usually self-employed, much of their success depends on the amount and type of work created, the drive and determination in selling the artwork, and the interest or readiness of the public to appreciate and purchase the work.

Success for an artist, however, is difficult to quantify. Individual artists may consider themselves successful as their talent matures and they are better able to present their vision in their work. This type of success goes beyond financial considerations. Few artists enter this field for the money. Financial success depends on a great deal of factors, many of which have nothing to do with the artist or his or her work. Artists with good marketing skills will likely be the most successful in selling their work.

For More Information

For general information on ceramic arts study, contact:

- **National Art Education Association**
  1916 Association Drive
  Reston, VA 22091-1590
  Tel: 703-860-8000
  Web: http://www.cedarnet.org/emig

The following organization helps artists market and sell their art. It offers marketing tools, a newsletter, a directory of artists, and reference resources.

- **National Association of Fine Artists**
  ArtNetwork
  PO Box 1360
  Nevada City, CA 95959
  530-470-0862
  Email: info@artmarketing.com
  Web: http://www.artmarketing.com

This government agency supports art programs and offers grants to individual artists and to agencies. It has a list of state and regional arts agencies, and other resources.

- **National Endowment for the Arts**
  Nancy Hanks Center
  Arts and Education
  Education and Access Division
  1100 Pennsylvania Avenue, NW
  Washington, DC 20506-0001
  Tel: 202-682-5426
  Email: webmgr@arts.endow.gov
  Web: http://arts.endow.gov

Paralegals

School Subjects: English, Government
Personal Skills: Communication/ideas, Following instructions
Work Environment: Primarily indoors, Primarily multiple locations
Salary Range: $23,800 to $32,700 to $40,000+
Certification or Licensing: Voluntary
Outlook: Faster than the average

The Job

Paralegals support lawyers in a variety of ways, including assisting in trial preparations, investigating facts, and preparing documents such as affidavits and pleadings. Although the lawyer assumes responsibility for the paralegal's work, the paralegal may take on all the duties of the lawyer except for setting fees, appearing in court, accepting cases, and giving legal advice.

Paralegals spend much of their time in law libraries, researching laws and previous cases, and compiling facts to help lawyers prepare for trial. Paralegals often interview witnesses as part of their research as well. After analyzing the laws and facts that have been compiled for a particular client, the paralegal often writes a report that the lawyer may use to determine how to proceed with the case. If a case is brought to trial, the paralegal helps prepare legal arguments and draft pleadings to be filed in court. They also organize and store files and correspondence related to cases.

Professional and Personal Requirements

The National Association of Legal Assistants Certifying Board offers certification, which is voluntary. Certification is available for Certified Legal Assistants (CLAs) and Registered Paralegals (RPs); the latter recognizes paralegals with bachelor's degrees and at least two years' experience.

Communication skills, both verbal and written, are vital to working as a paralegal. A paralegal must be able to think logically and learn new laws and regulations quickly. Research skills, computer skills, and people skills are necessary for success as a paralegal.

Starting Out

Most employers prefer to hire individuals who have completed paralegal programs. To have the best opportunity at getting a quality job in the paralegal field, students should attend a school that offers training in paralegal studies. In addition to providing a solid background in paralegal studies, most schools help graduates find jobs.

The National Federation of Paralegal Associations recommends using job banks that are sponsored by paralegal associations across the country. Many jobs for paralegals are posted on the Internet as well.

Earnings

According to 1997 statistics from the National Federation of Paralegal Associations, beginning paralegals average about $23,800 a year. Paralegals with 7 to 10 years' experience earn about $32,900. Top paralegals in large offices can earn as much as $40,000 a year, and paralegal supervisors, $40,000 to $50,000. Many paralegals receive year-end bonuses, some averaging $1,900 or more.

Paralegals employed by the federal government averaged $44,000 annually in 1997, as reported by the U.S. Department of Labor.

Employment Outlook

The employment outlook for paralegals through 2006 is excellent, representing one of the fastest-growing professions in the country. In the private sector, paralegals can work in banks, insurance companies, real estate firms, and corporate legal departments. In the public sector, there is a growing need for paralegals in the courts and community legal service programs, government agencies, and consumer organizations.

For More Information

For information regarding accredited educational facilities, contact:

- **American Association for Paralegal Education**
  2965 Flowers Road South, Suite 105
  Atlanta, GA 30341
  Tel: 770-452-9877
  Web: http://www.aafpe.org

For general information about careers in the law field, contact:

- **American Bar Association**
  750 North Lake Shore Drive
  Chicago, IL 60611
  Tel: 312-988-5000
  Web: http://www.abanet.org

For information about educational and licensing programs, contact:

- **National Association of Legal Assistants**
  1516 South Boston Avenue, Suite 200
  Tulsa, OK 74119
  Tel: 918-587-6828
  Web: http://www.nala.org

For brochures about almost every aspect of becoming a paralegal, contact:

- **National Federation of Paralegal Associations**
  PO Box 33108
  Kansas City, MO 64114-0108
  Tel: 816-941-4000
  Web: http://www.paralegals.org

For information about employment networks and school listings, contact:

- **National Paralegal Association**
  PO Box 406
  Solebury, PA 18963
  Tel: 215-297-8333
  Web: http://www.nationalparalegal.org

Pedorthists

School Subjects: Biology, Technical/Shop
Personal Skills: Helping/teaching, Mechanical/manipulative
Work Environment: Primarily indoors, Primarily one location
Salary Range: $20,000 to $32,500 to $65,000
Certification or Licensing: Voluntary
Outlook: Much faster than the average

The Job

Pedorthists treat patients' foot problems by designing and fitting therapeutic footwear based on doctors' prescriptions. They examine and make impressions of patients' feet to get the exact measurements and contours.

If the foot problem can be corrected by using footwear that has already been created, pedorthists will make minor adjustments to this ready-made device to fit the patient's needs. Sometimes, pedorthists must design new footwear that meets the specific needs of the patient. After pedorthists have followed this process, they must evaluate the footwear or device to make sure it was made correctly and will function as it was intended. They try the footwear or device on the patient to make sure the fit is correct. Often, pedorthists must oversee several trial fittings, making numerous adjustments, to be sure the footwear is absolutely correct. They also must keep precise, detailed records which are used to create reports for patients' doctors.

Many pedorthists specialize in a variety of areas, including adult foot deformities; amputations; arthritis; congenital deformities; diabetes; geriatrics; overuse injuries; pediatrics; sports-related injuries; and trauma.

Professional and Personal Requirements

Certification, which is voluntary, is offered by the Board for Certification in Pedorthics.

Pedorthist work closely with patients, physicians and other health care workers. Because of this, they need strong written and oral communication skills. They must also be in good physical condition since they repeatedly kneel, sit, or stand as they work with patients.

Starting Out

The most direct way to enter this field is to earn at least a two-year degree with summer internships built in. These internships often turn into jobs or into leads to other possible job opportunities.

The Pedorthic Footwear Association sponsors several national and regional seminars each year. These events provide many educational opportunities for the beginning pedorthist and allow the beginner to meet and talk with experienced pedorthists.

Earnings

Pedorthists just entering the field will usually start out making $20,000 to $28,000 a year, according to the Board for Certification in Pedorthics. With certification and hands-on experience, pedorthists can make $30,000 to $35,000 a year. Those at the top of their field may earn up to $65,000.

Pedorthists working in shoe stores and clinics usually receive paid sick days, holidays, vacation days, and some level of insurance. Retirement savings plans are usually offered as well. Most hospitals provide insurance and other benefits, including discounted or free medical services to their employees.

Employment Outlook

Jobs are abundant for pedorthists for many reasons. Two of the main reasons for the high demand for pedorthists are the aging elderly population and the popularity of sports and fitness. As people grow older, they tend to have increased foot problems which require special footwear. The sports and fitness boom shows no signs of declining. Many people involved in different sports activities will need special braces, inserts, and devices to maintain a high level of activity. Also, sports-related injuries are increasingly common, so skilled pedorthists able to treat such injuries will be in high demand.

For More Information

For information about the pedorthist profession and free brochures, contact:

- **Pedorthic Footwear Association**
  7150 Columbia Gateway Drive, Suite G
  Columbia, MD 21046-1151
  Web: http://pedorthics.org/

For certification information, and a free certification handbook, contact:

- **Board for Certification in Pedorthics**
  7150 Columbia Gateway Drive, Suite G
  Columbia, MD 21046-1151
  Web: http://www.cpeds.org/

Perfusionists

School Subjects: Biology, Mathematics

Personal Skills: Helping/teaching, Technical/scientific

Work Environment: Primarily indoors, Primarily one location

Salary Range: $42,000 to $55,000 to $125,000

Certification or Licensing: Recommended

Outlook: Faster than the average

The Job

Perfusionists operate equipment that literally takes over the functioning of patients' hearts and lungs during surgery and in cases of respiratory failure. When surgeons pierce the patient's breast bone and the envelope surrounding the heart, which is known as the pericardial sac, they must transfer the functions of the patient's heart and lungs to the heart-lung machine before any surgery can begin on the heart itself. The heart-lung machine is activated by inserting two tubes into the heart; one circulates blood from the heart to the machine and the other circulates blood from the machine back into the heart. It is necessary during this procedure not only to maintain circulation and pumping action but also to maintain the appropriate oxygen, carbon dioxide, and other blood gas levels. In addition, perfusionists must effectively control the patient's body temperature because the flow of blood through the body greatly influences body temperature. Perfusionists use various probes within the body to monitor body temperature, blood gases, kidney functioning, electrolytes, and blood pressure.

Professional and Personal Requirements

Certification currently is not an absolute requirement for perfusionists, but it is rapidly becoming a practical requirement. Currently, more than two-thirds of perfusionists nationally are certified.

Perfusionists should have good judgment, an ability to concentrate for long periods of time, and a strong sense of responsibility for the welfare of their patients. They must be able to respond to stressful situations in an intelligent and decisive manner. Perfusionists also need good communication and teamwork skills.

Starting Out

The most important prerequisite for entering the field of perfusion technology is acceptance at an accredited school that offers such a program. Once you have entered a program you should begin to investigate the field first through your professors and teachers and then through the American Society of Extracorporeal Technology. This professional society of perfusion technologists has an active student membership division that hosts meetings and conferences and is a good source of advice and information concerning various job openings in the field.

Earnings

Salaries for perfusion technologists compare favorably with those of other health technicians. The national range of salaries in the late-1990s starts at about $42,000 per year for entering perfusionists and rises to an average of $55,000 per year for more experienced professionals. Some perfusionists earn as much as $125,000 annually, but those earning higher salaries are typically employed directly by a physician or are self-employed.

Employment Outlook

The perfusion field is highly specialized and employs approximately 3,000 individuals nationwide. These professionals work in approximately 750 hospitals with open-heart surgery departments. Employment in this area is expected to grow at a rate faster than the average for all occupations through the year 2006. As with many medical fields, advancing technology calls for additional professionals as these procedures are performed on a more regular basis. The field of open-heart surgery and the expanded scope of extracorporeal technology grew dramatically during the 1980s and is expected to continue to expand, so the job opportunities and job stability for perfusionists are expected to be excellent.

For More Information

For information about the career of perfusionist, contact:

- **American Society of Extracorporeal Technology**
  National Office
  503 Carlisle Drive, Suite 125
  Herndon, VA 20170
  Tel: 703-435-8556
  Web: http://www.amsect.org

For information about certification, contact:

- **American Board of Cardiovascular Perfusion**
  207 North 25th Avenue
  Hattiesburg, MS 39401
  Tel: 601-582-3309

For information on medical careers, contact:

- **American Medical Association**
  515 North State Street
  Chicago, IL 60610
  Tel: 312-464-5000
  Web: http://www.ama-assn.org

For information on accredited schools, contact:

- **Accreditation Committee for Perfusion Education**
  7108-C South Alton Way
  Englewood, CO 80112-2106
  Tel: 303-741-3598

Pharmacy Technicians

The Job

Pharmacy technicians provide technical assistance for registered pharmacists and work under their direct supervision. They usually work in chain or independent drug stores, hospitals, community ambulatory care centers, home health care agencies, nursing homes, and the pharmaceutical industry. They maintain patient records; count, package, and label medication doses; prepare and distribute sterile products; and fill and dispense routine orders for stock supplies such as over-the-counter products.

As their roles increase, trained technicians have become more specialized. Some specialized types of pharmacy technicians include narcotics control pharmacy technicians, operating room pharmacy technicians, emergency room pharmacy technicians, nuclear pharmacy technicians, and home health care pharmacy technicians. Specially trained pharmacy technicians are also employed as data entry technicians, lead technicians, supervisors, and technician managers.

Professional and Personal Requirements

At least three states license pharmacy technicians and all 50 states have adopted a written, standardized test for voluntary certification of technicians. Some states, including Texas and Louisiana, require certification of pharmacy technicians.

Pharmacy technicians must be precision-minded, honest, and mature as they are depended on for accuracy and high levels of quality control, especially in hospitals. They must be able to precisely follow written or oral instructions as a wide variety of people, including physicians, nurses, pharmacists, and patients, rely on their actions. Technicians also need computer aptitude in order to effectively record pharmaceutical data.

Starting Out

In some cases pharmacy technicians may be able to pursue education and certification while they are employed. Some chain drugstores are paying the certification fees for their techs, and are also rewarding certified techs with higher hourly pay. This practice will probably increase; industry experts predict a shortage of pharmacists and technicians as more chain drugstores open across the country and more pharmacies offer 24-hour service.

Pharmacy technicians often are hired by the hospital or agency where they interned. If employment is not found this way, aspiring technicians can use employment agencies or newspaper ads to help locate job openings.

Earnings

Most technicians are paid by the hour, and certified technicians can expect to make more than those without certification. In 1997, the Hospital and Healthcare Report found that pharmacist assistants made between $5.90 and $15.41 an hour, with a national average of $9.54 an hour. Richland College, a Dallas County community college that offers allied health certificate programs, estimates the entry level salary for a technician is $6.25 to $7.00 an hour in retail; $7.50 to $8.50 in hospitals; $9.00 to $10.00 in home health care.

Benefits generally include medical and dental insurance, retirement savings plans, and paid sick, personal, and vacation days.

Employment Outlook

As the role of the pharmacist shifts to consultation, more technicians will be needed to assemble and dispense medications. Because of more complex medications and new drug therapies on the market, more education may be necessary for certification in the future. Mechanical advances in the pharmaceutical field, such as robot-picking devices and automatic counting equipment, may eradicate some of the duties pharmacy technicians previously performed, but there will remain a need for skilled technicians to clean and maintain such devices.

For More Information

To learn more about certification and training, contact:

- **Pharmacy Technician Certification Board**
  2215 Constitution Avenue, NW
  Washington, DC 20037-2985
  Tel: 202-429-7576
  Web: http://www.ptcb.org

To obtain a copy of The Journal of Pharmacy Technology, *which lists opportunities for pharmacy technicians and developments in technology, and the* PTEC Directory, *which lists pharmacy tech training programs in the United States and Canada, contact:*

- **Pharmacy Technology Educators Council (PTEC)**
  Harvey Whitney Book Publishing
  PO Box 42696
  Cincinnati, OH 45242
  Tel: 513-793-3555

To learn about membership, contact:

- **Association of Pharmacy Technicians**
  PO Box 1447
  Greensboro, NC 27402
  Tel: 336-275-1700
  Email: aapt@bellsouth.net
  Web: http://pharmacytechnician.com

Phlebotomy Technicians

School Subjects: Biology, Chemistry
Personal Skills: Helping/teaching, Technical/scientific
Work Environment: Primarily indoors, Primarily one location
Salary Range: $16,000 to $25,000 to $38,000
Certification or Licensing: Required by certain states
Outlook: About as fast as the average

The Job

Phlebotomy technicians draw blood from patients or donors in hospitals, blood banks, clinics, physicians' offices, or other facilities. They assemble equipment, verify patient identification numbers, and withdraw blood either by puncturing a person's finger, or by extracting blood from a vein or artery with a needle syringe. They label, transport, and store blood for analysis or for other medical purposes.

The first step a phlebotomy technician performs when drawing blood is to take the patient's medical history, temperature and pulse, and match the physician's testing order with the amount of blood to be drawn. Next, the site of the withdrawal is located and blood is carefully and systematically withdrawn.

After collection, the phlebotomy technician labels the blood, coordinates its number with the worksheet order, and transports the blood to a storage facility or to another laboratory worker. The phlebotomy technician also checks to make sure that the patient is all right, notes any adverse reactions, and administers first aid or other medical assistance when necessary.

Professional and Personal Requirements

Certification and licensing for phlebotomy technicians varies according to state and employer. Several agencies grant certification. To be eligible to take the qualifying examination from the American

Society of Phlebotomy Technicians, or from the Board of Registry of the American Society of Clinical Pathologists, there are several criteria. Applicants must have worked as a full-time phlebotomist for six months or as a part-time phlebotomist for one year, or have completed an accredited phlebotomy training program. American Medical Technologists also offers certification to phlebotomy technicians.

Phlebotomy technicians should enjoy working with people and be effective communicators and a good listeners. They should also be attentive to detail and be able to work under pressure. In addition, phlebotomy technicians should have patience and good manual dexterity.

Starting Out

Many of the publications serving health care professionals list job advertisements, as do daily newspapers. In addition, some employers actively recruit employees by contacting students who are graduating from accredited programs. Some programs offer job placement assistance, as well.

Earnings

Experience, level of education, employer, and work performed determine the salary ranges for phlebotomy technicians. Beginning full-time phlebotomy technicians have median annual salaries of around $16,000. The median annual salary for more experienced workers is around $18,000. Pay rates are highest in the Northeast and West. They are lowest in the central United States. A specialist in blood bank technology with a bachelor's degree and advanced training can usually expect a starting salary of approximately $38,000 a year.

Benefits such as vacation time, sick leave, insurance, and other fringe benefits vary by employer, but are usually consistent with other full-time health care workers.

Employment Outlook

The demand for phlebotomy technicians in the United States is highest in small hospitals. As the percentage of our population aged

65 or older continues to rise, the demand for all kinds of health care professionals will increase as well. There is a demand for workers who are qualified to draw blood at the bedside of patients. The growing number of patients with certain diseases, such as HIV and AIDS, also increases the need for phlebotomy technicians.

For More Information

For more information on educational programs and scholarships, contact:

- **American Association of Blood Banks**
  8101 Glenbrook Road
  Bethesda, MD 20814
  Tel: 301-907-6977
  Web: http://www.aabb.org/

For information on certification and continuing education, contact:

- **American Medical Technologists**
  710 Higgins Road
  Park Ridge, IL 60068-5765
  Tel: 847-823-5169
  Web: http://www.amt1.com/

For information on certification, contact:

- **American Society of Phlebotomy Technicians, Inc.**
  1109 2nd Avenue, SW
  Hickory, NC 28602-2545
  Tel: 704-322-1334

For information on certification and education, contact:

- **American Society of Clinical Pathologists**
  2100 West Harrison Street
  Chicago, IL 60612
  Tel: 312-738-1336
  Web: http://www.ascp.org/

For a list of accredited training programs, contact:

- **National Accrediting Agency for Clinical Laboratory Sciences**
  8410 West Bryn Mawr, Suite 670
  Chicago, IL 60631-3402
  Tel: 773-714-8880
  Web: http://www.naacls.org/

Photographers

School Subjects: Art, Chemistry
Personal Skills: Artistic, Communication/ideas
Work Environment: Indoors and outdoors, Primarily multiple locations
Salary Range: $16,500 to $25,000 to $37,000+
Certification or Licensing: None available
Outlook: About as fast as the average

The Job

Photographers take and sometimes develop and print pictures of people, places, objects, and events, using a variety of cameras and photographic equipment. They work in publishing, advertising, public relations, science, and business, as well as in personal photographic services. They may also work as fine artists.

Photography is both an artistic and technical occupation. Photographers must know how to use cameras and adjust focus, shutter speeds, aperture, lenses, and filters. They must understand the types and speeds of films and the use of light and shadow.

Some photographers send their film to laboratories, but some develop their own negatives and make their own prints. These processes require knowledge about chemicals such as developers and fixers and how to use enlarging equipment.

Professional and Personal Requirements

There is no certification or licensing available in this field.

Being a photographer requires good eyesight, manual dexterity, color vision, and artistic ability. Photographers need an eye for form and line and an appreciation of light and shadow. In addition, they should be patient and accurate and enjoy working with detail. Photographers who are self-employed need good business, marketing, management, and sales skills.

Starting Out

Some photographers enter the field as apprentices, trainees, or assistants. Trainees may work in a darkroom, camera shop, or developing laboratory. They may move lights and arrange backgrounds for a commercial or portrait photographer or motion picture photographer. Trainees may spend many months learning this kind of work before they move into a job behind a camera.

In many large cities, there are schools of photography. Some graduates go into business for themselves as soon as they have finished their formal education. Setting up a studio may not require a large capital outlay, but beginners may find that success does not come easily.

Earnings

In the late 1990s, photographers who handle routine work earned an average of about $25,000 a year. Photographers who do difficult or challenging work earned $37,000 or more a year.

In the 1990s, beginning photographers working for newspapers that have contracts with the Newspaper Guild earned a median salary of about $19,000 a year. Most earned between $16,500 and $22,500, with the top 10 percent receiving $26,500 or more. Experienced newspaper photographers earned a median of $30,700 a year.

Photographers in government service earned an average salary of about $29,500 a year. Self-employed photographers often earn more than salaried photographers, but their earnings depend on general business conditions, and they must provide their own benefits.

Employment Outlook

Employment of photographers will increase about as fast as the average for all occupations through the year 2006, according to the *Occupational Outlook Handbook*. The demand for new images should remain strong in education, communication, entertainment, marketing, and research. As more newspapers and magazines turn to electronic publishing, it will increase the need for photographs.

Photography is a highly competitive field. There are far more photographers than positions available. Only those who are extremely talented and highly skilled can support themselves as self-employed photographers. Many photographers take pictures as a sideline while working another job.

For More Information

The ASMP promotes the rights of photographers, educates its members in business practices, and promotes high standards of ethics.

- **American Society of Media Photographers (ASMP)**
  14 Washington Road, Suite 502
  Princeton Junction, NJ 08550-1033
  Tel: 609-799-8300
  Email: Mbr@ASMP.org
  Web: http://www.asmp.org

The NPPA maintains a job bank, provides educational information, and makes insurance available to its members. It also publishes News Photographer *magazine.*

- **National Press Photographers Association (NPPA)**
  3200 Croasdaile Drive, Suite 306
  Durham, NC 27705
  Tel: 800-289-6772
  Email: nppa@mindspring.com
  Web: http://metalab.unc.edu/nppa/index.html

The PPA provides training, publishes its own magazine, and offers various services for its members.

- **Professional Photographers of America (PPA)**
  229 Peachtree Street, NE, No. 2200
  Atlanta, GA 30303-2206
  Tel: 404-522-8600
  Email: membership@ppa.world.org
  Web: http://www.ppa-world.org

Physical Therapy Assistants

School Subjects: Biology, Health
Personal Skills: Helping/teaching, Mechanical/manipulative
Work Environment: Primarily indoors, Primarily one location
Salary Range: $20,000 to $30,000 to $35,000+
Certification or Licensing: Required in most states
Outlook: Much faster than the average

The Job

Physical therapy assistants are skilled health care workers who assist physical therapists in a variety of techniques (such as exercise, massage, heat, and water therapy) to help restore physical function in people with injury, birth defects, or disease.

Physical therapy assistants work directly under the supervision of physical therapists. They teach and help patients improve functional activities required in their daily lives, such as walking, climbing, and moving from one place to another. The assistants observe patients during treatments, record the patients' responses and progress, and report these to the physical therapist, either orally or in writing. They fit patients for and teach them to use braces, artificial limbs, crutches, canes, walkers, wheelchairs, and other devices. They may make physical measurements to assess the effects of treatments or to evaluate patients' range of motion, length and girth of body parts, and vital signs. Physical therapy assistants act as members of a team and regularly confer with other members of the physical therapy staff.

Professional and Personal Requirements

Licensure for physical therapy assistants is currently mandatory in 44 states. Licensure requirements vary from state to state, but all require graduation from an American Physical Therapy Association-accred-

266

ited two-year associate degree program and passing a written examination administered by the state.

Physical therapy assistants must have stamina, patience, and
determination, and they should genuinely like and understand people. Physical therapy assistants must be reasonably strong and enjoy
physical activity. Manual dexterity and good coordination are needed
to adjust equipment and assist patients. Assistants should be able to
lift, climb, stoop, and kneel.

Starting Out

The student's school placement office is probably the best place to find
a job. Alternatively, assistants can apply to the physical therapy
departments of local hospitals, rehabilitation centers, extended-
care facilities, and other potential employers. Openings are listed in
the classified ads of newspapers, professional journals, and with
private and public employment agencies. In locales where training
programs have produced many physical therapy assistants, competition for jobs may be keen. In such cases, assistants may want to
widen their search to areas where there is less competition, especially
suburban and rural areas.

Earnings

Salaries for physical therapy assistants vary considerably depending
on geographical location, employer, and level of experience. According
to the *Occupational Outlook Handbook,* the income for a recently
graduated assistant averaged about $24,000 a year in 1996, while expe-
rienced physical therapy assistants averaged about $30,000. Fringe
benefits vary, although they usually include paid holidays and vacations, health insurance, and pension plans.

Employment Outlook

Employment prospects are very good for physical therapy assistants, with job growth projected around 80 percent through the
year 2006, according to the U.S. Department of Labor. Demand for
rehabilitation services is expected to continue to grow much more

rapidly than the average for all occupations, and the rate of turnover among workers is relatively high. Many new positions for physical therapy assistants are expected to open up as hospital programs that aid the disabled expand and as long-term facilities seek to offer residents more adequate services.

For More Information

For information on accredited training programs, contact:

- **American Physical Therapy Association**
  1111 North Fairfax Street
  Alexandria, VA 22314
  Tel: 800-999-2782
  Web: http://www.apta.org

Physician Assistants

School Subjects: Biology, Health
Personal Skills: Helping/teaching, Technical/scientific
Work Environment: Primarily indoors, Primarily multiple locations
Salary Range: $62,300 to $80,000 to $100,000
Certification or Licensing: Required
Outlook: Much faster than the average

The Job

Physician assistants (PAs) practice medicine under the supervision of licensed doctors of medicine or osteopathy, providing various health care services to patients. Much of the work they do was formerly limited to physicians. PAs may be assigned a variety of tasks; they may take medical histories of patients, do complete routine physical examinations, order laboratory tests, draw blood samples, give injections, make diagnoses, choose treatments, and assist in surgery. The extent of the PA's duties depends on the specific laws of the state and the practices of the supervising physician, as well as the experience and abilities of the PA. PAs work in a variety of health care settings, including hospitals, clinics, physician's offices, and federal, state, and local agencies.

About 50 percent of all PAs specialize in primary care medicine, such as family medicine, internal medicine, pediatrics, obstetrics and gynecology, and emergency medicine. Nineteen percent of all PAs work in surgery or surgical subspecialties. In 1998, 41 states and the District of Columbia allowed PAs to prescribe medicine to patients.

Professional and Personal Requirements

Currently, all states—except Mississippi—require that PAs be certified by the National Commission on Certification of Physician Assistants.

Physician assistants should be compassionate, confident, and emotionally stable.

Starting Out

PAs must complete their formal training programs before entering the job market. Once their studies are completed, the placement services of the schools may help them find jobs. PAs may also seek employment at hospitals, clinics, medical offices, or other health care settings. Information about jobs with the federal government can be obtained by contacting the Office of Personnel Management.

Earnings

Salaries of PAs vary according to experience, specialty, and employer. In 1998, PAs earned a starting average of $62,300 annually. Those working in hospitals and medical offices earn slightly more than those working in clinics. Experienced PAs have the potential to earn close to $100,000 a year. PAs working for the military averaged $50,300 a year. PAs are well compensated compared with other occupations that have similar training requirements. Most PAs receive health and life insurance among other benefits.

Employment Outlook

There were approximately 64,000 physician assistants employed in the United States in 1998. Employment for PAs, according to the U.S. Department of Labor, is expected to increase much faster than the average for all occupations. A 46.4 percent increase in the number of new jobs is projected through the year 2006. In fact, job growth is expected to outpace the number of potential employees entering this occupation by as much as 9 percent. This field was also mentioned in *U.S. News & World Report*'s 1998 article "Best Jobs for the Future."

The role of the PA in delivering health care has also expanded over the past decade. PAs have taken on new duties and responsibilities, and they now work in a variety of health care settings.

For More Information

The following organizations have information on physician assistant careers and education.

- **American Academy of Physician Assistants**
  950 North Washington Street
  Alexandria, VA 22314
  Tel: 703-836-2272
  Email: aapa@aapa.org
  Web: http://www.aapa.org

- **Association of Physician Assistant Programs**
  950 North Washington Street
  Alexandria, VA 22314
  Tel: 703-548-5538
  Email: apap@aapa.org
  Web: http://www.apap.org

For information on certification, contact:

- **National Commission on Certification of Physician Assistants**
  6849-B2 Peachtree Dunwoody Road
  Atlanta, GA 30328
  Tel: 404-493-9100
  Web:
  http://www.social.com/health/nhicdata/hr1300/hr1334.html

Pilots

School Subjects: Mathematics, Physics
Personal Skills: Leadership/management, Technical/scientific
Work Environment: Primarily indoors, Primarily multiple locations
Salary Range: $26,290 to $76,800 to $200,000
Certification or Licensing: Required
Outlook: About as fast as the average

The Job

Pilots operate aircraft for the transportation of passengers, freight, mail, or for other commercial purposes. In addition to actually flying the aircraft, pilots perform a variety of safety-related tasks. Before each flight, they must determine weather and flight conditions, ensure that sufficient fuel is on board to complete the flight safely, and verify the maintenance status of the aircraft. Pilots must also perform system operation checks to test the proper functioning of instrumentation, controls, and electronic and mechanical systems on the flight deck. During a flight, pilots monitor aircraft systems, keep a watchful eye on local weather conditions, perform checklists, and maintain constant communication with the air traffic controllers along the flight route. Pilots must also keep detailed logs of their flight hours, both for payroll purposes and to comply with Federal Aviation Administration (FAA) regulations.

In addition to airline pilots, there are various other types of pilots, including *business pilots,* or *executive pilots,* who fly for businesses that have their own planes. *Test pilots* test new models of planes and make sure they function properly. *Flight instructors* are pilots who teach others how to fly.

Professional and Personal Requirements

All pilots and copilots must be licensed by the FAA before they can do any type of commercial flying.

Sound physical and emotional health are essential requirements for aspiring pilots. Emotional stability is necessary because the safety of other people depends upon a pilot's remaining calm and level-headed. Physical health is equally important, as are excellent vision, hearing, and coordination.

Starting Out

A large percentage of commercial pilots have received their training in the armed forces. A military pilot who wants to apply for a commercial airplane pilot's license is required to pass only the Federal Aviation Regulations examination if application is made within a year after leaving the service.

Pilots possessing the necessary educational qualifications and license may apply directly to a commercial airline for a job.

Earnings

The 1996 average starting salary for airline pilots was about $15,000 at small turboprop airlines and $26,290 at larger, major airlines. Pilots with six years of experience made $28,000 a year at turboprop airlines and nearly $76,800 at the largest airlines. Senior captains on the largest aircraft earned as much as $200,000 a year.

Pilots with the airlines receive life and health insurance and retirement benefits. Pilots and their families usually may fly free or at reduced fares.

Employment Outlook

The employment prospects of airline pilots look very good into the next century. The airline industry expects passenger travel to grow by as much as 60 percent, and airlines will be adding more planes and more flights to accommodate passengers.

Competition is expected to diminish as the many pilots who were hired during the boom of the 1960s reach mandatory retirement age. In addition, because the military has increased its benefits and incentives, many pilots choose to remain in the service, further reducing the supply of pilots for civilian work. These factors are expected to create a shortage of qualified pilots.

For More Information

Contact the following organizations for information on a career as a pilot:

- **Air Line Pilots Association, International**
  PO Box 1169
  Herndon, VA 22070
  Tel: 703-689-2270
  Web: http://www.alpa.org/

- **Air Transport Association of America**
  1301 Pennsylvania Avenue, NW, Suite 1100
  Washington, DC 20004-1707
  Tel: 202-626-4000
  Web: http://www.air-transport.org/

- **Federal Aviation Administration**
  Flight Standards Division
  Fitzgerald Federal Building
  John F. Kennedy International Airport
  Jamaica, NY 11430

- **Future Aviation Professionals of America**
  4959 Massachusetts Blvd.
  Atlanta, Georgia 30337
  Phone: 404-997-8097

Plastics Technicians

School Subjects: Chemistry, Mathematics
Personal Skills: Mechanical/manipulative, Technical/scientific
Work Environment: Primarily indoors, Primarily one location
Salary Range: $16,000 to $31,000 to $39,500
Certification or Licensing: Voluntary
Outlook: Much faster than the average

The Job

Plastics technicians are skilled professionals who help design engineers, scientists, research groups, and manufacturers develop, manufacture, and market plastics products.

The duties of plastics technicians can be grouped into five general categories: research and development, mold and tool making, manufacturing, sales and service, and related technical tasks. Plastics technicians in research and development work in laboratories to create new materials or improve existing ones. They may monitor chemical reactions, test, evaluate test results, keep records, and submit reports. Mold and tool making is a specialized division of plastics manufacturing. Technicians in plastics manufacturing work in molding, laminating, or fabricating. Sales and service work encompasses a wide variety of jobs for plastics technicians. These technicians are needed in the sales departments of materials suppliers, machinery manufacturers, molding companies, laminators, and fabricators.

Plastics technicians are also important and valued employees in certain related fields. For example, companies that make computers, appliances, electronic devices, aircraft, and other products that incorporate plastics components rely heavily on plastics technicians to specify, design, purchase, and integrate plastics in the manufacture of the company's major product line.

Professional and Personal Requirements

Certification isn't required of plastics technicians, but is available through the Society of the Plastics Industry (SPI) in four areas: blow molding, extrusion, injection molding, or thermoforming.

Plastics technicians need good hand-eye coordination and manual dexterity to perform a variety of tasks, especially building laminated structures. They should have normal eyesight, good communication skills, and the ability to follow instructions precisely.

Starting Out

Technical schools provide the best means for getting started in the field. Personnel managers maintain contact with schools that have ongoing plastics programs, and recruiting agents visit graduating technicians to acquaint them with current opportunities. Also, experts in various fields are regularly invited to lecture at technical schools and colleges. Their advice and information can provide good ideas about finding entry-level employment.

Visits to plants and laboratories can give prospective technicians a broad overview of the many manufacturing processes. During these tours, students can observe working conditions and discuss employment possibilities.

Earnings

According to 1997 wage surveys conducted by SPI, machine operators in the plastics industry earn between $16,000 and $22,000 a year. Quality assurance inspectors make around $21,000 a year. Computer-aided design (CAD) specialists earn between $31,000 and $39,500 a year.

Benefits often include paid vacations, health and dental insurance, pension plans, credit union services, production bonuses, stock options, and industry-sponsored education. These benefits will vary with the size and nature of the company.

Employment Outlook

The plastics industry encompasses so many employment categories that employment is virtually assured for any qualified graduate of a technical program. Worldwide expansion of this industry is expected to continue through the year 2006. This expansion is expected to create a strong demand for technicians who can meet the challenges of this changing industry. Those who pursue advanced education and who acquire a variety of skills and talents will have the best employment opportunities. SPI ranks the top plastics industry states by employment: in 1996, the top five states were California, Ohio, Michigan, Illinois, and Texas.

For More Information

For a career brochure and information about education and certification, contact:

- **Society of the Plastics Industry**
  1801 K Street, NW, Suite 600K
  Washington, DC 20006-1301
  Tel: 202-974-5200
  Web: http://www.socplas.org

The APC is a trade industry that offers a great deal of information about the plastics industry, and maintains an informative Web site:

- **American Plastics Council (APC)**
  1801 K Street, NW, Suite 701-L
  Washington, DC 20006-1301
  Tel: 800-243-5790
  Web: http://www.plastics.org

For information about scholarships, seminars, and training, contact:

- **Plastics Institute of America**
  University of Massachusetts-Lowell
  333 Aiken Street
  Lowell, MA 01854
  Tel: 978-934-3130
  Web: http://www.eng.uml.edu/dept/PIA/index.html

For information on student membership, contact:

- **Society of Plastics Engineers**
  PO Box 403
  Brookfield, CT 06804-0403
  Tel: 203-775-0471
  Web: http://www.4spe.org

Plumbers and Pipefitters

School Subjects: Chemistry, Physics
Personal Skills: Following instructions, Mechanical/manipulative
Work Environment: Primarily indoors, Primarily multiple locations
Salary Range: $14,976 to $30,730 to $50,256
Certification or Licensing: Required for certain positions
Outlook: Little change or more slowly than the average

The Job

Plumbers and pipefitters assemble, install, alter, and repair pipes and pipe systems that carry water, steam, air, or other liquids and gases for sanitation and industrial purposes as well as other uses. Plumbers also install plumbing fixtures, appliances, and heating and refrigerating units.

Because little difference exists between the work of the plumber and the pipefitter in most cases, the two are often considered to be one trade. However, some craftsworkers specialize in one field or the other, especially in large cities.

The work of pipefitters differs from that of plumbers mainly in its location and the variety and size of pipes used. Plumbers work primarily in residential and commercial buildings, whereas pipefitters are generally employed by large industrial concerns—such as oil refineries, refrigeration plants, and defense establishments—where more complex systems of piping are used. Plumbers assemble, install, and repair heating, water, and drainage systems, especially those that must be connected to public utilities systems. Some of their jobs include replacing burst pipes and installing and repairing sinks, bathtubs, water heaters, hot water tanks, garbage disposal units, dishwashers, and water softeners. Plumbers also may work on septic tanks, cesspools, and sewers. During the final construction stages of both commercial and residential buildings, plumbers install heating and air-conditioning units and connect radiators, water heaters, and plumbing fixtures.

Professional and Personal Requirements

A license is required for plumbers in many places. To obtain this license, plumbers must pass a special examination to demonstrate their knowledge of local building codes as well as their all-around knowledge of the trade. To become a plumbing contractor in most places, a master plumber's license must be obtained.

Those who would be successful and contented plumbers should like to solve a variety of problems and should not object to being called on during evenings, weekends, or holidays to perform emergency repairs. As in most service occupations, plumbers should be able to get along well with all kinds of people. The plumber should be a person who works well alone, but who can also direct the work of helpers and enjoy the company of those in the other construction trades.

Starting Out

Applicants who wish to become apprentices usually contact local plumbing, heating, and air-conditioning contractors who employ plumbers, the state employment service bureau, or the local branch of the United Association of Journeymen and Apprentices of the Plumbing and Pipe Fitting Industry of the United States and Canada. Individual contractors or contractor associations often sponsor local apprenticeship programs. Apprentices very commonly go on to permanent employment with the firms with which they apprenticed.

Earnings

The annual median salary for plumbers who are not self-employed is $30,730, according to the *Occupational Outlook Handbook*. Wages vary, however, according to location. Monthly wages for plumbers range from $1,248 to $4,188. Hourly pay rates for apprentices usually start at 50 percent of the experienced worker's rate, and increase by 5 percent every six months until a rate of 95 percent is reached. Benefits for union workers usually include health insurance, sick time, and vacation pay, as well as pension plans.

Employment Outlook

The U.S. Department of Labor predicts slower than average growth for plumbers and pipefitters through the year 2006. Despite this prediction, there will be many job openings for qualified workers. There are several reasons for this outlook. First, and foremost, increased construction activity has created a demand for qualified workers; a demand that far exceeds the current supply. Second, plumbing and heating work in new homes is expected to include the installation of sprinkler systems, more bathrooms per house, washing machines, waste disposals, air-conditioning equipment, and solar heating devices. Third, because pipework is becoming more important in large industries, more workers will be needed for installation and maintenance work, especially where refrigeration and air-conditioning equipment are used. Fourth, thousands of job openings each year are created by those who leave the field.

For More Information

For general information on plumbing and pipefitting careers, contact:

- National Association of Plumbing-Heating-Cooling Contractors
  PO Box 6808
  180 South Washington Street
  Falls Church, VA 22040
  Tel: 800-533-7694
  Web: http://www.naphcc.org/

For information on union membership, contact:

- United Association of Journeymen and Apprentices of the Plumbing and Pipe Fitting Industry of the United States and Canada
  901 Massachusetts Avenue, NW
  Washington, DC 20001
  Tel: 202-628-5823
  Web: http://www.ua.org/

Police Officers

School Subjects: Physical education, Psychology
Personal Skills: Leadership/management
Work Environment: Indoors and outdoors, Primarily multiple locations
Salary Range: $19,200 to $34,700 to $58,500+
Certification or Licensing: None available
Outlook: About as fast as the average

The Job

Police officers perform many duties relating to public safety. Their responsibilities include not only preserving the peace, preventing criminal acts, enforcing the law, investigating crimes, and arresting those who violate the law but also directing traffic, community relations work, and controlling crowds at public events. If police officers patrol a beat or work in small communities, their duties may be many and varied. In large city departments, their work may be highly specialized. Police officers are employed at the federal, state, county, and city level. They are under oath to uphold the law 24-hours a day.

Specific positions within this field include *internal affairs investigators* (who police the police); *specialized officers* (who supervise in special situations, such as missing persons or fraud); *police clerks* (who perform clerical and community-oriented tasks); and *state police officers* (who patrol highways and enforce the laws and regulations that govern the use of those highways, in addition to performing general police work).

Professional and Personal Requirements

There is no certification or licensing available in this field. Candidates in this field must satisfy a number of requirements as to intelligence, age, vision, hearing, weight, fitness level, and background and personal history.

Prospective police officers should enjoy working with people and be able to cooperate with others. They must have a strong degree of emotional control and the ability to think clearly and logically during emergency situations.

Starting Out

Applicants interested in police work should apply directly to local civil service offices or examining boards. In smaller communities that do not follow civil service methods, applicants should apply directly to the police department or city government offices in the communities where they reside. Those interested in becoming state police officers may apply directly to their state civil service commissions or state police headquarters.

Earnings

According to the U.S. Department of Labor, police officers in 1996 earned an annual average salary of $34,700; the lowest 10 percent earned less than $19,200 a year, while the highest 10 percent earned over $58,500 annually. Police officers in supervisory positions earned median salaries of $41,200 a year in 1996, with a low of $22,500 and a high of over $64,500. Sheriffs and other law enforcement officers earned median annual salaries of $26,700 in 1996.

Police officers usually receive generous benefits, including health insurance and paid vacation and sick leave, and enjoy increased job security. In addition, most police departments offer retirement plans and retirement after 20 or 25 years of service, usually at half pay.

Employment Outlook

Employment of police officers is expected to increase about as fast as the average for all occupations through the year 2006, according to the U.S. Department of Labor. Federal "tough-on-crime" legislation passed in the mid-1990s has created a short-term increase of new jobs in police departments at the federal, state, and local levels. The opportunities that become available, however, may be affected by technological, scientific, and other changes occurring today in police work.

This occupation has a very low turnover rate. However, new positions will open as current officers retire, leave the force, or move into higher positions. Retirement ages are relatively low in police work compared to other occupations.

For More Information

The educational arm of the American Federation of Police and the National Association of Chiefs of Police, the American Police Academy compiles statistics, operates a placement service and a speaker's bureau, and offers home study programs. For more information, contact:

■ **American Police Academy**
1000 Connecticut Avenue, NW, Suite 9
Washington, DC 20036
Tel: 202-293-9088

The following association maintains a speaker's bureau, conducts educational programs, and offers both recognition and scholarship awards. For more information, contact:

■ **National Police Officers Association of America**
PO Box 22129
Louisville, KY 40252-0129
Tel: 800-467-6762

The following organization compiles statistics, operates a hotline, hall of fame, and speaker's bureau, offers children's services, and sponsors competitions and scholarships:

■ **National United Law Enforcement Officers Association**
256 East McLemore Avenue
Memphis, TN 38106
Tel: 800-533-4649

Pollution Control Technicians

School Subjects: Biology, Chemistry
Personal Skills: Mechanical/manipulative, Technical/scientific
Work Environment: Indoors and outdoors, One location with some travel
Salary Range: $15,500 to $28,500 to $49,500
Certification or Licensing: Required for certain positions
Outlook: About as fast as the average

The Job

Pollution control technicians, also known as *environmental technicians,* conduct tests and field investigations to obtain samples and data required by engineers, scientists, and others to clean up, monitor, control, or prevent pollution. They apply principles and methods of engineering, chemistry, meteorology, agriculture, or other disciplines in their work. A pollution control technician usually specializes in air, water, or soil pollution. Although work differs by employer and specialty, technicians generally collect samples for laboratory analysis, using specialized instruments and equipment; monitor pollution control devices and systems, such as smokestack air "scrubbers"; and perform various other tests and investigations to evaluate pollution problems. They follow strict procedures in collecting and recording data in order to meet the requirements of environmental laws.

In general, pollution control technicians do not operate the equipment and systems designed to prevent pollution or remove pollutants. Instead, they test environmental conditions. In addition, some analyze and report on their findings.

Professional and Personal Requirements

Certification or licensing is required for some positions in pollution control, especially those in which sanitation, public health, a public water supply, or a sewage treatment system is involved. The

American Society of Certified Engineering Technicians and the Air and Waste Management Association offer certification to pollution control technicians.

Pollution control technicians should be patient, detail-oriented, and capable of following instructions. They should be able to read and understand technical materials, charts, maps, and diagrams. Computer skills are also helpful. Good physical condition is a requirement for some activities, such as climbing up smoke stacks to take emission samples.

Starting Out

Graduates of two-year pollution control technology or related programs are often employed during their final term by recruiters who visit their schools. When they first start out, technicians may find the greatest number of positions available in state or local government agencies.

Most schools can provide job-hunting advice and assistance. Direct application to state or local environmental agencies, employment agencies, or potential employers can also be a productive approach.

Earnings

Government entry-level salaries for pollution control technicians are about $15,500 to $19,500 per year, depending on education and experience. The average is $28,500 per year. Technicians who move up to become managers or supervisors can make up to $49,500 per year or more.

No matter which area they specialize in, pollution control technicians generally enjoy health insurance benefits, paid vacation, holidays and sick time, and employer paid training.

Employment Outlook

Employment for technicians is expected to increase about as fast as the average through 2006. Demand will be higher in some areas of the country than others depending on specialty; for example, air pollution control technicians will be especially in demand in large cities facing pressure to comply with national air quality standards, such as Los Angeles and New York. Amount of industrialization, stringency of state and local pollution control enforcement, local economy, and other factors also will affect demand by region and specialty. Perhaps the single greatest factor affecting all pollution control work is continued mandates for pollution control by the federal government. As long as the federal government is supporting pollution control, the pollution control industry will continue to grow and technicians will be needed.

For More Information

For information on certification, contact:

- **Air and Waste Management Association**
  One Gateway Center, Third Floor
  Pittsburgh, PA 15222
  Web: http://www.awma.org

The following group is affiliated with the National Society of Professional Engineers and is a source of technician certification:

- **American Society of Certified Engineering Technicians**
  PO Box 1348
  Flowery Branch, GA 30542-1348
  Web: http://www.nmsu.edu/~ascet/ASCET

Following is the national organization. For your state's Environmental Protection Agency, check the government listings in your phone book:

- **Environmental Protection Agency**
  401 M Street, SW
  Washington, DC 20460
  Web: http://www.epa.gov

The following organization is an environmental careers resource for high school and college students:

- **Environmental Careers Organization**
  179 South Street
  Boston, MA 02111
  Tel: 617-426-4375
  Web: http://www.eco.org

Preschool Teachers

School Subjects: Art, English
Personal Skills: Communication/ideas, Helping/teaching
Work Environment: Primarily indoors, Primarily one location
Salary Range: $12,710 to $21,000 to $38,611
Certification or Licensing: Required by certain states
Outlook: Faster than the average

The Job

Preschool teachers promote the education of children under age five in all areas. They help students develop physically, socially, and emotionally, work with them on language and communications skills, and help cultivate their cognitive abilities. They also work with families to support parents in raising their young children and reinforcing skills at home. They plan and lead activities developed in accordance with the specific ages and needs of the children. It is the goal of all preschool teachers to help students develop the skills, interests, and individual creativity that they will use for the rest of their lives.

Many schools and districts consider kindergarten teachers, who teach students five years of age, to be preschool teachers. Kindergarten teachers usually have their own classrooms, made up exclusively of five-year-olds, and they usually spend more time helping students with academic skills than do other preschool teachers.

Professional and Personal Requirements

In some states, licensure may be required. Kindergarten teachers working in public elementary schools almost always need teaching certification similar to that required by other elementary school teachers in the school.

Because young children look up to adults and learn through example, it is especially important that a preschool teacher be a good role model. Everything they say and do effects the children they teach. Patience, a sense of humor, and respect for children are essential qualities in a preschool teacher.

Starting Out

Aspiring preschool teachers should contact child care centers, nursery schools, Head Start programs, and other preschool facilities to identify job opportunities. Often jobs for preschool teachers are listed in the classified section of newspapers. In addition, many school districts and state boards of education maintain job listings of available teaching positions. If no permanent positions are available at preschools, beginners may be able to find opportunities to work as a substitute teacher. Most preschools and kindergartens maintain a substitute list and refer to it frequently.

Earnings

According to the Bureau of Labor Statistics, preschool teachers made about $404 a week in 1998. A 1997 report from the National Education Association estimated the annual average salary for all teachers to be $38,611.

Because some preschool programs are only in the morning or afternoon, many preschool teachers work only part time. As part-time workers, they often do not receive medical insurance or other benefits and may get paid minimum wage to start.

Employment Outlook

According to the U.S. Department of Labor, employment opportunities for preschool teachers are expected to increase through 2006. Jobs should be available at private child care centers, nursery schools, Head Start facilities, public and private kindergartens, and laboratory schools connected with universities and colleges.

One-third of all childcare workers leave their centers each year, often because of the low pay and lack of benefits. This will mean plenty of job openings for preschool teachers and possibly improved benefit plans, as centers attempt to maintain qualified preschool teachers.

For More Information

For information about certification, contact:

■ **Council for Early Childhood Professional Recognition**
2460 16th Street, NW
Washington, DC 20009
Tel: 800-424-4310
Web: http://www.cdacouncil.org

For information on training programs, contact:

■ **American Montessori Society**
281 Park Avenue South, 6th Floor
New York, NY 10010-6102
Tel: 212-358-1250
Web: http://www.amshq.org

For general information on preschool teaching careers, contact:

■ **National Association for the Education of Young Children**
1509 16th Street, NW
Washington, DC 20036
Tel: 800-424-2460
Web: http://www.naeyc.org

For information about student memberships and training opportunities, contact:

■ **National Association of Child Care Professionals**
304-A Roanoke Street
Christiansburg, VA 24073
Tel: 800-537-1118
Web: http://www.naccp.org

Quality Control Technicians

School Subjects: Mathematics, Physics
Personal Skills: Mechanical/manipulative, Technical/scientific
Work Environment: Primarily indoors, Primarily one location
Salary Range: $17,000 to $28,500 to $70,000
Certification or Licensing: Voluntary
Outlook: About as fast as the average

The Job

Quality control technicians work with quality control engineers in designing, implementing, and maintaining quality systems. They test and inspect materials and products during all phases of production in order to ensure they meet specified levels of quality. They may test random samples of products or monitor automated equipment and production workers that inspect products during manufacturing. Using engineering blueprints, drawings, and specifications, they measure and inspect parts for dimensions, performance, and mechanical, electrical, and chemical properties. They establish *tolerances,* or acceptable deviations from engineering specifications, and direct manufacturing personnel in identifying rejects and items that need to be reworked. They monitor production processes to be sure that machinery and equipment are working properly and set to established specifications.

Quality control technicians also record and evaluate test data. Using statistical quality control procedures, technicians prepare charts and write summaries about how well a product conforms to existing standards. Most important, they offer suggestions to quality control engineers on how to modify existing quality standards and manufacturing procedures. This helps to achieve the optimum product quality from existing or proposed new equipment.

Professional and Personal Requirements

Certification is voluntary and offered through professional associations, such as the American Society for Quality.

Quality control technicians need scientific and mathematical aptitudes. They should have good eyesight and good manual skills, including the ability to use hand tools. They should be able to follow technical instructions and to make sound judgments about technical matters.

Starting Out

Students enrolled in two-year technical schools may learn of openings for quality control technicians through their schools' job placement services. In many cases, employers prefer to hire engineers who have some work experience in their particular industry. For this reason, applicants who have had summer or part-time employment or participated in a work-study or internship program may have greater job opportunities.

Students may also learn about openings through help wanted ads or by using the services of state and private employment services. They also may apply directly to companies that employ quality control engineers and technicians.

Earnings

Most beginning quality control technicians who are graduates of two-year technical programs earn salaries ranging from $17,000 to $21,000 a year. Experienced technicians with two-year degrees earn salaries that average $28,500 a year. Some senior technicians with special skills or experience may earn as much as $70,000 a year.

Most companies offer benefits that include paid vacations, paid holidays, and health insurance. Other benefits may include pension plans, profit sharing, 401(k) plans, and tuition assistance programs.

Employment Outlook

The employment outlook depends, to some degree, on general economic conditions. Although many economists forecast low to moderate growth in manufacturing operations through the year 2006, employment opportunities for quality control personnel should remain steady or slightly increase as many companies place increased emphasis on quality control activities. Opportunities for quality control technicians should be good in the food and beverage industries, pharmaceutical firms, electronics companies, and chemical companies. Declines in employment in some industries may occur because of the increased use of automated equipment that tests and inspects parts during production operations.

For More Information

For information on certification, contact:

■ **American Society for Quality**
PO Box 3005
Milwaukee, WI 53201-3005
Tel: 800-248-1946
Web: http://www.asqc.org/

Radiologic Technologists

School Subjects: Biology, Health
Personal Skills: Helping/teaching, Technical/scientific
Work Environment: Primarily indoors, Primarily one location
Salary Range: $23,400 to $27,700 to $33,300
Certification or Licensing: Recommended
Outlook: Faster than the average

The Job

Radiologic technologists operate equipment that creates images of the body's tissues, organs, and bones for medical diagnoses and therapy. Before an X-ray examination, radiologic technologists may administer drugs or chemical mixtures to the patient to better highlight internal organs. They then place the patient in the correct position between the X-ray source and film and protect body areas that are not to be exposed to radiation. After determining the proper duration and intensity of the exposure, they operate the controls to beam X rays through the patient and expose the photographic film. They may also operate computer-aided imaging equipment that does not involve X rays and may help to treat diseased or affected areas of the body by exposing the patient to specified concentrations of radiation for prescribed times.

Professional and Personal Requirements

Radiologic technologists may register with the American Registry of Radiologic Technologists after graduating from an accredited program in radiography, radiation therapy, or nuclear medicine. Although registration and certification are voluntary, many jobs are open only to technologists who have acquired these credentials.

In 1997, licenses were needed by radiologic technologists in 36 states.

Radiologic technologists should be responsible individuals with a mature and caring nature. They should be personable and compassionate and should enjoy interacting with all types of people, including those who are very ill.

Starting Out

With more states regulating the practice of radiologic technology, certification by the appropriate accreditation body for a given specialty is quickly becoming a necessity for employment. Persons who acquire training in schools that have not been accredited, or who learn on the job, may have difficulty in qualifying for many positions, especially those with a wide range of assignments. Students enrolled in hospital educational programs often work for the hospital upon completion of the program. Those who attend degree programs can get help finding jobs through their schools' placement offices.

Earnings

The starting salary in a hospital or medical center averages about $23,400 a year for radiologic technologists, according to the U.S. Department of Labor. With experience, technologists earn average salaries of about $29,100 a year.

Technologists with specialized skills may earn larger incomes. Radiation therapists earn about $30,700 to start, and the average salary for experienced employees is about $34,300. In ultrasound technology, the average pay for graduates of an accredited program is $27,700 for beginning technologists and about $33,300 for those with experience.

Most technologists are covered by the same vacation and sick leave provisions as other employees in the organizations that employ them, and some receive free medical care and pension benefits.

Employment Outlook

The number of people working in the field of radiologic technology has stabilized. Although enrollments in accredited schools have equalized in recent years, the demand for qualified people in some areas of the country far exceeds the supply. This shortage is particularly acute in rural areas and small towns.

In the years to come, increasing numbers of radiologic technologists will be employed in nonhospital settings, such as physicians' offices, clinics, health maintenance organizations, laboratories, government agencies, and diagnostic imaging centers. However, hospitals will remain the major employers for the near future.

For More Information

The following organization has information about radiologic technologists, a catalog of educational products, and a job bank.

- **American Society of Radiologic Technologists**
  15000 Central Avenue, SE
  Albuquerque, NM 87123
  Tel: 505-298-4500
  Web: http://www.asrt.org

For information on accreditation, contact:

- **American Cancer Society**
  1599 Clifton Road
  Atlanta, GA 30329
  Tel: 404-320-3333
  Web: http://www.cancer.org

For information on registration, contact:

- **American Registry of Radiologic Technologists**
  1255 Northland Drive
  St. Paul, MN 55120
  Tel: 612-687-0048
  Web: http://www.arrt.org/

Real Estate Agents and Brokers

School Subjects: Business, English, Mathematics
Personal Skills: Communication/ideas, Helping/teaching
Work Environment: Primarily indoors, Primarily multiple locations
Salary Range: $20,000 to $31,500 to $100,000
Certification or Licensing: Required
Outlook: Little change or more slowly than the average

The Job

The primary responsibility of *real estate brokers and agents* is to help clients buy, sell, rent, or lease a piece of real estate. A main duty is to actively solicit listings for the agency. Once the listing is obtained, real estate brokers must analyze the property to best present it to prospective buyers. Frequently, the broker counsels the owner about the asking price for the property. When the property is ready to be shown, agents in the office review their files to identify prospective buyers. As potential buyers are contacted, the agent arranges a convenient time for them to see the property. When the buyer finds an affordable and desirable property, the agent must bring the buyer and seller together at terms agreeable to both. Once both parties have signed the contract, the broker or agent must see to it that all special terms of the contract are carried out before the closing date.

Professional and Personal Requirements

Every state and the District of Columbia require that real estate agents and brokers be licensed.

Brokers and agents should possess a pleasant personality and a neat appearance. Agents must work with many different types of people and inspire their trust and confidence. They must be knowledgeable, organized, and detail-oriented, and they should have a good mem-

296

ory for names, faces, and business details, such as taxes, zoning regulations, and local land-use laws.

Starting Out

The typical entry position in this field is as an agent working for a broker with an established office. Another opportunity may be in inside sales with a construction firm that is building a new housing development. Beginners usually apply directly to local real estate firms or may be referred through public and private employment services. Brokers looking to hire agents may run newspaper advertisements. People often contact firms in their own communities, where their knowledge of local neighborhoods is an advantage.

Earnings

Commissions range from 5 to 10 percent of the selling price, averaging about 7 percent. Agents usually split commissions with the brokers who employ them.

Full-time residential real estate agents earn an average of about $31,500 per year in 1996, according to the *Occupational Outlook Handbook*. Commercial agents usually earn $50,000 or more annually. Brokers earn a median gross personal annual income (after expenses) of about $50,000 in residential real estate and about $100,000 in commercial real estate. The most successful people in the field earn much more.

Agents typically are considered independent from the firms they work with, so they often don't receive traditional benefits.

Employment Outlook

The U.S. Department of Labor predicts that employment in this field is expected to grow more slowly than the average through 2006. However, as the average age of real estate agents and brokers is considerably higher than for workers in many other occupations, many opportunities for new agents will be made available because of agents retiring or transferring to other types of work. Because of this high job turnover, tens of thousands of real estate openings are expected yearly. Also, growing affluence and continuing mobility among Americans will result in increasing numbers of property owners.

For More Information

For information on professional designations, real estate courses, and publications, contact:

- **National Association of Realtors**
  430 North Michigan Avenue
  Chicago, IL 60611
  Tel: 312-329-8200
  Web: http://nar.realtor.com

For information on industrial and office real estate, contact:

- **Society of Industrial and Office Realtors**
  700 11th Street, NW, Suite 510
  Washington, DC 20001
  Tel: 202-737-1150
  Web: http://www.sior.com

Recreation Workers

School Subjects: Physical education, Theater/Dance
Personal Skills: Following instructions, Helping/teaching
Work Environment: Indoors and outdoors, Primarily one location
Salary Range: $16,000 to $18,700 to $37,500+
Certification or Licensing: Required by certain states
Outlook: Faster than the average

The Job

Recreation workers help people, as groups and as individuals, enjoy and use their leisure time constructively. They organize and administer physical, social, and cultural programs.

Recreation workers employed by local governments and voluntary agencies include *recreation supervisors* who coordinate recreation center directors, who in turn supervise recreation leaders and aides. With the help of volunteer workers, they plan and carry out programs at community centers, neighborhood playgrounds, recreational and rehabilitation centers, prisons, hospitals, and homes for children and the elderly, often working in cooperation with social workers and sponsors of the various centers. Programs may include arts and crafts, dramatics, music, dancing, swimming, games, camping, nature study, and other pastimes. Special events may include festivals, contests, pet and hobby shows, and various outings. Supervisors have overall responsibility for coordinating the work of the recreation workers who carry out the programs and supervise several recreation centers or an entire region.

Other positions in the field include recreation center directors; recreation leaders; recreation aides; camp counselors; camp directors; and social directors.

Professional and Personal Requirements

Many recreation professionals apply for certification as evidence of their professional competence. The National Recreation and Park Association (NRPA), the American Camping Association, and the National Employee Services and Recreation Association award certificates to individuals who meet their standards. More than 40 states have adopted NRPA standards for park/recreation professionals.

Personal qualifications for recreation work include a desire to work with people, an outgoing personality, an even temperament, and an ability to lead and influence others. Recreation workers should have good health and stamina and should be able to stay calm and think clearly and quickly in emergencies.

Starting Out

College placement offices are useful in helping graduates find employment. Most college graduates begin as either recreation leaders or specialists and, after several years of experience, may become recreation directors. A few enter trainee programs leading directly to recreation administration within a year or so. Those with graduate training may start as recreation directors.

Earnings

Full-time recreation workers earned an average of $18,700 a year in 1996, according to the *Occupational Outlook Handbook*. Some earned up to $37,500 or more, depending on job responsibilities and experience. Some top level managers can make considerably more.

Salaries in industrial recreation are higher. Newly hired recreation workers in industry have starting salaries of about $18,000 to $24,000 a year. Camp directors average about $1,600 per month in municipally operated camps; in private camps, earnings are higher. Camp counselors employed seasonally are paid anywhere from $200 to $800 a month. Recreation workers in the federal government start at about $16,000 a year.

Employment Outlook

The U.S. Department of Labor predicts that employment opportunities for recreation workers will increase faster than the average through the year 2006. The expected expansion in the recreation field will result from increased leisure time and income for the population as a whole combined with a continuing interest in fitness and health and a growing elderly population in nursing homes, senior centers, and retirement communities. There also is a demand for recreation workers to conduct activity programs for special needs groups. Two areas promising the most favorable opportunities for recreation workers are the commercial recreation and social service industries.

For More Information

For information regarding industry trends, education, and scholarships, or for a copy of Leisure Today, *contact:*

■ **American Association for Leisure and Recreation**
1900 Association Drive
Reston, VA 20191
Web: http://www.aahperd.org

For information on the recreation industry, career opportunities, and certification qualifications, contact:

■ **National Recreation and Park Association**
22377 Belmont Ridge Road
Ashburn, VA 20148
Web: http://www.nrpa.org

For information on certification qualifications, contact:

■ **American Camping Association**
5000 State Road, 67 North
Martinsville, IN 46151-7902
Web: http://www.acacamps.org/

For information on certification qualifications, contact:

■ **National Employee Services and Recreation Association**
2211 York Road, Suite 207
Oak Brook, IL 60523-2371
Tel: 630-368-1280
Web: http://www.nesra.org/

Registered Nurses

School Subjects: Biology, Chemistry
Personal Skills: Helping/teaching, Technical/scientific
Work Environment: Primarily indoors, Primarily multiple locations
Salary Range: $28,777 to $36,244 to $54,028+
Certification or Licensing: Required
Outlook: Faster than the average

The Job

Registered nurses (RNs) help individuals, families, and groups to achieve health and prevent disease. They care for the sick and injured in hospitals and other health care facilities, physicians' offices, private homes, public health agencies, schools, camps, and industry. Some registered nurses are employed in private practice.

Registered nurses work under the direct supervision of nursing departments and in collaboration with physicians. Two-thirds of all nurses work in hospitals. There are many different kinds of RNs, such as general duty nurses; surgical nurses; maternity nurses; head nurses and supervisors; nursing service directors; private duty nurses; office nurses; occupational health (or industrial) nurses; school nurses; community health (or public health) nurses; and advanced practice nurses.

Professional and Personal Requirements

All states and the District of Columbia require a license to practice nursing. To obtain a license, graduates of approved nursing schools must pass a national examination. Nurses may be licensed by more than one state. In some states, continuing education is a condition for license renewal. Different titles require different education and training levels.

Stamina, both physical and mental, is a must for this occupation. Nurses spend much of the day on their feet, either walking or standing. Handling patients who are ill or infirm can also be very exhausting. Sick persons are often very demanding, or they may be depressed or irritable. Despite this, the registered nurse must retain her or his composure and should be cheerful to help the patient achieve emotional balance. Registered nurses must also be patient, and have a caring, nurturing attitude. As part of a health care team, they must be able to follow orders and work under close supervision.

Starting Out

The only way to become a registered nurse is through completion of one of the three kinds of educational programs, plus passing the licensing examination. Registered nurses may apply for employment directly to hospitals, nursing homes, companies, and government agencies that hire nurses. Jobs can also be obtained through school placement offices, or by signing up with employment agencies specializing in placement of nursing personnel, or through the state employment office. Other sources of jobs include nurses' associations, professional journals, and newspaper want ads.

Earnings

According to the *Occupation Outlook Handbook,* registered nurses earned an average of $36,244 annually in 1996. Fifty percent earned between $29,692 and $45,136. The top 10 percent made over $54,028 a year.

Salary is determined by several factors: setting, education, and work experience. Most full time nurses are given flexible work schedules, health and life insurance; some are offered education reimbursement and year-end bonuses. A staff nurse's salary is limited only by the amount of work one is willing to take on. Many nurses take advantage of overtime work and shift differentials. About 10 percent of all nurses hold more than one job.

Employment Outlook

In the late 1990s, there were almost two million nurses employed in the United States—making this field the largest of all health care occupations. Employment prospects for nurses look good. The U.S. Department of Labor projects registered nurses to be one of the top 25 occupations with fastest growth, high pay, and low unemployment. In fact, it is predicted that there will be about 425,000 additional jobs available through the year 2006.

Employment in nursing homes is expected to grow faster than jobs in hospitals. Though more people are living well into their 80s and 90s, many need the kind of long term care available at a nursing home.

Nursing specialties will be in great demand. There are in addition many part-time employment possibilities—approximately 30 percent of all nurses work on a part-time basis.

For More Information

For information on careers in nursing, a financial aid fact sheet, and a listing of AACN-member schools, contact:

- **American Association of Colleges of Nursing (AACN)**
  1 Dupont Circle, Suite 530
  Washington, DC 20036
  Tel: 202-463-6930
  Web: http://www.aacn.nche.edu

For information about opportunities as an RN, contact:

- **American Nurses' Association**
  600 Maryland Avenue, SW, Suite 100W
  Washington, DC 20024-2571
  Web: http://www.nursingworld.org

For information about state-approved programs and information on nursing, contact:

- **National Association for Practical Nurse Education and Service, Inc.**
  1400 Spring Street, Suite 310
  Silver Spring, MD 20910
  Tel: 301-588-2491
  Web: http://www.aoa.dhhs.gov/aoa

Respiratory Therapists

School Subjects: Health, Mathematics
Personal Skills: Helping/teaching, Technical/scientific
Work Environment: Primarily indoors, Primarily one location
Salary Range: $19,084 to $33,072 to $50,856
Certification or Licensing: Required by certain states
Outlook: Much faster than the average

The Job

Respiratory therapists evaluate, treat, and care for patients with deficiencies or abnormalities of the cardiopulmonary (heart/lung) system, either providing temporary relief from chronic ailments or administering emergency care where life is threatened.

Working under a physician's direction, these workers set up and operate respirators, mechanical ventilators, and other devices. They monitor the functioning of the equipment and the patients' response to the therapy and maintain the patients' charts. They also assist patients with breathing exercises, and inspect, test, and order repairs for respiratory therapy equipment.

Respiratory therapy workers include therapists, technicians, and assistants. The duties of therapists and technicians are essentially the same, although therapists are expected to have a higher level of expertise, and their responsibilities often include teaching and supervising other workers. Assistants clean, sterilize, store, and generally take care of the equipment but have very little contact with patients.

Professional and Personal Requirements

Thirty-seven states license respiratory care personnel. The National Board for Respiratory Care offers certification at two levels: Certified Respiratory Therapy Technician (CRRT) and Registered Respiratory

Therapist (RRT). The latter designates CRRTs who meet certain education and experience requirements.

Respiratory therapists must enjoy working with people. They need to be sensitive to patients' physical and psychological needs. They must pay strict attention to detail, remain cool in emergencies, and be able to follow instructions and work as part of a team. Mechanical ability and manual dexterity are necessary to operate much of the respiratory equipment.

Starting Out

Graduates of accredited respiratory therapy training programs may have the school's placement service to aid them in finding a job. Otherwise, they may apply directly to the individual local health care facilities.

High school graduates may apply directly to local hospitals for jobs as respiratory therapy assistants. If their goal is to become a therapist or technician, however, they would do better to enroll in a formal respiratory therapy educational program.

Earnings

In 1996, the overall median salary for respiratory therapists was $33,072, according to the U.S. Department of Labor. Therapists fresh out of training programs earned an average of $19,084, while the most experienced therapists earned as much as $50,856. Part-time therapists earned an average of $14.55 per hour.

Hospital workers receive benefits that include health insurance, paid vacations and sick leave, and pension plans. Some institutions provide additional benefits, such as uniforms and parking, and offer free courses or tuition reimbursement for job-related courses.

Employment Outlook

The U.S. Department of Labor predicts that employment growth for respiratory therapists is expected to be much faster than the average for all occupations through the year 2006, despite the fact that efforts to control rising health care costs have reduced the number of job opportunities in hospitals.

The increasing demand for therapists is the result of several factors. The fields of neonatal care and gerontology are growing. Also, there is a greater incidence of cardiopulmonary and AIDS-related diseases, coupled with more advanced methods of diagnosing and treating them. The field of home health care is growing as well, which will provide additional opportunities for therapists. There also should be numerous openings for respiratory therapists in equipment rental companies and in firms that provide respiratory care on a contract basis.

For More Information

For information on scholarships, continuing education, job listings, and other resources, contact:

■ **American Association for Respiratory Care**
11030 Ables Lane
Dallas, TX 75229
Tel: 214-243-2272
Web: http://www.aarc.org

For information on licensing and certification, contact:

■ **National Board for Respiratory Care**
8310 Nieman Road
Lenexa, KS 66214
Tel: 913-599-4200
Web: http://www.nbrc.org

For information on accredited schools, contact:

■ **Commission on Accreditation of Allied Health Education Programs**
American Medical Association
515 North State Street, Suite 7530
Chicago, IL 60610
Tel: 312-464-4625
Web: http://www.caahep.org

Restaurant and Food Service Managers

School Subjects: Business, Health
Personal Skills: Communication/ideas, Leadership/management
Work Environment: Primarily indoors, Primarily one location
Salary Range: $21,000 to $30,000 to $50,000+
Certification or Licensing: None available
Outlook: Faster than the average

The Job

Restaurant and food service managers work in restaurants ranging from fast food restaurants to elegant hotel dining rooms. They also may work in food service facilities ranging from school cafeterias to hospital food services. Whatever the setting, these managers coordinate and direct the work of the employees who prepare and serve food and perform other related functions. Restaurant managers set work schedules for wait staff and host staff. Food service managers are responsible for buying the food and equipment necessary for the operation of the restaurant or facility, and they may help with menu planning. They inspect the premises periodically to ensure compliance with health and sanitation regulations. Restaurant and food service managers perform many clerical and financial duties, such as keeping records, directing payroll operations, handling large sums of money, and taking inventories. Their work usually involves much contact with customers and vendors. Restaurant managers generally supervise any advertising or sales promotions for their operations.

Professional and Personal Requirements

There is no certification or licensing available in this field.

Experience in all areas of restaurant and food service work is an important requirement for successful managers. Business knowledge and technical, industry-related knowledge are also necessary for restaurant managers, as is stamina to endure long, often irregular hours. Desirable personality characteristics include poise, self-confidence, and an ability to get along with people.

Starting Out

Many restaurants and food service facilities provide self-sponsored, on-the-job training for prospective managers. There are still cases in which people work hard and move up the ladder within the organization's workforce, finally arriving at the managerial position. More and more, people with advanced education and specialized training move directly into manager-trainee positions and then on to managerial positions.

Earnings

According to a 1995 salary survey conducted by the National Restaurant Association, manager-trainees earned an average salary of $21,000 a year. Those working in larger restaurants and food service facilities received about $30,000. Experienced managers received an average of approximately $30,000 a year. Those in charge of the largest restaurants and institutional food service facilities often earned over $50,000. Managers of fast-food restaurants averaged about $21,000 per year. In addition to a base salary, most managers receive bonuses based on profits, which can increase their annual salaries by several thousand dollars.

Employment Outlook

The industry is rapidly growing and employs about 493,000 professional managers. According to the U.S. Department of Labor, opportunities for well-qualified restaurant and food service managers appear to be excellent through 2006, especially for those with bachelor's or associate degrees.

Many job openings will arise from the need to replace managers retiring from the workforce. Also, population growth will result in an increased demand for eating establishments and, in turn, a need for managers to oversee them. As the elderly population increases, managers will be needed to staff dining rooms located in hospitals and nursing homes.

Economic downswings have a great effect on eating and drinking establishments. During a recession, people have less money to spend on luxuries such as dining out, thus hurting the restaurant business. However, greater numbers of working parents and their families are finding it convenient to eat out or purchase carryout food from a restaurant.

For More Information

For information on careers and education, contact the following organization:

- **National Restaurant Association Educational Foundation**
  250 South Wacker Drive, Suite 1400
  Chicago, IL 60606-5834
  Tel: 800-765-2122
  Email: info@foodtrain.org
  Web: http://www.edfound.org

For a list of schools offering hotel and restaurant management and food service, contact:

- **Council on Hotel, Restaurant and Institutional Education**
  1200 17th Street, NW
  Washington, DC 20036-3097
  Tel: 202-331-5990
  Web: http://chrie.org/

Retail Managers

School Subjects: Business, Mathematics
Personal Skills: Helping/teaching, Leadership/management
Work Environment: Primarily indoors, Primarily one location
Salary Range: $12,900 to $40,000 to $100,000+
Certification or Licensing: None available
Outlook: Little change or more slowly than the average

The Job

Retail managers are responsible for the profitable operation of retail trade establishments. They oversee the selling of food, clothing, furniture, sporting goods, novelties, and many other items. Their primary duties include hiring, training, and supervising other employees; maintaining the physical facilities; managing inventory; monitoring expenditures and receipts; and maintaining good public relations. Other duties vary according to the type of merchandise sold, size of store, and number of employees. In small, owner-operated stores, managers often are involved in accounting, data processing, marketing, research, sales, and shipping. In large retail corporations, however, managers may be involved in only one or two activities.

Professional and Personal Requirements

There is no certification or licensing available for this field.

A retail manager should have good communication skills and enjoy working with and supervising people. Diplomacy often is necessary when creating schedules for workers and in disciplinary matters. There is a great deal of responsibility in retail management and such positions often are stressful. A calm disposition and ability to handle stress will serve the manager well.

Starting Out

Many new community college graduates are able to find managerial positions through their schools' placement service. Some of the large retail chains engage in campus recruitment.

Not all store managers, however, are college graduates. Many store managers are promoted to their positions from jobs of less responsibility within the organization. Some may be in the retail industry for more than a dozen years before being promoted. Those with more education often receive promotions faster.

Earnings

Salaries depend on the size of the store, the responsibilities of the job, and the number of customers served. Some managers earn as little as $12,900, but median earnings are about $24,400. Experienced managers average about $40,000, and the top 10 percent earn more than $50,400. Salaries in smaller stores are lower. Those who oversee an entire region for a retail chain can earn more than $100,000.

In addition to a salary, some stores offer their managers special bonuses, or commissions, which are typically connected to the store's performance. Many stores also offer employee discounts on store merchandise.

Employment Outlook

Although some retailers have reduced their management staff to cut costs and make operations more efficient, there still are good opportunities in retailing. There is high turnover in this field as experienced managers move into higher positions, transfer to other occupations, or retire. However, competition for jobs probably will continue to increase, and computerized systems for inventory control may reduce the need for some managers. Applicants with the best educational backgrounds and work experience will have the best chances of finding jobs.

For More Information

For materials on educational programs in the retail industry, contact:

- **National Retail Federation**
  325 7th Street, NW, Suite 1000
  Washington, DC 20004
  Tel: 202-783-7971
  Web: http://www.nrf.com

For a copy of How Many People Does It Take to Sell a Lightbulb?, *which describes jobs in retail, contact:*

- **International Mass Retail Association**
  1700 North Moore Street, Suite 2250
  Arlington, VA 22209
  Tel: 703-841-2300
  Web: http://www.impra.org
  or http://www.massretailcareers.com

Robotics Technicians

School Subjects: Computer science, Mathematics
Personal Skills: Mechanical/manipulative, Technical/scientific
Work Environment: Primarily indoors, Primarily one location
Salary Range: $20,000 to $36,000 to $45,000+
Certification or Licensing: None available
Outlook: About as fast as the average

The Job

Robotics technicians assist robotics engineers in a wide variety of tasks relating to the design, development, production, testing, operation, repair, and maintenance of robots and robotic devices. The majority of robotics technicians work within the field of computer-integrated manufacturing or programmable automation.

Robotics technicians who install, repair, and maintain robots and robotic equipment need knowledge of electronics, electrical circuitry, mechanics, pneumatics, hydraulics, and computer programming. They use hand and power tools, testing instruments, manuals, schematic diagrams, and blueprints.

Robotics technicians may also be referred to as electromechanical technicians; manufacturing technicians; robot mechanics; robotics repairmen; robot service technicians; and installation robotics technicians. Specific jobs within this field include robot field technicians; robotics design technicians; robot assemblers; materials handling technicians; mechanical assembly technicians; electrical assembly technicians; robot operators; and robotics trainers.

Professional and Personal Requirements

There is no certification or licensing available in this field.

People interested in becoming robotics technicians need manual dexterity, good hand-eye coordination, and mechanical and electrical aptitudes. They should also be willing to continue their education and training to remain competitive in this constantly changing field.

Starting Out

Many people entered robotics technician positions in the 1980s and early 1990s who were formerly employed as automotive workers, machinists, millwrights, computer repair technicians, and computer operators. Because of the trend to retrain employees rather than hire new workers, entry-level applicants without any work experience may have difficulty finding their first jobs. Students who have participated in a cooperative work program or internship have the advantage of some work experience.

Graduates of two- and four-year programs may learn about available openings through their schools' job placement services.

Earnings

Robotics technicians who are graduates of a two-year technical program earn between $22,000 and $26,000 a year. With increased training and experience, technicians can earn much more. Technicians with special skills, extensive experience, or added responsibilities can earn $36,000 or more. Technicians involved in design and training generally earn the highest salaries, with experienced workers earning $45,000 or more a year; those involved with maintenance and repair earn relatively less, with some beginning at salaries around $20,000 a year.

Employers offer a variety of benefits that can include the following: paid holidays, vacations, personal days, and sick leave; medical, dental, disability, and life insurance; 401(k) plans, pension and retirement plans; profit sharing; and educational assistance programs.

Employment Outlook

During the late 1980s and early 1990s, the robotics market suffered because of a lack of orders for robots and robotic equipment and intense foreign competition, especially from Japanese manufacturers. However, in the mid 1990s, U.S. robot manufacturers shipped record numbers of robots and robotic equipment. In addition, some Japanese robot builders shifted production to U.S. facilities. After a slump of several years, it is expected that the robotics industry will once again pick up. Some robotics industry experts are predicting that during the next decade there will be a robotics boom and robotics sales will double.

For More Information

To purchase a copy of Robotics and Vision Supplier Directory *and for information on educational programs and student membership in the International Service Robot Association and Global Automation Information Network, contact:*

■ **Robotic Industries Association**
  PO Box 3724
  Ann Arbor, MI 48106
  Tel: 313-994-6088
  Web: http://www.robotics.org

For information on educational programs, competitions, and student membership in SME, Robotics International, or Machine Vision Association, contact:

■ **Society of Manufacturing Engineers (SME)**
  Education Department
  PO Box 930
  Dearborn, MI 48121-0930
  Tel: 313-271-1500
  Web: http://www.sme.org

Security Technicians

School Subjects: Business, Psychology
Personal Skills: Communication/ideas, Following instructions
Work Environment: Indoors and outdoors, One location with some travel
Salary Range: $11,440 to $22,900 to $35,600
Certification or Licensing: Recommended
Outlook: Faster than the average

The Job

Security technicians are responsible for protecting public and private property against theft, fire, vandalism, illegal entry, and acts of violence. They may work for a variety of clients, including large stores, art museums, factories, laboratories, data processing centers, and political candidates.

Some security technicians work for government agencies or for private companies hired by government agencies. Their task is usually to guard secret or restricted installations domestically or in foreign countries. They spend much of their time patrolling areas, which they may do on foot, on horseback, or in automobiles or aircraft. They may monitor activities in an area through the use of surveillance cameras and video screens. Their assignments usually include detecting and preventing unauthorized activities, searching for explosive devices, standing watch during secret and hazardous experiments, and performing other routine police duties within government installations.

Security technicians are usually armed and may be required to use their weapons or other kinds of physical force to prevent certain kinds of activities.

Specific jobs within this field include security officers; security guards; bouncers; golf-course rangers; gate tenders; and bank guards.

Professional and Personal Requirements

Certification, which is recommended though not required, is offered by the American Society for Industrial Security. Virtually every state has licensing or registration requirements for security guards who work for contract security agencies.

Good general health (especially vision and hearing), alertness, emotional stability, and the ability to follow directions are important characteristics in security technicians. Many jobs stipulate that technicians meet certain criteria related to height, weight, and physical fitness. Military service and experience in local or state police departments are assets. Prospective guards should have clean police records.

Starting Out

People interested in careers in security services generally apply directly to security companies. Some jobs may be available through state or private employment services. People interested in security technician positions should apply directly to government agencies.

Earnings

Starting salaries for security guards and technicians generally ranged between $5.50 and $11.73 per hour in 1996, according to the U.S. Department of Labor. Experienced security guards average as high as $35,600 per year, with those employed in manufacturing facilities receiving the highest wages.

Security guards and technicians employed by federal government agencies earn starting salaries of $15,500 or $17,500 per year, and they average $22,900 per year with experience. Government employees typically enjoy good job security and generous benefits. Benefits for positions with private companies vary significantly.

Employment Outlook

The U.S. Department of Labor predicts that employment for guards and other security personnel is expected to increase faster than the average through the year 2006, as crime rates rise with the overall population growth. Many job openings will be created as a result of the high turnover of workers in this field.

A factor adding to this demand is the trend for private security firms to perform duties previously handled by police officers, such as courtroom security and crowd control in airports. Private security companies employ security technicians to guard many government sites, such as nuclear testing facilities. Private companies also operate many training facilities for government security technicians and guards, in addition to providing police services for some communities.

For More Information

For information on union membership, contact the following:

- **International Security Officers' Police and Guard Union**
  321 86th Street
  Brooklyn, NY 11209
  Tel: 718-836-3508

- **International Union of Security Officers**
  2404 Merced Street
  San Leandro, CA 94577
  Tel: 510-895-9905

For information on professional development and certification, contact:

- **American Society for Industrial Security**
  1625 Prince Street
  Alexandria, VA 22314-2818
  Tel: 703-519-6200
  Web: http://www.asisonline.org

Semiconductor Technicians

School Subjects: Chemistry, Mathematics, Physics
Personal Skills: Communication/ideas, Technical/scientific
Work Environment: Primarily indoors, Primarily one location
Salary Range: $25,000 to $43,750 to $62,000
Certification or Licensing: Voluntary
Outlook: About as fast as the average

The Job

Semiconductor technicians are highly skilled workers who test new kinds of semiconductor devices being designed for use in modern electronic equipment. They may also test samples of devices already in production to assess production techniques. Moreover, they help develop and evaluate the test equipment used to gather information about the semiconductor devices. Working under the direction provided by engineers in research laboratory settings, they assist in the design and planning for later production or help to improve production yields. They are responsible for ensuring that each step of the process precisely meets test specifications and for identifying flaws and problems in the material and design. Technicians may also assist in designing and building new test equipment, and in communicating test data and production instructions for large-scale manufacture. Some technicians may be responsible for maintaining the equipment and for training operators on their use.

Professional and Personal Requirements

The International Society of Certified Electronics Technicians offers certification, which is voluntary, at various levels and fields of electronics.

A thorough understanding of semiconductors, electronics, and the production process is necessary for semiconductor technicians, as are investigative and research skills and a basic knowledge of computers and computer programs. Other important qualities include patience, perseverance, and attention to detail.

Starting Out

Semiconductor technician positions can be located through the job placement office of a community college or vocational training school. Many of these degree programs provide students with job interviews and introductions to companies in the community who are looking for qualified workers. Job listings in the newspaper or at local employment agencies are also good places for locating opportunities.

Earnings

Because of the stringent requirements, qualified semiconductor technicians command salaries which tend to be higher than many other professions. According to a 1998 salary survey by *Circuits Magazine*, the average technician with a two-year degree earned $43,750, with starting salaries at about $25,000 and upper salaries of $62,000. The highest salaries go to technicians with a great deal of education and experience.

Employment Outlook

The semiconductor industry is expected to remain a strong source of employment into the next century, but dramatic increases in technical positions are not expected. A variety of factors will affect employment levels. The increasing demand for semiconductors and related devices in most areas of industry, manufacturing, and consumer services will mean the steady need for personnel trained in their development and processing. New applications for semiconductor technology are continually being created, and these too will spur the demand for trained technical staff. Advancements in technology will require increased and continuing educational requirements for persons seeking and holding positions in this industry.

For More Information

For certification information, contact:

- **International Society of Certified Electronics Technicians**
  2708 West Berry Street
  Fort Worth, TX 76109-2356
  Tel: 817-921-9101
  Email: iscetFW@aol.com
  Web: http://www.iscet.org/

For industry information and educational programs, contact:

- **Semiconductor Equipment and Materials International**
  805 East Middlefield Road
  Mountain View, CA 94043-4080
  Tel: 605-964-5111
  Email: semihq@semi.org
  Web: http://www.semi.org/

For industry information, contact:

- **Semiconductor Industry Association**
  181 Metro Drive, Suite 450
  San Jose, CA 95110
  Tel: 408-436-6600
  Web: http://www.semichips.org/

SEMATECH, a non-profit research and development consortium of U.S. semiconductor manufacturers, sponsors the Discover a New World of Opportunity Web site. Visit the site to get information on careers, associate degrees and certification programs, and profiles of workers in the field. Additionally, the site has a FAQ section and a Glossary of semiconductor industry terms:

- **Discover a New World of Opportunity**
  Web: http://www.4chipjobs.com/index.html

Surgical Technologists

School Subjects: Biology, Health
Personal Skills: Helping/teaching, Technical/scientific
Work Environment: Primarily indoors, Primarily one location
Salary Range: $20,900 to $25,000 to $28,000+
Certification or Licensing: Recommended
Outlook: Faster than the average

The Job

Surgical technologists, also called *surgical technicians* or *operating room technicians,* are members of the surgical team who work in the operating room with surgeons, nurses, anesthesiologists, and other personnel before, during, and after surgery. They perform functions that ensure a safe and sterile environment. To prepare a patient for surgery, they may wash, shave, and disinfect the area where the incision will be made. They arrange the equipment, instruments, and supplies in the operating room according to the preference of the surgeons and nurses. During the operation, they adjust lights and other equipment as needed. They count sponges, needles, and instruments used during the operation, hand instruments and supplies to the surgeon, and hold retractors and cut sutures as directed. They maintain specified supplies of fluids such as saline, plasma, blood, and glucose and may assist in administering these fluids. Following the operation, they may clean and restock the operating room and wash and sterilize the used equipment using germicides, autoclaves, and sterilizers, although in most larger hospitals these tasks are done by other central service personnel.

Professional and Personal Requirements

Voluntary professional certification is available from the Liaison Council on Certification for the Surgical Technologist. Technologists can earn the Certified Surgical Technologist (CST) designation by grad-uating from a formal educational program (accredited by the Commission on Accreditation of Allied Health Education Programs) and passing a nationally administered certifying examination. Increasing numbers of hospitals are requiring certification as a con-dition of employment.

Surgical technologists must possess an educational background in the medical sciences, a strong sense of responsibility, a concern for order, and an ability to integrate a number of tasks at the same time. They need good manual dexterity to handle awkward surgical instruments with speed and agility. In addition, they need physical stamina to stand through long surgical procedures.

Starting Out

Graduates of programs are often offered jobs in the same hospital in which they received their clinical training. Programs usually coop-erate closely with hospitals in the area, which are usually eager to employ technologists educated in local programs. Available positions are also advertised in newspaper want ads.

Earnings

According to the Association of Surgical Technologists, the average salary for surgical technologists was about $25,000 in 1996. New tech-nologists earned $20,900 annually, while the most experienced technologists earned about $28,000 a year. Some technologists with experience earn much more. Most surgical technologists are required to be periodically on call and can earn overtime from such work. Graduates of educational programs usually receive salaries higher than technologists without formal education.

Employment Outlook

Job opportunities for competent surgical technologists far exceed the supply. According to the *Occupational Outlook Handbook,* the field of surgical technology is projected to experience rapid job growth through the year 2006. Population growth, longevity, and improvement in medical and surgical procedures have all contributed to a growing demand for surgical services and hence for surgical technologists.

Staffing patterns are also changing in response to the need to control costs. Hospitals are employing more allied health professionals, such as surgical technologists, who can provide cost-effective care. Hospitals are also increasing their use of multiskilled workers who can handle a wide variety of tasks in different areas of the hospital. A number of health care workers, including surgical technologists, are being asked by their employers to participate in training programs to become multiskilled.

For More Information

For information on education programs and certification, contact:

- **Association of Surgical Technologists**
  7108-C South Alton Way, Suite 100
  Englewood, CO 80112-2106
  Tel: 303-694-9130
  Web: http://www.ast.org

For information on certification, contact:

- **Liaison Council on Certification for the Surgical Technologist**
  7790 East Arapahoe Road, Suite 240
  Englewood, CO 80112-1274
  Tel: 800-707-0057
  Web: http://www.lcc-st.org/

Systems Set Up Specialists

School Subjects: Business, Computer science
Personal Skills: Mechanical/manipulative, Technical/scientific
Work Environment: Primarily indoors, Primarily one location
Salary Range: $26,130 to $32,300 to $40,000
Certification or Licensing: None available
Outlook: Faster than the average

The Job

Systems set up specialists are responsible for installing new computer systems and upgrading existing ones to meet the specifications of the client. They install hardware, such as memory, sound cards, fax/modems, fans, microprocessors, and systems boards. They also load software and configure the hard drive appropriately. Some systems set up specialists install computer systems at the client's location. Installation might include normal hard drive or network server configurations as well as connecting peripherals like printers, phones, fax machines, modems, and numerous terminals. They might also be involved with technical support in providing initial training to users. Systems set up specialists are employed by computer manufacturing companies or computer service companies nationwide, or may be employed as part of the technical support department of many businesses. Systems set up specialists are sometimes called *technical support technicians, desk top analyst/specialists,* and *PC set up specialists.*

Professional and Personal Requirements

There is no certification or licensing available in this field.

Systems set up specialists need good manual dexterity and a curiosity about how things work. Patience and problem-solving skills are important attributes.

Starting Out

Most positions in systems set up are considered entry level. Workers who plan to enter this field without a postsecondary education but with computer skills and experience will need to network with working computer professionals for potential employment opportunities. Jobs are advertised in the newspaper every week; in fact, many papers devote entire sections to computer-related positions.

Graduates of two-year educational programs should work closely with their school's placement office. Many firms looking for computer professionals inform schools first, since they are assured of meeting candidates with a certain level of proficiency in the field.

Earnings

According to a 1997 Technical Support Salary Survey, systems set up specialists with entry-level customer service responsibilities earned an annual average of $26,130; those with experience earned an averaged annual salary of about $32,300. Senior level set up specialists with superior technical skills and work experience earned an average salary of about $40,000.

Most full-time set up specialists work for companies that provide a full range of benefits, including health insurance, sick leave, and paid vacation.

Employment Outlook

The demand for systems set up specialists is expected to grow faster than the average through 2006, according to the *Occupational Outlook Handbook*. Most jobs in the computer industry, especially those that provide a special or unique service to computer customers, will enjoy increased demand.

The ability to network and share information within the company allows businesses to be productive and work more efficiently. As new technology is developed, companies may upgrade, or replace their systems altogether. Skilled workers will be in demand by companies to staff their technical support departments and provide services ranging from set up and installation to diagnostics.

For More Information

For information regarding industry salary expectations or employment opportunities nationwide, contact:

■ **Association of Support Professionals**
17 Main Street
Watertown, MA 02172-4491
Tel: 617-924-3944, ext. 14
Web: http://www.asponline.com/

For information regarding the industry, career opportunities, or membership requirements, contact:

■ **Association of Computing Machinery**
1515 Broadway, 17th Floor
New York, NY 10036-5701
Tel: 212-869-7440
Email: SIGS@acm.org
Web: http://www.acm.org

For information on technical careers, scholarships, or a copy of Computer Magazine, contact:

■ **The Computer Society**
1730 Massachusetts Avenue, NW
Washington, DC 20036-1992
Tel: 202-371-0101
Web: http://www.computer.org

For employment information and online career sites for computer professionals, contact:

■ **Institute of Electronic and Electrical Engineers**
3 Park Avenue, 17th Floor
New York, NY 10016-5997
Tel: 212-419-7900
Web: http://www.ieee.org

Teacher Aides

School Subjects: Art, English
Personal Skills: Helping/teaching, Leadership/management
Work Environment: Primarily indoors, Primarily one location
Salary Range: $12,710 to $13,000 to $16,000
Certification or Licensing: None available
Outlook: Much faster than the average

The Job

Teacher aides perform a wide variety of duties to help teachers run a classroom. Teacher aides prepare instructional materials, help students with classroom work, and supervise students in the library, on the playground, and at lunch. They perform administrative duties such as photocopying, keeping attendance records, and grading papers.

Teacher aides work in public, private, and parochial preschools and elementary and secondary schools. Duties vary depending on the classroom teacher, school, and school district. Some teacher aides specialize in one subject and some work in a specific type of school setting. These settings include bilingual classrooms, gifted and talented programs, classes for learning disabled students and those with unique physical needs, and multi-age classrooms. They conduct the same type of classroom work as other teacher aides, but may provide more individual assistance to students.

Professional and Personal Requirements

There is no certification or licensing available in this field.

Teacher aides must enjoy working with children and be able to handle their demands, problems, and questions with patience and fairness. They must be willing and able to follow instructions, but should also be able to take the initiative in projects. Flexibility, cre-activity, and a cheerful outlook are definite assets for anyone working with children.

Starting Out

New graduates should apply directly to schools and school districts for teacher aide positions. Many school districts and state departments of education maintain job listings, bulletin boards, and hot lines that list available job openings. Teacher aide jobs are often advertised in the classified section of the newspaper.

Earnings

Teacher aides are usually paid on an hourly basis and usually only during the nine or 10 months of the school calendar. Some teacher aides may earn as little as minimum wage while others earn up to $15.00 an hour. A study by the Educational Research Service found that the average wage of an aide with teaching responsibilities was $9.04 an hour in 1996; those without teaching responsibilities earned $8.52 an hour.

Benefits such as health insurance and vacation or sick leave may also depend upon the school or district as well as the number of hours a teacher aide works. Many schools employ teacher aides only part time and do not offer such benefits. Other teacher aides may receive the same health and pension benefits as the teachers in their school and be covered under collective bargaining agreements.

Employment Outlook

Growth in this field is expected to be much faster than the average into the next century because of an expected increase in the number of school-age children. As the number of students in schools increases, new schools and classrooms will be added and more teachers and teacher aides will be hired. A shortage of teachers will find administrators hiring more aides to help with larger classrooms. Also, the specific areas of day care and special education are expected to grow particularly rapidly, providing many employment opportunities.

For More Information

To learn about current issues effecting paraprofessionals in education, visit the AFT Web site or contact:

- **American Federation of Teachers, Paraprofessionals, and School-Related Personnel**
  555 New Jersey Avenue, NW
  Washington, DC 20001
  Tel: 202-879-4400
  Web: http://www.aft.org

To order publications and to read current research and other information, visit the ACEI Web site, or contact:

- **Association for Childhood Education International (ACEI)**
  17904 Georgia Avenue, Suite 215
  Olney, MD 20832
  Tel: 301-570-2111
  Web: http://www.udel/bateman/acei

For information about training programs and other resources, contact:

- **National Resource Center for Paraprofessionals in Education and Related Services**
  CASE-SUNY
  25 West 43rd Street, Room 620
  New York, NY 10036
  Tel: 212-642-2948

Technical Support Specialists

School Subjects: Computer science, English, Mathematics
Personal Skills: Helping/teaching, Technical/scientific
Work Environment: Primarily indoors, Primarily one location
Salary Range: $20,000 to $30,750 to $50,000+
Certification or Licensing: Voluntary
Outlook: Much faster than the average

The Job

Technical support specialists investigate and resolve problems in computer functioning. They listen to customer complaints, walk customers through possible solutions, and write technical reports based on these events. Technical support specialists have different duties depending on whom they assist and what they fix. Regardless of specialty, all technical support specialists must be very knowledgeable about the products with which they work and be able to communicate effectively with users from different technical backgrounds. They must be patient with frustrated users and be able to perform well under stress. Technical support is basically like solving mysteries, so support specialists should enjoy the challenge of problem solving and have strong analytical thinking skills.

Professional and Personal Requirements

Computer associations, such as the Institute for Certification of Computing Professionals, offer many different kinds of voluntary certifications to people working in computer technical support.

Technical support specialists should be patient, enjoy challenges of problem solving, and think logically. They should work well under stress and demonstrate effective communication skills. They should be naturally curious and enthusiastic about learning new technologies as they are developed.

Starting Out

Most technical support positions are considered entry-level. They are found mainly in computer companies and large corporations. Individuals interested in obtaining a job in this field should scan the classified ads for openings in local businesses and may want to work with an employment agency for help finding out about opportunities. Since many job openings are publicized by word of mouth, it is also very important to speak with as many working computer professionals as possible. They tend to be aware of job openings before anyone else and may be able to offer a recommendation to the hiring committee.

If students of computer technology are seeking a position in technical support, they should work closely with their school's placement office. Many employers inform placement offices at nearby schools of openings before ads are run in the newspaper. In addition, placement office staffs are generally very helpful with resume and interviewing techniques.

Earnings

Technical support specialist jobs are plentiful in areas where clusters of computer companies are located, such as northern California and Seattle, Washington. According to Robert Half International, Inc., the average technical support specialist earns between $25,000 to $36,500 a year. Those with more education, responsibility, and expertise have the potential to earn much more. Most technical support specialists work for companies that offer a full range of benefits, including health insurance, paid vacation, and sick leave.

Employment Outlook

The U.S. Department of Labor predicts that technical support specialists will be one of the fastest growing of all occupations through the year 2006. The U.S. Department of Labor forecasts huge growth— about 115 percent—of additional support jobs through the year 2006. Every time a new computer product is released on the market or another system is installed, there is a need for technical support specialists. Since technology changes so rapidly, it is very important for these professionals to keep up-to-date on advances.

For More Information

For information on student membership and Crossroads, *the ACM student magazine, contact:*

- **The Association for Computing Machinery**
  One Astor Plaza
  1515 Broadway
  New York, NY 10036
  Tel: 212-869-7440
  Email: ACMHELP@acm.org
  Web: http://www.acm.org

For information on colleges and computer careers, student membership, or to obtain the student newsletter, looking.forward, *contact:*

- **IEEE Computer Society**
  1730 Massachusetts Avenue, NW
  Washington, DC 20036-1992
  Tel: 202-371-0101
  Web: http://computer.org

For certification information, contact:

- **Institute for Certification of Computing Professionals**
  2200 East Devon Avenue, Suite 247
  Des Plaines, IL 60018-4503
  Tel: 847-299-4227
  Web: http://www.iccp.org

Veterinary Technicians

School Subjects: Biology, Chemistry
Personal Skills: Following instructions, Technical/scientific
Work Environment: Primarily indoors, Primarily one location
Salary Range: $15,000 to $25,000 to $40,000
Certification or Licensing: Required by certain states
Outlook: Faster than the average

The Job

A *veterinary technician* is the person who performs much of the laboratory testing procedures commonly associated with veterinary care. In fact, approximately 50 percent of a veterinary technician's duties involves laboratory testing. A veterinary technician may also assist the veterinarian with necropsies in an effort to determine the cause of an animal's death.

In a clinic or private practice, a veterinary technician assists the veterinarian with surgical procedures. This generally entails preparing the animal for surgery, administering and monitoring anesthesia, tracking surgical instruments, and monitoring vital signs. If an animal is very ill and has no chance for survival or an overcrowded animal shelter is unable to find a home for a donated or stray animal, the veterinary technician may be required to assist in euthanizing it.

During routine examinations and check ups, veterinary technicians help restrain the animals. They may perform ear cleaning and nail clipping procedures as part of regular animal care. Outside the examination and surgery rooms, veterinary technicians may record, replenish, and maintain pharmaceutical equipment and other supplies.

Professional and Personal Requirements

Although the American Veterinary Medical Association (AVMA) determines the majority of the national codes for veterinary technicians, state codes and laws vary. Most states offer registration or certification, and graduation from an AVMA-accredited program is usually a prerequisite.

A veterinary technician must be an effective communicator and proficient in basic computer applications. In clinical or private practice, it is usually the veterinary technician who conveys and explains treatment and subsequent animal care to the animal's owner. In most practical veterinary settings, the veterinary technician must record various information on a computer.

Starting Out

Veterinary technicians who complete an accredited program and become certified or registered by the state in which they plan to practice are often able to receive assistance in finding a job through their college placement offices. Students who have completed internships may receive job offers from the place where they interned.

Veterinary technician graduates may also learn of clinic openings through classified ads in newspapers, and industry periodicals such as *Veterinary Technician Magazine* and *AZVT News,* a newsletter published by the Association of Zoo Veterinary Technicians.

Earnings

Earnings are generally low for veterinary technicians in private practices and clinics, but pay scales are steadily climbing due to the increasing demand. About 70 percent of veterinary technicians are employed in private or clinical practice and research, and salaries range from $15,000 for recent graduates to $40,000 for experienced graduates working in supervisory positions. Earnings for zoo veterinary technicians range from $17,000 to $35,000. Benefits vary and depend on each employer's policies.

Employment Outlook

The employment outlook for veterinary technicians is very good through the year 2006, according to the U.S. Department of Labor. Veterinary technicians are constantly in demand. Veterinary medicine is a field that is not adversely affected by the economy, so it does offer stability.

In 1996, there were 27,000 veterinary technicians employed in the United States. Currently, there is a shortage of veterinary technicians. The public's love for pets coupled with higher disposable incomes will raise the demand for this occupation.

For More Information

For more information on careers, schools, and resources, write to the American Veterinary Medical Association. In addition, check out the AVMA's Web page for career and education information, especially the "NetVet" link that provides access to information on specialties, organizations, publications, and fun sites.

- **American Veterinary Medical Association (AVMA)**
  Education and Research Division
  1931 North Meacham Road, Suite 100
  Schaumburg, IL 60173-4360
  Tel: 800-248-2862 or 847-925-8070
  Web: http://www.avma.org

For general information on the career of veterinary technician, contact:

- **North American Veterinary Technician Association**
  PO Box 224
  Battle Ground, IN 47920
  Web: http://www.avma.org/navta/default.htm

For more information on zoo veterinary technology and positions, contact:

- **Association of Zoo Veterinary Technicians**
  c/o Louisville Zoo
  PO Box 37250
  Louisville, KY 40233
  Web: http://www.worldzoo.org/azvt/

Wastewater Treatment Plant Technicians

School Subjects: Chemistry, Mathematics
Personal Skills: Mechanical/manipulative, Technical/scientific
Work Environment: Indoors and outdoors, Primarily one location
Salary Range: $17,420 to $34,736 to $53,678+
Certification or Licensing: Required by certain states
Outlook: Faster than the average

The Job

Wastewater treatment plant technicians work under the supervision of wastewater treatment plant operators. Technicians take samples and monitor treatment to ensure treated water is safe for its intended use. Depending on the level of treatment, water is used for human consumption or for nonconsumptive purposes, such as field irrigation or discharge into natural water sources.

Wastewater treatment plant technicians' duties may include regulating flow of wastewater by adjusting pumps, valves, and other equipment; monitoring purification processes; collecting water samples and conducting laboratory tests; logging data to be supervised and monitored by plant operators; performing maintenance and minor repairs to equipment such as valves and pumps; surveying streams and studying basin areas; preparing graphs, tables, and diagrams to illustrate survey data answering public inquiries; and training new personnel.

Professional and Personal Requirements

In most states, workers who control operations at wastewater treatment plants must be certified by the state. Many states issue several classes of certification, depending on the size of the plant the worker is qualified to control.

Technicians must be familiar with the provisions of the Federal Clean Water Act and various state and local regulations that apply to their work. In larger cities and towns especially, job applicants may have to take a civil service exam or other tests that assess their aptitudes and abilities.

Starting Out

Graduates of most postsecondary technical programs and some high schools can get help in locating job openings from the placement office of the school they attended. Another source of information is the local office of the state employment service. Job seekers may also directly contact state and local water pollution control agencies and the personnel offices of wastewater treatment facilities in desired locations.

Earnings

According to the *Occupational Outlook Handbook,* entry-level plant technicians and operators can expect to make at least $17,420 per year. Average earnings in the profession are $34,736 per year. Experienced certified workers can make over $53,768 depending on the size of the plant and staff they supervise. In addition to their pay, most operators and technicians receive benefits such as life and health insurance, a pension plan, and reimbursement for education and training related to their job.

Employment Outlook

Over the next 10 to 15 years employment in this field is expected to grow at a faster rate than average for all occupations. The growth in demand for wastewater treatment will be related to the overall growth of the nation's population and economy. New treatment plants will probably be built, and existing ones will be upgraded, requiring additional trained personnel to manage their operations. Other openings will arise when experienced workers retire or transfer to new occupations. Technicians with formal training will have the best chances for new positions and promotions.

Workers in wastewater treatment plants are rarely laid off, even during a recession, because wastewater treatment is essential to public health and welfare.

For More Information

For current information on the field of wastewater management, contact:

- **American Water Works Association**
  6666 West Quincy Avenue
  Denver, CO 80235
  Tel: 303-794-7711
  Web: http://www.awwa.org

For information on education and training, contact:

- **Coalition of Environmental Training Centers**
  c/o National Environmental Training Association
  2930 East Camelback Road, Suite 185
  Phoenix, AZ 85016
  Tel: 602-956-6099

For information on environment-related careers, contact:

- **Environmental Careers Organization**
  179 South Street
  Boston, MA 02111
  Tel: 617-426-4375
  Web: http://www.eco.org

The following is a professional organization monitoring developments in the field of wastewater management:

- **Water Environment Federation**
  601 Wythe Street
  Alexandria, VA 22314-1994
  Tel: 703-684-2452
  Web: http://www.wef.org

Webmasters

School Subjects: Computer science, Mathematics
Personal Skills: Communication/ideas, Technical/scientific
Work Environment: Primarily indoors, Primarily one location
Salary Range: $25,000 to $35,000 to $100,000
Certification or Licensing: Voluntary
Outlook: Faster than the average

The Job

Webmasters design, implement, and maintain World Wide Web sites for corporations, educational institutions, not-for-profit organizations, government agencies, or other institutions. Webmasters should have working knowledge of network configurations, interface, graphic design, software development, business, writing, marketing, and project management. Because the function of a webmaster encompasses so many different responsibilities, in a large organization, the position is often held by a team of individuals, rather than a single person. Duties may include securing space on the Web for new sites by contracting with an Internet service provider; developing the actual Web site; coding text in HyperText Markup Language (HTML); designing the graphic elements to the site; maintaining and updating pages and hyperlinks; and monitoring and reporting on Web site "hits."

Professional and Personal Requirements

Certification is voluntary and is available at many colleges, universities, and technical schools throughout the United States, as well as through the International Webmasters Association.

Webmasters should be creative. Good writing skills and an aptitude for marketing are also excellent qualities for anyone considering a career in Web site design. Of course, a strong knowledge of computer technology is necessary, and employers usually require at least two years of experience with World Wide Web technologies.

Starting Out

Most people become webmasters by moving into the position from another computer-related position within the same company. Another way that individuals find jobs in this field is through on-line postings of job openings. Many companies post webmaster position openings on-line because the candidates they hope to attract are very likely to use the Internet for a job search. Therefore, the prospective webmaster should use the World Wide Web to check job-related newsgroups.

Earnings

According to *U.S. News & World Report,* salaries for the position of webmaster range from $50,000 to $100,000 per year. Most webmasters, however, have merely moved into the position from another position within their company or have taken on the task in addition to other duties. According to the 1998 Webmaster Survey, the majority of webmasters earn under $50,000. Nineteen percent of all webmasters earned from $25,000 to $40,999 annually; 17 percent earned less than $25,000.

A typical benefits package includes paid vacations and holidays, medical insurance, and perhaps a pension plan.

Employment Outlook

There can be no doubt that computer—and specifically on-line—technology will continue its rapid growth for the next several years. The World Organization of Webmasters projects an explosion of jobs available through the year 2006—well over 8 million. Growth will be largest for Internet content developers—webmasters responsible for the information displayed on a Web site.

One thing to keep in mind, however, is that when technology advances extremely rapidly, it tends to make old methods of doing things obsolete. It is possible that in the next few years, changes in technology will make the Web sites we are now familiar with a thing of the past. Another possibility is that user-friendly software programs will make Web site design so easy and efficient that it no longer requires an "expert" to do it well. These factors may influence the outlook for webmasters.

For More Information

The Association of Internet Professionals represents the worldwide community of people employed in Internet-related fields.

- **Association of Internet Professionals**
  9200 Sunset Boulevard, Suite 710
  Los Angeles, CA 90069
  Tel: 800-JOIN-AIP
  Email: info@association.org
  Web: http://www.association.org/index.html

For information on its newsletter, Webreference Update, *and information regarding its voluntary certification program, contact:*

- **International Webmasters Association**
  119 East Union Street, Suite #E
  Pasadena, California 91103
  Tel: 626-449-3709
  Web: http://www.iwanet.org

For information on education and certification, contact:

- **World Organization of Webmasters**
  9580 Oak Avenue Parkway, Suite 7-177
  Folsom, CA 95630
  Tel: 916-929-6557
  Email: info@world-webmasters.org
  Web: http://www.world-webmasters.org/

Wireless Service Technicians

School Subjects: Computer science, Physics
Personal Skills: Mechanical/manipulative, Technical/scientific
Work Environment: Primarily indoors, Primarily multiple locations
Salary Range: $35,000 to $45,000 to $53,000
Certification or Licensing: None available
Outlook: Much faster than the average

The Job

Wireless service technicians are responsible for maintaining a specified group of cell sites, including the radio towers, cell site equipment, and often the building and grounds for the sites. Technicians routinely visit and monitor the functioning of the on-site equipment, performing preventive testing and maintenance. They are also responsible for troubleshooting and remedying problems that might arise with any of their sites. Most wireless service technicians spend their work time at various locations, visiting each of their cell sites as necessary.

In addition to routine maintenance and troubleshooting responsibilities, wireless service technicians may have a range of other duties. They may test the wireless system by driving around the coverage area while using a mobile phone. They also may work with technicians in the switching center to incorporate new cell sites into the network and make sure that the wireless calls are smoothly transmitted from one cell to another.

Professional and Personal Requirements

There is no certification or licensing available in this field.

The ability to work independently is one of the most important characteristics of a good wireless service technician. Most technicians work on their own, traveling from site to site and performing their duties with little or no supervision, so they must have a high degree of self-discipline and responsibility. Also necessary are a valid driver's license and good driving record.

Starting Out

One of the best ways to start looking for a job as a wireless service technician is to visit the Web sites of several wireless providers. Many wireless companies maintain job sections on their sites, which list available positions. Industry magazines also often contain jobs postings. Another way to find a job is to look for and attend technical job fairs, expos, or exchanges. Finally, college placement offices are an excellent source of job leads. Many wireless companies visit schools that offer the appropriate degree programs to recruit qualified students for employees.

Earnings

According to *U.S. News and World Report*'s 1998 Career Guide, the entry-level technician might average around $35,000 annually. With a bit more experience and a proven record of success, he or she could expect to earn $45,000. At the high end of the salary scale, wireless service technicians can make as much as $53,000.

Benefit packages often include health insurance, paid vacation, holiday, and sick days, and a pension or 401(k) plan. Other perks may include the use of company vehicles, cellular phones, and laptop computers.

Employment Outlook

Job opportunities for wireless service technicians are expected to grow much faster than the average for all other occupations through the year 2006. The main reason for this increase is the growth of the number of cellular service users. Other factors contributing to the growth of this industry include the steady decrease in prices for cellular service, expanding coverage areas, the continuous improvement in cellular phones and services due to technological advances, and the growing number of wireless companies. This competition has created a large number of technicians' jobs, and is expected to continue to do so.

For More Information

For job postings, links to wireless industry recruiters, industry news, and training information, contact or visit the Web site of:

- **Cellular Telecommunications Industry Association**
  1250 Connecticut Avenue, NW, Suite 200
  Washington, DC 20036
  Tel: 202-785-0081
  Web: http://www.wow-com.com

For the latest on the wireless industry, job information, and information about Wireless Magazine, *contact or visit the Web site of:*

- **Wireless Industry Association**
  9746 Tappenbeck Drive
  Houston, TX 77055
  Tel: 800-624-6918
  Web: http://wirelessdealers.com

Chapter V

RELATED RESOURCES

The American Association of Community Colleges (AACC) "works with other higher education associations, the federal government, Congress, and other national associations that represent the public and private sectors to promote the goals of community colleges and higher education."

- **American Association of Community Colleges (AACC)**
  One Dupont Circle, NW, Suite 410
  Washington, DC 20036
  Tel: 202-728-0200
  Web: http://www.aacc.nche.edu

AACC has teamed up with U.S. News & World Report *to create a helpful Web site which will help you locate a community college that matches your interests and needs. You can search for schools by name or use an interactive work sheet to locate schools based on location, distance from your home, programs, or student services. The site provides links to over 1,200 two-year schools.*

- **Find Your Community College**
  Web: http://www.gseis.ucla.edu/ERIC/finderset.html

The League's Web site offers links to community and technical colleges in the United States, Canada, and selected foreign countries. The site also offers links to community and technical college resources including professional associations, instructional resources, distance education, education-related publications, information about the Web itself, and a variety of Web search tools.

- **League for Innovation in the Community College**
  26522 La Alameda, Suite 370
  Mission Viejo, CA 92691
  Tel: 949-367-2884
  Web: http://www.league.org/

ERIC is a "national information system designed to provide users with ready access to an extensive body of education-related literature," including community college-related topics.

- **ERIC Clearinghouse for Community Colleges**
  University of California, Los Angeles
  3051 Moore Hall, Box 951521
  Los Angeles, CA 90095-1521
  Web: http://www.gseis.ucla.edu/ERIC/eric.html

DETC serves as a clearinghouse of information on distance learning. It also sponsors a nationally recognized accrediting agency, the Accrediting Commission of the Distance Education and Training Council. DETC also offers a free Directory of Accredited Institutions. *Contact:*

- **Distance Education and Training Council (DETC)**
  1601 18th Street, NW
  Washington, DC 20009-2529
  Tel: 202-234-5100
  Web: http://www.detc.org

Embark.com offers students practical information and advice on topics ranging from financial aid to college majors and careers to the everyday issues of college life. The site also lists information for over 6,000 two- and four-year colleges. An added plus: students who visit this site can apply electronically to selected colleges.

- **Embark.com**
  Web: http://www.embark.com/

Offers links to over 1,000 community colleges in the United States, Canada, and other selected foreign countries. There are also links to over 130 other resources relating to community college education.

- **Community College Web**
  Web: http://www.mcli.dist.maricopa.edu/cc/

The My Future Web site aims to provide high school students with information about alternatives to four-year colleges, such as apprenticeships; internships; military opportunities; and enrollment at community, technical, and vocational colleges.

- **My Future**
  Web: http://www.myfuture.com/

INDEX